The Temple
Cleveland, Ohio

IN MANY WORLDS

IN MANY WORLDS

by Jacob M. Alkow

SHENGOLD PUBLISHERS, INC.
New York

ISBN 0-88400-111-3
Library of Congress Catalog Card Number: 84-52110
Copyright © 1985 by Jacob M. Alkow

All rights reserved

Published by Shengold Publishers, Inc.
New York, N.Y.

Printed in the United States of America

To Virginia

CONTENTS

I	Shumsk	9
II	New York	23
III	Boyle Heights	31
IV	Hollywood	34
V	Decision	44
VI	On the Way to Palestine	47
VII	Tel Aviv	51
VIII	Jerusalem	56
IX	Galilee	60
X	Paris	67
XI	America—1929	72
XII	San Bernardino	83
XIII	Egypt and Palestine—1936	96
XIV	Russia	101
XV	Berlin	115
XVI	Japan	123
XVII	China	129
XVIII	The War Era	162
XIX	Television 1946–1953	175
XX	Z.O.A. House 1953–1955	190
XXI	Wall Street	205
XXII	A New Life	226

ACKNOWLEDGMENTS

I am grateful to two people who encouraged me in writing this book, my wife, Virginia, and my friend, Dr. Ira Eisenstein.

I extend my appreciation to Miranda Konyuk for her help and guidance and my thanks to Eleanor Lieb, who assisted in the preparation of the manuscript.

I
SHUMSK

In the third year of this century I made my appearance in the small town of Shumsk, thirty miles from Vilna, the chief city of Lithuania. An additional child for a family that already had six children was no particular event. The first three migrated to America when I was still a small child, and a last child, my younger brother Harry, appeared two years after me.

Shumsk was a pleasant place to live in. Surrounded by ancient forests, undulating hills, vast meadows, wheat fields, and a winding river, its climate was ideal in both summer and winter. Although the population numbered no more than forty families, it had two colorful churches, the larger being the old Russian Orthodox church with its spacious grounds, which was directly opposite our house. The other, newer church was Polish Catholic. On the highest hill stood the courthouse. A few hundred meters farther were the grounds used for the lively county fairs.

Under the restrictive Czarist laws, Jews were prohibited from living in the county seats. My parents and my father's widowed sister had to obtain special permission to live in Shumsk. My parents had come from the nearby Jewish town of Kenna four miles away. After their marriage, they built their home in Shumsk on land allocated by the Russian Church. My father, who was held in great esteem by the mixed population of Russians and Poles, was often called in to serve as arbitrator in the petty, local squabbles and disputes. With his knowledge of both Russian and Polish, he was friendly with most of the residents. He had a special, comradely attachment to the bearded Russian priest and we were always invited to the annual Christmas party held in the main chamber of the courthouse; we were the only non-Russians there.

Even though we faithfully retained our traditional Jewish way of life, our family had, fortunately, escaped the effects of the oppressive, Czarist, anti-Jewish laws. My father would wryly tell the people of his synagogue that so far as we were concerned, God, in his kindness, had forgotten to include us in the punishment of *galut*, the deep awareness of living in exile. *Galut* was a source of continuous, unmitigated Jewish torment for countless generations. Lest they forget, Mother Russia reminded the Jews periodically that they were in exile.

Unlike those members of the family who devoted their free time to the study of the Talmud, my father loved to read the Bible and the Jewish historians, Graetz and Dubnow. He was a self-educated man and his reactions and interpretations of what he read were, at times, quite startling.

When asked how he felt about living and raising a family in a totally non-Jewish atmosphere, he said that he felt like the Gibeonites of old. In the Bible the Gibeonites were the hewers of wood and the drawers of water, a ragged tribe of Canaanites who, through deception, had led Joshua to enter into a treaty of peace with them. For my father the Gibeonites appeared in an altogether different light. For him they were an exemplary group in history. "For 1,500 years," he pointed out, "they lived in close contact with the Jewish people, in peace and in harmony." Despite the Gibeonites' distinctive way of life, the Jews accorded them all the rights of free citizenship, and when the Babylonian Jewish exiles returned to their ancient homeland, the Gibeonites were among the first to volunteer in the rebuilding of the walls of Jerusalem.

The historical analogy my father drew between the Gibeonites, as he saw them, and our peaceful life in the midst of the Russian and Polish communities, where we were the minority, may not have impressed his scholarly listeners. But it left an indelible impression on me.

In Kenna, to which my father's ancestors had migrated about the time of Napoleon's invasion of Russia, there was an old wooden synagogue with a large courtyard. Within the synagogue there was a customary place for storing old Hebrew books and scrolls which were out of use. Because of their sanctity, the scrolls and books could not be destroyed. It was through some of these books and the handwritten records on their front and back pages that we traced the origin of the migrations and the history of the Jewish people of the area. From this source we learned that my father's ancestors had lived in parts of Lithuania for many generations before Lithuania was annexed by Poland in 1712; it came under the heels of Russian domination in 1785.

Unlike other Jewish settlements in Russia and Poland, Kenna was always relatively prosperous. It had a modern railroad station with a sizable waiting room, a fire department, and some rooming houses for vacationers from Vilna, who filled every available accommodation in summer.

Kenna had a small population of no more than a hundred Jewish families. Among them were my well-to-do uncles, aunts, and older cousins. The two largest homes were owned by my father's sister and his younger brother. His sister's husband was the wealthiest Jew outside of Vilna. He was known as "King of the Tarf." (In Russia, tarf, a hardened kind of peat cut out of the ground, is a heating substitute for coal.) With the death and decay of trees in the vast surrounding forests, the ground offered an unlimited supply of the cut bricks, which my uncle exported to heat the homes and factories of Germany. The Russian government encouraged this exploitation of its natural wealth and had even awarded my uncle some medals and other honors in appreciation for his work.

My uncle was also a scholarly man. My grandfather selected him as a son-in-law in the hope that he would become a rabbi. But my uncle found opportunities in Kenna and did not hesitate to proclaim that he was much happier in the successful role of "first-class, honorable merchant of Russia." He endowed his front seat in the synagogue with greater prominence than the seat near the eastern wall, which my father had inherited from his father. My father and his devoted younger brother could never forgive my uncle for his arrogance. Nevertheless, both of them showed their brother-in-law considerable respect, though to the sorrow of their sister, they refused to associate with him too intimately. When people of the town told my father how his wealthy brother-in-law was invited to visit with the Minister of Commerce in St. Petersburg, my father acidly answered, "Oh, yes, and the Minister put two lumps of sugar in his tea!" Privately, when he spoke of his prosperous brother-in-law, my father would say, "Erudition and wealth, when not accompanied by modesty, are no more than an empty eggshell." Hearing this, the rabbi of the synagogue quietly said that my father was right.

Kenna was in some respects a rural suburb of Vilna. It was Vilna which gave Kenna its newspapers, periodicals, books, religious items, clothes, and medical care, and it was to the old cemetery of Vilna that my parents' ancestors and my own little sister were brought to be buried.

My seven-year-old sister had been scalded by boiling water from a large basin which had been set at the edge of our table; she died in my father's arms while he was rushing her to the emergency hospital in Vilna. My sister was at that time my father's most loving, comforting child. After the failure of his desperate effort to save her life, his hair turned gray.

Though their faculties are not developed for any thought about death, children have the greatest fear of it. Death deprives the child of something he trusted and loved. What is this horrible thing that robs him? Death, the darkest evil of all. Such were the feelings I had when I was seven and my mother wrapped me in a blanket and told me that my dear grandfather was dead.

It was a cold, clammy, November evening. It was dark, but through the darkness and the whispering I sensed my mother's tears. When we arrived at the courtyard of the synagogue, dimly lit by lamps, candles, and lanterns, my aunts, uncles, and cousins had already gathered there. Then more people came—every member of the community. The courtyard was filled to capacity and some people had to stand outside the gate.

The wooden coffin was brought to the center while the cantor was chanting the psalm "What is man that Thou takest notice of him and the son of man who is dirt and ashes." Then the rabbi spoke, bringing tears to the eyes of the mourners. Shivers passed through my spine when he said, "A great and mighty oak has fallen." The words "mighty oak" rang in my ears. He went on to say that the great and mighty oak had spread its rich foliage to protect and shade a generation from the bitter onslaughts of a hard world, and he ended by saying, "Now his sons will accompany him on his last voyage to our ancient cemetery in Vilna."

When the echoes of the weeping subsided, the coffin was placed on a wagon in deep silence. My father, his younger brother from Kenna, and older brother from Vilna climbed into another wagon. As the procession of the two wagons started on their seven-hour journey into the night, I tore myself away from my mother and ran after the wagons. When stopped, I wept bitterly.

From the time I was six years old my parents had only three children to look after: my older sister, Sarah, who was very kind to me, myself, and my younger brother who was my steady companion for many years.

My first six months of schooling were under the tutelage of my mother's father in Gur, an agricultural village situated on the highest hill adjacent to Vilna. My grandfather was a renowned Talmudic scholar and lived with my mother's youngest sister, her husband, and their four children, one of whom was my age.

Except for the affectionate attention of my grandfather and the joyous sleigh rides on the pure, white, snowy hills around the house, I remember very little. My mother, who was loathe to part with me for too long a time, soon brought me back home to be taught by private tutors.

The first tutor who came to live in our home had only two pupils—my sister Sarah and myself. The two that followed him taught my brother also and were young men who, having encountered some political difficulties in the city, sought relief in the beautiful, natural surroundings and pure air of the country. My grown-up sister, Libby, fell in love with the first of them and joined him in America, where they were married.

My favorite teacher was the third and last tutor, who had been under surveillance by the police of Vilna for revolutionary activities. Penniless and jobless, he found in Shumsk the ideal hideout. My father was greatly impressed with his learning and the manner in which he imparted his knowledge to my sister, myself, and my younger brother. This tutor was responsible for my lasting love of Hebrew poetry and most of the books of the Bible. The impression that this young, swarthy, emaciated, unkempt teacher made on me was more profound than that of any teacher I subsequently encountered in any of the universities of the world.

Toward the end of his contractual year, my teacher seemed to change. He became restless and secretive. Then sums of cash began to disappear from the tills and other places in our house. The accusing finger was first pointed at some of the servants, but when he was eventually caught in the act, my favorite, inspiring teacher was unceremoniously thrown out of the house. Nearly everyone in our neighboring town of Kenna was shocked at the unprecedented event of a brilliant, learned, Hebrew teacher behaving like a common thief.

After this experience my parents decided to send my brother and me to my father's older sister in Kenna. With her children married, settled, and scattered throughout the world, my aunt instigated the move. She told my parents she was very lonely in her large house and its numerous servants. When not absorbed with his international trade, her husband was immersed in his studies.

Sad to leave our parents, our fine horses, our happy surroundings, the blooming apple-and-cherry orchard, we were, nevertheless, at first easily conciliated with our new environment. I was happy to find friends my own age and felt comfortable in my father's warm, solicitous family.

But as the months passed, I began to grow more and more unhappy. My passionate interest in learning waned. I couldn't adjust to a formal classroom filled with over twenty children of varied ages in an ill-equipped schoolroom supervised by a harried teacher. I could hardly wait for Friday, when after the morning lesson on the weekly scriptural reading of the Law, we were driven home.

No sooner did I reach Shumsk in the summer than I shed my shoes and stockings to allow my bare feet to roam alongside the wheat fields in the back of our house up to the forest, with its mushrooms and blackberries, and down to the winding river past all my familiar childhood sites. My mother disapproved of my running around barefooted like the children of the peasants, but my kind sister, who was charged to watch over us, never betrayed us. She hid our shoes so that my mother would never know.

During the late spring and summer, when it seemed to me the weather was more beautiful than anywhere in the world, my father and I would walk the four miles separating our home from the synagogue in Kenna. Attending the synagogue was a part of life that diverted one's attention from worldly pursuits to matters of the spirit. Temporarily forgetting their mundane cares, the people were imbued with hope and strength. Many who quarreled and abused each other during the week underwent a change of heart as they passed over the threshold of the old synagogue. Heine compared the Jew on his Sabbath day to "a beggar turned into a prince."

Our Saturday morning walks to and from the synagogue created a strong bond between my father and myself. In a mood of great patience and relaxation my father bent his attentive ear to absorb all I had to say about my experiences. He had heard about my unhappy adjustment to schoolwork. His promise to make some favorable changes consoled me and heightened my ability to endure life at school. Little did he think at the time that the changes he contemplated for my good would take place sooner than anyone could have anticipated.

On our weekly visits to Shumsk I was always glad to visit my father's widowed sister and her three unwed daughters, who lived near us. They were in straitened circumstances. The two older girls were seamstresses and the younger one helped her mother in the little store which my father had set up for them. It was a poor little store for indigent peasants who couldn't afford to buy anything more expensive than needles, candles, kerosene, rope, and similar items.

Our visits to my aunt's house on Sabbath afternoon always created great excitement. They helped to break the loneliness and monotony of the girls' isolated and friendless lives. Detached from the hub of any community life, they had no money for dowries and no matchmaker had taken notice of them. The oldest was already past twenty-four, and my aunt's tears were bottomless.

One evening a strange, unknown matchmaker appeared at my aunt's house. He assured her that he had a brilliant match for her older daughter with a fine, hardworking, upright man who was only ten years older than my cousin. There was, however, a slight drawback. The proposed bridegroom was a hunchback.

My aunt was overcome by mixed feelings and felt both relief and sorrow over what fate had meted out for her child. With tears streaming from her eyes she ran to my father for guidance and advice. We children were all shooed from the room during the lengthy discussions that ensued. My father reassured my aunt that the family would never regard her daughter's marriage to a hunchback as anything demeaning. What was important and significant, he told her, was that the bridegroom had picked my cousin for a wife and that he was a good and honorable man.

Her fears and anxieties assuaged, my aunt was now overjoyed. In addition, my father promised new clothes for her and for her daughters, as well as a tidy sum for a suitable wedding and the establishment of a modest household for the couple. Among the warmest embraces between my mother and my aunt, and endless felicitations of *mazel tov*, we children were invited back to the living room, where we found our aunt transformed and radiant.

I recall the frantic preparations in my aunt's house before the wedding. The sadness and despair that prevailed prior to the matchmaker's arrival gave way to a joyous mood of expectancy. Everyone was busy doing something important and urgent. Emissaries ran to and from my mother for advice and counseling. My sister Sarah, then fifteen years old, was infected with the overall excitement and joined my cousins in their laughter and songs of cheerful Yiddish melodies, which replaced the sorrowful laments of poverty, exile, and loneliness. One of Sarah's deepest regrets was that my father, mother, and we three children had to leave Shumsk before the wedding.

The marriage was ill-fated. The hunchback lived only seven years, and when he died his wife was left with two young children. My cousin showed symptoms of tuberculosis and was advised not to keep the children with her. She sent them to her brother Boris, who was living in a small city in Germany. Several years earlier he had married a German woman who converted to Judaism. The couple was childless and glad to adopt the two orphaned children. Both boys were well looked after by their uncle and aunt. They graduated from the university in Germany with promising careers in professions which they would later be forbidden to practice. Twenty-eight years later, when I went to Paris, I met the eldest son, who was one of the first refugees fleeing from the virulent anti-Semitism of Nazi Germany.

The intolerance woven into the fabric of Russian society was, to a smaller extent, also true of the enclosed Jewish society. Among themselves, Jews were intolerant of different modes of prayer, dress, and adherences to certain rabbis. However, Kenna, fortunately, free of an oppressive, ultra-orthodox rigidity, was an emancipated and friendly town.

A well-established Jewish merchant in Vilna surprised the community with his decision to move his home and business to Kenna. He bought the large, general store which my uncle and his wife had established and enlarged throughout the years. The merchant had a beautiful wife, but no children. Dressed in the latest fashion, the merchant's wife would often replace her husband in running the store while he was away on business. People liked and admired the gentle and affable lady of the store.

One who grew to admire her, however, more than anyone else, was my second cousin. Recently returned to his parents after completing four years of military service, he was an attractive, robust, athletic man with an excellent knowledge of Russian literature. This and his pleasant voice had, in spite of his Jewishness, won him the friendship of some officers of his brigade.

Despite the restraint of the lady of the store, people could not fail to notice the development of the relationship. Some began to talk of the considerable time my cousin spent near the counter of the store whenever the head of the store was gone. This, it was generally agreed, was highly inappropriate. The injunction of "You shall not covet your neighbor's wife" was just one step below "You shall not commit adultery."

In spite of its liberalism, Kenna had never deviated from a strict, traditional adherence to the Jewish concept of the sanctity of the home. While the community often shut one of its eyes to the indiscretions of young men and women, it never tolerated any promiscuous behavior on the part of married men or women.

One day the town was in an uproar. One townsman rushed to another to gossip or hear of an event that had never occurred before. The story was told in hushed voices calculated not to reach our young ears. The lady of the store and my second cousin were found naked in my cousin's bed!

The whole thing might never have been discovered were it not for a headache that compelled my cousin's mother and her sister-in-law to return from the fair sooner than expected. Unable to control their horror, they burst into screams that attracted some of the neighbors. Although the neighbors saw very little, they embellished the story, to the outrage and delight of the residents and visitors in town.

On the following days there were all sorts of rumors and talk of revenge. Though the younger ones were kept at a distance, my friends and I found a pretext to go to the store for some purchase so that we could look for the long, sharp knife, which people said was hidden by the storekeeper in the bin of groats.

When the talk of revenge and foul play began to be taken seriously, the rabbi was asked to intervene to cool the tempers and return the town to sanity. It was not the rabbi's custom to preach every week or even every month. But now it was announced that the rabbi would deliver a sermon on the forthcoming Sabbath afternoon. My mother didn't think I should go, but my father convinced her I was old enough to be included even if I failed to understand everything.

The rabbi began with a discussion of the portion of the week which was read from the Torah at the morning services. The second part of the reading dealt with the death of Aaron, the High Priest, who was "a lover of peace and a pursuer of peace." The rabbi connected the story of Aaron with the story of Jephthah, which was read in the supplementary reading of the *haphtorah*.

There was a great warrior and patriot called Jephthah, said the rabbi, and the people accepted him, the Bible tells us, even though Jephthah, the Gileadite, was the son of a whore. His half-brothers chased him out of the house because of his lowly birth. Jephthah also consorted with vain fellows. All of this, however, was overlooked by the elders of Gilead, who said to him, "Come and be our chief."

In spite of his bravery and great love for his people, the rabbi went on with the sermon, Jephthah was a rash and proud man. "When the spirit of the Lord came upon him in the deliverance of Israel from the children of Ammon, he made a vow that whatsoever will come forth from the doors of his house to meet him on his return in peace, he would offer as a sacrifice." And it was Jephthah's only, beloved daughter who was the first to come forth. This criminal vow, our rabbis say, could have been annulled, if not for the pride and vanity of two men.

According to the *Midrash*, the High Priest, Pinchas, could have nullified the vow if he had gone to Jephthah to do so. Instead, he declared, "Let Jephthah come to me." Jephthah retorted, "I, the prince of the land, should not humiliate myself before my subjects," and refused to approach the man he disliked.

Both sinned grievously before God and both were punished. Jephthah, after he sacrificed his daughter, died a horrible death, and Pinchas was punished when the holy spirit departed from him. No one wept, continued the rabbi, for Pinchas, but for Aaron, who made peace between man and man, and husband and wife—no matter how much they had injured each other—the whole community wept. Aaron would go first to one and then to another and tell each party how the other was sorry and harbored no thought of revenge or harm.

"This is our lesson from our Torah," he said, "humility, repentance, and forgiveness. If anyone dares to harbor thoughts of sinful revenge, let him remember that 'Mine is the vengeance,' saith the Lord, and God's vengeance is different from man's."

The congregation, which had been hungry to hear these words, quickly returned to the pursuits of everyday life. My cousin left the town on the following day and I never saw him again.

My father left the supervision of our general store in Shumsk in the hands of my capable mother. His main interest was in forestry and the export of lumber to Germany and other western countries. His younger brother, a leading resident in Kenna, was closely associated with him in all his business ventures and both men and their wives lived on amicable terms.

There was yet another Jewish-owned store in Shumsk. Some relatives of ours obtained permission to live there by paying a sizable sum to the Russian authorities. Helping out with the business was seventeen-year-old Aaron, the brother of the widow who owned it. He was a likeable, shy boy, who was great friends with my fifteen-year-old sister, Sarah. After his year's sojourn in Shumsk, he could not forget her, and five years later when he met my sister again in New York, they were married.

We liked Aaron because he would play with us, so it was a treat when my mother sent me to Vilna with Aaron to buy a watermelon for the High Holidays. A round watermelon symbolized the round, sweet year, which the Jews prayed for on Rosh Hashanah, the Jewish New Year.

Aaron and I took the horses and wagon to Kenna, where we tied up the horses at the railway station. From there it was an hour's train ride to Vilna. This was the eve of the holiday, and in the Vilna market the atmosphere was charged with excitement. People were haggling with merchants about prices and rushing about to get everything ready for the festival. The market-place and its rich displays of food, its noise and its bustle, fascinated us. I wanted to remain there longer, but Aaron had selected two ripe, round watermelons and was ready to go for lunch to a restaurant in Vilna owned by my uncle. We two boys ate heartily and were each given a large cake to take home for the holidays.

On the way back to the railroad station, I asked Aaron if he had ever seen the Vilna Synagogue. I knew he had been in Vilna only once before. The Vilna Synagogue was the most unusual synagogue in modern, Jewish history because it was built in 1573 through the initiative of the Polish King, Zigmund August. The king himself brought the best-known Polish architects from Cracow. They drew up the most ambitious plans of any religious building during that period.

Aaron couldn't resist this temptation. We detoured to the great synagogue. He gaped in wonder at the four round pillars beside the *biemah*, which supported the stately cupola. We counted the fifteen steps which led to the entrance of the building, symbolizing the fifteen verses of the psalm "From the depths I have called upon You, my Lord." I had been to the synagogue with my parents, but this was Aaron's first time, and I enjoyed watching the impression it made on the seventeen-year-old boy.

On this day before the New Year hundreds of worshippers kept coming in and out for special morning and afternoon services. Everyone appeared to be in an elated mood, and the sounds of the prayers were accompanied by the clinking of coins dropped into the charity boxes by each one entering the building.

It was hard to tear Aaron away, but we were burdened with our watermelons and cakes and had to get them home. We entered the third-class coach and Aaron secured the melons on the upper racks with empty sacks and bundles. The train pulled out of the station slowly and gained speed. Then it suddenly jerked to a stop, throwing everyone off balance, including my watermelon, which was on the right side. Aaron's watermelon remained on the rack. Mine rolled off, hit the floor, and shattered to smithereens.

I couldn't help crying. All the passengers tried to console me, but it did no good. When we arrived in Shumsk, I returned home carrying only the cake. Aaron took his melon to his sister in the store.

I hardly had time to tell my parents what had happened when Aaron's sister came running to our house with the watermelon. "This is yours," she said to my mother. "It was my brother's fault that the other watermelon fell down."

My father finally convinced the poor widow that she was mistaken and that the watermelon was really hers. When Aaron's sister left, my father told us it didn't matter whose melon remained. What did matter was that the widow and her three orphans needed it more than we did.

On the High Holidays my parents packed and moved into the spacious home of my uncle in Kenna. Since there were too many of us to eat together, we had our own private dining room for the five in our family. My uncle and his loving wife had turned their living room into a dining room for themselves and their five children.

After the evening services in the synagogue and the festive dinners, both families merged into one. Asleep, we children had to be carried out to our bedroom, while the brothers and their wives continued their endless family talk until late in the night.

On the following morning, either my father or his brother chanted the *Shachris*, the early part of the service; they took turns on both days of Rosh Hashanah. On Yom Kippur they also alternated before and after the moving, soulful prayers by an indigent cantor. Burdened with a large family, the cantor earned pitifully little in this provincial community. Only Vilna and other large cities could afford good, professional cantors.

With a voice that was not very strong, though adequate for a small synagogue, the poor cantor in Kenna reached the depth of my heart more than any other cantor or operatic singer I've heard since. When he wrapped his prayer shawl over his head and began very softly with *Hineni Heani*, "Lo, I am the poorest and least worthy to stand before You and to pray for Your people," a cry emanating from the women's section began to roll, wave after wave, and engulfed me and all others in blinding tears.

During our last year in Russia, my father encountered some unprecedented hostility from a Polish duke, who was the largest landowner outside of Vilna. As an heir of the landed Polish nobility, the duke assumed control of the lands and forests when his mother, the old duchess, died.

My father had been on relatively good terms with the old duchess. He often visited her palatial home, which was outside of Shumsk and surrounded by numerous cottages, buildings, and stables. There was a special, private jail for penal laborers, whom she received from the government to work on her lands. Every Passover eve my mother would send my sister, myself, and a servant with matzohs and special Passover dishes for the few Jewish inmates who found their unhappy way to the gangs of prison labor camp. I watched the eyes of a Jewish convict when we told him of the preparations we were making for the *seder*. I will never forget his expression of sadness and nostalgia.

All this changed abruptly on our last Passover in Europe. We were strictly warned not to come too close to the duchess's grounds. The duke had his eye on the forests and intended to encroach on the land which my father had leased to cut and export timber. The duke even refused to recognize the signed documents, thereby abrogating my father's legal rights. His animosity was seconded by a newly arrived, fiery, red-headed Polish priest, who carried with him an inveterate hatred for both Russians and Jews. Most of the humble, honest, Polish peasants, who had known my father since their childhood, resented the venomous sermons preached by the priest on Catholic holidays. They also hated the duke, in whom they saw a return to power of the old, rich, Polish exploiters of their land and lives. The loyalty and devotion of the simple peasants to Jews further intensified the enmity shown by the duke and the priest.

Aware of my father's temper and his uncompromising intolerance of injustice, my uncle and other heads of the family begged him to be cautious. We are still not as free as you think we are, was the admonition.

"Give him what he wants, give him the forests, give him everything," my mother pleaded, "your life is worth more than all your possessions." But these attempts at forewarning elicited no more than an off-handed acknowledgment from my father.

In addition to this, my father had innocently implicated himself in another way. Besides the general store my parents also had a license and a distributorship of Vilna's famous Lipsky beer. Once the timber-cutting season was over, the many peasants employed by my father were treated with a few kegs of the excellent beer. As often happened among the repressed, joyless, hard-working peasants after a release of their tensions, there was a brawl. One of the constables who had nothing much to do would frequently join in the festivities. When a sizable fight followed such a festivity, the constable would assume full authority as an officer of the law and prepare a report for his superiors. These insignificant reports were invariably dismissed in the crowded, inefficient, bribe-ridden offices. One report, however, was seized upon by the conniving duke. No one was aware of it for a long time.

One afternoon the superintendent of my father's work force came running to my father. The duke's hirelings demanded that the laborers leave the forest where they were working. When the peasants refused to obey, the duke's servants unleashed fierce dogs. There was panic. Axes were swung at the dogs and a few peasants who didn't run for their lives were attacked and badly bitten.

My father jumped on his horse and rushed to the scene. He found that the laborers and the dogs had already retreated. He immediately set out for the duke's palace, and on the way, encountered the duke himself, astride his horse. At this point my father heeded his wife's plea and the admonitions of his family and asked for some reasonable truce.

In a confrontation of two people, one with an innate pride and an unimpeachable sense of justice, and the other with an inborn, domineering arrogance and closed mind, little harmony can be expected. Instead of accepting my father's offer, the duke dismissed him in the most insulting and humiliating manner, calling him a filthy Jew. My father's temper prevailed over any reason, and he lashed the duke across the face with his whip. The duke, shocked, confused, and frightened by the unanticipated impudence of a Jew, wiped the blood from his face and galloped back to his estate. The constables, who knew the mood of the peasants, advised the duke against any precipitous action.

Two days later there was a police inquiry. From the testimony of some of the peasants and superintendents, a senior Russian police official, who hated Poles, told my father that he had never thought that a Jew could do such a nice thing! My parents and my father's family were greatly relieved.

This state of euphoria lasted only twenty-four hours. A trusted government official rushed from Vilna to warn my father to leave the country immediately. Grave charges were being prepared against him for assaulting a close relative of the Governor General of Vilna, and for inciting the peasants through drunkenness to rebel against the Church and the Czar. With the influence my father had, he hurriedly arranged for passports, and at ten in the evening, my aunt bundled the children in blankets and two of her servants helped bring us to the railroad station in Kenna, where my father, mother, and sister awaited us. As the train pulled out of the station, my aunt stood silent and alone on the platform. I knew she was crying.

Sitting in a second-class compartment on the way to the border, we remained quiet, bundled up in our quilts. Forewarned against the Russian Secret Police, we tried to be inconspicuous. Though valid, our passports brought no assurance that we would not be questioned. No one said very much until we were told to leave the train and cross the border to the German side. There we were told to walk into an empty compartment in the German train.

As soon as we were settled in the new train, my mother broke into sobs. When I looked at my father I saw tears welling up in his eyes too. We three children joined them. They were tears of relief. Then as the train pulled away from the station on its way to Hamburg, the tears gave way to laughter and rejoicing. We embraced, kissed, and hugged each other again and again.

It was not long before my mother, exhausted, fell into a deep sleep. My father, too, closed his eyes, and only we three children were awake when the train pulled into Hamburg.

We took rooms at a pension in a quiet, middle-class neighborhood. Our two large rooms with their bay windows faced a large courtyard with trees different from those we had known. They were trees we had never seen before.

The sight of the ocean and of the great ships with sailors from all parts of the world did a great deal to bolster my father's morale. For us it was our first view of the sea, and my parents could scarcely tear us away from gazing in fascination at its limitless horizon.

In the late afternoons we would all go to the park and listen to the daily orchestra concerts. At the concert, we sensed a strange atmosphere of festivity, restlessness, and an urgency that the loud music was unable to drown out. It was not long before my father realized that we had entered Germany in a period of intense war hysteria. After the concerts ended we listened to speeches about the greatness of the Kaiser, the Germany Army, and the German Navy. Of course we understood very little of this but our father took care to explain the bombastic, patriotic rhetoric.

The woe of many, say the Jewish sages, is half a comfort. Absorbed in the excitement and preparations for war, my father forgot much of his own troubles.

However, toward the end of our happy interlude in Germany, we received word that my father had had an unusually quick trial; he was fined, in absentia, to a large sum of money and sentenced to five years' hard labor in Siberia. With this news we boarded the boat for America.

After a week at sea the captain made an important announcement: the outbreak of World War I. The German Admiralty gave the captain a choice of turning back to the harbor in Hamburg or proceeding as planned to Boston. Passengers and immigrants of all nationalities fell on their knees in thankful prayer when the captain decided to hold his course for America.

II
NEW YORK

My father was the one most adversely affected by our new life in America. He felt at a loss and could not forget what he had left behind.

The dairy business in the State of New York was largely controlled by my uncle and five of my mother's first cousins. Like most of the newly arrived members of our family, my father was taken into the business. With determination and the encouragement of his children and relatives, he eventually managed to become more or less adjusted to his new surroundings.

My brother Izzie, who had come to America earlier by himself to escape being drafted into the Russian Army, was already employed and had been assigned a route in the Williamsburgh section of Brooklyn. Each company of the family had its own territory and was strongly protected from the threats of the underworld. Occasional attacks by the gangsters of the burgeoning Mafia had strengthened, rather than weakened, the united family in its struggle for existence. The corrupt Democratic Party, the venal judges appointed by Tammany Hall, and a police force which fattened on bribery could not be counted on for protection. Great stamina, muscle, and smart maneuvering were required to survive.

Since the outbreak of the First World War, the world demand for American dairy products had become very great. Booming affluence in the dairy trade attracted the Mafia and other underworld mobs. When my family rejected their demands for protection payoffs, some delivery wagons were attacked and the drivers robbed and beaten. My brother was one of their victims. Later they burned some of my uncle's stables. A watchman was killed and fifty horses were lost in the flames.

To meet this grave challenge, all members of the dairy companies were summoned to an emergency meeting. My brother and father were among those present. Immediate measures were adoped to protect life and property. All horses and wagons were replaced by the newest trucks produced in Detroit. In the strong, well-enclosed forward cabs of these trucks, there was room for a driver and an armed assistant. As a result, the battle for the safe operation of the industry was won more quickly than expected. The relatively new immigrants had set an example for the entire city. Banks were impressed, and lent the necessary funds for trucks and new equipment.

The New York I knew as a youngster in America was a jungle. The masses which the Statue of Liberty welcomed to its kind shores never ceased to be teeming, tired, and oppressed. The sweatshops and their filthy surroundings sucked in most of the new arrivals and paid them a pittance. Special milk stations were established on the East Side to help sustain the lives of the wretched children. Many of the immigrants, unable to withstand twelve hours a day in dusty, airless factories, became victims of tuberculosis.

"A curse on Columbus" accompanied their bitter complaints against the overcrowded, bug-infested living quarters in the tenements. During the hot nights of the summer only the rusty fire escapes provided relief. The fire escapes and streets were the only places one could meet one's neighbors, aside from the small, badly vented synagogues in some of the cellars.

Nevertheless, New York, which so greatly diminished an entire generation's *joie de vivre*, was for me a joy and a song. I used to stand near the approach to the Williamsburgh Bridge and watch the cars, horses, and wagons ascend the first half of the curved span. I marveled at the roads, held up by the steel ropes of the mightily built towers, the car tracks, and the street-cars. Gradually I moved from the bottom of the bridge to its center, half-way between Williamsburgh and Delancey Street, on the Lower East Side of New York. I felt the same emotions Thomas Wolfe or Walt Whitman might have felt, watching the bridge above the stream of muticolored boats below. I extended my walks, and by the time I reached bar mitzvah age I knew every pushcart on Orchard Street.

When I was twelve years old, every Saturday after sunset I joined the ranks of newsboys selling the Yiddish Sunday morning newspapers. With the training I had in the fields of Shumsk, I was able to run faster than the others, and on receiving my load of papers on East Broadway, I would race through the streets leading to the Yiddish theatrical district on Second Avenue, shouting, "*Forwards, Varheit, Tageblat, Tag!*"

Selling papers was followed by other youthful enterprises. One was hawking apples, oranges, and Park and Tilford candies in the Italian Opera House on the Bowery. I loved the opera more than the money I earned, and I loved the simple, poor Italian opera-goers most of all. Eating their salami sandwiches during the intermissions, the opera enthusiasts on my balcony showed little interest in the wares I had to sell. Here and there someone would buy an apple or an orange and would, sometimes, add a penny. I didn't need the pennies but I loved the people who gave them to me.

I tried one venture after another, including pushing racks of dresses along the streets of Seventh Avenue, but soon lost interest in money-making activities. The novelty had worn off, and at fifteen I felt that the commercial world had lost its attractions.

I never developed any liking for the dairy business. All the talk about cottage cheese, pot cheese, and cream cheese had led me to dislike the dairy products which filled our icebox. When I was seventeen, my uncle told my father he should be happy that my natural inclinations weren't mercenary. "Business," he said, "can never give one the fulfillment to be found in the pursuit of learning." My uncle had once been a learned man before he became absorbed in business, and despite his success, he deeply regretted abandoning the scholar's life.

With all my passionate interest in learning and countless happy hours spent in the 42nd Street Library, at ages sixteen and seventeen I was not a particularly good student. My academic life was all ups and downs. I changed schools and teachers often, and I was easily bored. But when an inspired teacher appeared in preparatory school, and later in college and in the Jewish Theological Seminary, my absorption in what he taught was a thrilling experience. I would study and review every word I had heard in the classroom.

The opportunities that lured me after I bought my first razor were those of learning and working for a cause. At sixteen I was elected president of the Theodore Herzl Zionist Club, which had been founded by one of America's

Jacob Alkow at age 15.

most brilliant orators, Dr. Abba Hillel Silver. He served as its first president until he left New York to study for the rabbinate in Cincinnati. I never changed or abandoned the ideals emanating from those meetings of the Zionist club in the Educational Alliance on East Broadway.

From the very beginning Zionism meant much more to me than the founding of a home for homeless people or the establishment of a state on its ancestral land. It was more than just the ingathering of the persecuted Jewish people. It was the means by which Jews could make their lives more beautiful. The building of a new country on the ancient soil of the prophets and kings of Israel was not the end in itself but a process that could lift people to greater heights and restore their dignity, crushed by oppression and homelessness.

At sixteen I began to appear as a speaker at meetings in the streets and halls of the East Side and Williamsburgh. During this period I was working part-time after school in the mimeograph room of the Jewish National Fund on East 23rd Street. Through a benevolent fate I was one of the first Jews in America to read the cablegram sent by the British Foreign Minister to Lord Rothschild, containing the electrifying, historic message—in short, the Balfour Declaration.

After nervously mimeographing a large quantity of the Declaration, I stuffed half a dozen copies in my pocket and ran to my evening Hebrew class on East Broadway to bring the glad tidings to my school. All classwork stopped. My teachers, Daniel Persky and Moshe Feinstein, embraced me and all the other students with shouts of "mazel tov."

The news crackled through the Jewish streets and we drank *l'chaim* while tears of joy ran down our young faces. Then, we formed a long line that took us dancing through the streets. It was a clear, cool night and people came from all directions to join us, singing and dancing. Soon the auditorium of our school opened its doors, and by the time the speeches started, it was crammed full. There was not an empty seat as prominent Jewish leaders addressed us on the historical significance of the Declaration and the fulfillment of a two-thousand-year-old dream. I returned home very late, but my parents and relatives were waiting up for me to share in the excitement of the momentous night.

One Sunday afternoon in Central Park, I walked alone from the lake through the park, surrounded by the skycrapers of central Manhattan. As I wandered along the Fifth Avenue side, I chanced upon a massive gray building, which somehow I had never noticed. It was the Metropolitan Museum of Art.

On entering the building and turning to its different wings, I was overcome with awe. I had been foolish enough to believe that I knew much about man's supreme achievements, but standing in the great foyer of the Metropolitan Museum of Art, I realized that I knew very little. At the age of sixteen I could realistically say that I knew a little about world literature, and a little about music, but nothing whatever about art.

This was typical of the immigrant world of New York in those days. Young intellectuals in this milieu knew literature and music, but were wholly ignorant of what went on in the field of art. This phenomenon was to last until after the Second World War.

Like my friends who returned to Carnegie Hall for refreshment of the soul, I kept returning to the Metropolitan Museum to see, to learn, to love more and more the countless treasures which it contains.

Desiring to continue my Hebraic studies, I entered the Jewish Theological Seminary. There I met Dr. Cyrus Adler, the friendliest and most cheeful head of a school of higher learning that I have ever encountered. My education and intellectual contacts had been with Ashkenazic Jews from eastern Europe or with those who were outside the Jewish fold. Dr. Adler was the first Sephardic Jew I got to know.

Though religiously conservative, he was a modern man who enjoyed life. I heard that he loved to drink a whisky and soda, an enjoyment which was unheard of among the scholars of the Jewish Theological Seminary and Dropsie College, the two institutions over which he presided. Though he circulated among great scholars of world renown, Dr. Adler, better known for his administrative acumen than for his scholarship, did not appear to be a lonely man in the seminary. He loved good conversation, and had an infectious laugh which won the friendship and trust of young people.

He knew about my precocious Zionist activities and asked me on more than one occasion to drop into his office for a chat.

I was surprised to find some students in the second and third year of Rabbinical college with a very limited knowledge of the Hebrew language, Bible, and related subjects. I soon learned, however, that this was not the fault of the seminary or its excellent teachers, among whom were Professors Louis Ginsburg, Israel Davidson, Alexander Marx, and Mordecai Kaplan. It was largely owing to the substantial number of students who were bent on becoming successful rabbis, not scholars. In this respect the seminary was not different from other schools of higher learning, where the school was a means to an end rather than an end in itself. The Jewish Theological Seminary was a young institution and, to a degree, had become utilitarian, a *kardom lachpor bo*, "a hatchet with which to dig." This had never been the function of a Jewish school of learning in the lands of the dispersion. The one and only aim had been the study of Torah. "For a Jew," said Dr. Kaplan, "the study of Torah is what Bertrand Russell said about the study of higher mathematics: the true spirit of delight, the exaltation, the sense of being more than a man, which is the touchstone of the highest excellence."

Until recently, there were no professional Jewish colleges, since Jews traditionally viewed education as a self-fulfilling pursuit. There was no Jewish counterpart to the priestly seminary, as found in the Catholic church. For Jews, the one and only purpose of a yeshiva was to enrich the soul and widen one's horizon. Of those who acquired sufficient learning, some were occasionally chosen to serve as rabbis. For each rabbi selected by a recognized authority, there were, at times, as many as ten scholars equally qualified.

Now, with the rapid social and religious changes sweeping the Jews of western Europe and America, there arose a need for a new type of yeshiva or school of higher learning. The seminary was one of the youngest institutions that adopted a dual role—one for the training of Conservative rabbis and the other for the enhancement of Jewish learning and research. Among those who were concerned with the posts and salaries which awaited them on graduation was a small group of brilliant students, for whom careers were a secondary matter.

The teachers who made the deepest impression on me were Professors Davidson, Kotkov, and Kaplan. I felt closest to the relatively young Dr. Kotkov, and was overwhelmed with grief when, on his way from the seminary, Dr. Kotkov was robbed and then murdered. For days I was unable to study.

From Professor Davidson I learned to penetrate and appreciate the riches of medieval Hebrew literature. However, of all my teachers Dr. Mordecai Kaplan was most responsible for the molding of my religious and philosophic outlook on life.

Dr. Mordecai Kaplan was born in Lithuania in 1881 and came to New York at the age of ten. What he learned until that age, he once told me, he only elaborated on later on. After having been ordained as rabbi by the Orthodox Chief Rabbi Jacob Joseph in New York, he freed himself from the straight-jacket of orthodoxy and became a leading teacher at the Jewish Theological Seminary. In the academically free and tolerant atmosphere of the Jewish Theological Seminary, he was able to evolve a new approach to Judaism. For the first time a great religious teacher announced that Judaism is more than a religion.

In his new, reconstructed approach, religion is no more than one spoke in a wheel which includes "history, Zionism, literature, and folk sanctions." Peoplehood, religion, and culture are "so enmeshed in one another," said Dr. Kaplan, "as to be incapable of being dealt with separately." Professor Kaplan exorcised the mythology from supernatural theology and turned it into a humanistic theology. He spoke out both against the "rugged individualism," and the "total collectivism" of the times. He called for ethical and moral values as guideposts to our personal, national, and international relations.

"This world is not a vestibule before the world to come," he claimed. Otherworldliness had no place in his religious outlook, and he found nothing miraculous in the miracles which attracted people to religion. His ideas of God were different from those of other Jewish theologians. "The God idea should be found in the field of natural experience," he said. "The true pragmatic test of an ideal is not the facility with which people are persuaded to accept it, but what it does to their lives once they accept it."

Like Spinoza, Dr. Kaplan had also excluded "the traditional attribute of Providence." He was in total disagreement with "the philosophers and theologians who assumed man's nature, rather than the condition of life, requires transformations."

Of his many books, the one which received the greatest acclaim was a 600-page volume, *Judaism as a Civilization*. It was hailed as "a Jewish classic, worthy of taking its place in the succession of great works which have made the Torah tradition a way of life for the Jewish people." Albert Einstein spoke of *Judaism as a Civilization* as "an objective exposition and interpretation of the Jewish problem."

To give form and substance to his religious philosophy, Dr. Kaplan enlisted the help of his son-in-law, Ira Eisenstein. Dr. Eisenstein has been devoting his life to the creation of a protective shell for the preservation of Dr. Kaplan's ideas. To these he had added another dimension.

"God," wrote Ira, "is the power within us to discover truth and abide by it when we find it." In order to discover that truth, Ira established the New Reconstructionist Rabbinical College. While in some other rabbinical colleges students were taught to accept the truths handed down to them, the students of the Reconstructionist College were urged to search and discover them anew.

All of Dr. Kaplan's acclaim and his books had the opposite effect in the Jewish Orthodox world. When his new, revised, Reconstructionist Prayer Book appeared in the early 30s, Orthodox rabbis denounced it as heresy and blasphemy. They were outraged by Dr. Kaplan's idea that the "Jews were not a chosen people," and that all the references to any of the miracles mentioned in the Bible were eliminated from the prayers. The prayerbook was also free of any priestly blessings, resurrection of the dead, or readings related to sacrificial offerings.

In the late 30s, on one of my periodic visits to New York, I read in a Yiddish morning paper that there would be a congregation of the faithful at the McAlpin Hotel for the purpose of excommunicating Mordecai Kaplan.

When I arrived, there was already a vast audience of mostly bearded and earlocked people, who filled the major hall of the hotel. No one was allowed to enter without a careful screening to assure that there would be no reporters, strangers, or nonbelievers. My dark hat, my railroad ticket, and the mention of an ultra-Orthodox rabbi in Los Angeles enabled me to get in and become a part of the excited, milling crowd. I went from one to another and listened to the exhortations and denunciations and vilification of my teacher. Pointing to the pages of Kaplan's prayerbook, the young zealots were the most vociferous and the most uncompromising. Anyone with moderate views advocating restraint was shouted down regardless of his age or status.

There was one elderly rabbi who moved me deeply. He seemed to be well known and respected by the older people. He ran from one group to another, pleading and crying, *Men tor nit*—it is forbidden to cut off a soul from its people, and it is forbidden to burn a Hebrew book that has in it the name of God. I followed the rabbi wherever he went and I saw that there were relatively few who were ready to listen. In the midst of the hysteria and fanaticism, one of the bitterest and most intolerant participants physically pushed and forced the rabbi out of his way. I rushed to his support when he seemed to have lost his balance.

"Rabbi, are you hurt?" I asked.

"Yes, I am hurt," he answered, "I am very hurt inside."

I remembered something that I once read about Thomas Jefferson. Jefferson was a great foe of intolerance, but he had at the same time an exceedingly placid temper. When he was in the company of the worst and most intolerant groups of men, he would say, "When you are in such a company, consider yourself as among the patients of Bedlam needing medical more than moral counsel." There are very few people who are able to feel as calm as Jefferson and emulate his noble behavior.

When the rabbi was rudely pushed by the excited fanatic, the temper I inherited from my father began to rise. With a pounding heart, I had to marshal all my strength to contain myself. I knew that if I didn't remain in control of my senses I would be thrown out.

After an hour of noise and excitement there was a deep silence. Black curtains covered all the windows. Lights were dimmed and several men ascended a platform carrying black candles and a *shofar*, the ram's horn which is blown on the High Holidays and during the Days of Penitence. On the table there was a large basin, and near it I could see the New Reconstructionist Prayer Book. The candles were lit and the ceremony and proceedings of the excommunication of Mordecai Kaplan began.

"In the name of the Lord of Hosts, the God of Israel who dwells on high. . . . May he be cursed with all the curses from the days of Moses until now. Cursed shall he be in the day and in the night. Cursed shall he be in his rising and in his lying down. Cursed shall he be in all his ways and in all his deeds. god of all spirits and all flesh, subdue him, destroy him, and cut him off. Let his path be black and slippery. . . ."

I couldn't bear to hear much more. I ran to a window for a little air, and across the room I saw the lowered head of the elderly rabbi as the ashes of the burning pages of the Prayer Book fell into the basin.

The excommunication of Mordecai Kaplan was exactly the same as that used against Baruch Spinoza and Uriel Acosta three hundred years ago.

III
BOYLE HEIGHTS

I was in the highest class in the Seminary when I fell ill. It began with a cold and developed into influenza and pneumonia. There were whisperings about my lungs possibly being affected, and my parents' anxiety increased. All too many immigrants and their children were victims of tuberculosis. Letters were rushed to Los Angeles where both my oldest sister, Lizzie, and my brother Sam, made their homes.

I remembered neither my sister nor my brother. They had left our home in Shumsk while I was still in my infancy. Though Lizzie had offered to send me a railroad ticket to come visit her, I never took advantage of the opportunity. Now my long-deferred visit had become a necessity.

My parents feared the ten-day trip to the coast would be too grueling and that I would become ill again en route. They were wrong. No medicine and no healing could have done as much for my health as the Art Institute in Chicago, Pike's Peak, or the Grand Canyon, all of which I discovered on my way west. I was met at the Los Angeles station by my sister, her husband, and my brother. They brought me to my sister's home in Alhambra.

The smell of orange blossoms, the large green lawn with two palm trees, and the eucalyptus trees bordering the property brought me back to an idyllic world I thought I had forgotten.

At the end of a full summer in California my good health returned completely, and I eagerly awaited enrolling at the university to complete my degree. I was also preparing for my first rabbinical work in Los Angeles, where I was to deliver four major sermons on the High Holidays.

Only once before had I delivered a sermon, and that was in Dr. Kaplan's class in homiletics. Dr. Kaplan had not been impressed. He demanded that his students never overlook the importance of the message that a sermon is to convey.

My speeches on the two days of the New Year were enthusiastically received in the synagogue, and I was sure my Yom Kippur eve delivery would be even better. But it was a failure. I talked over the heads of the congregation, and worse, my message for the new approach to religion alienated some of the older people.

Disappointed and unable to understand the reason for the cool reception, I worried about the sermon I was to give the following day. However, the faces of my audience indicated approval and satisfaction with my analysis of Jonah in the belly of the whale, and I parted on friendly terms with the members of the committee. In spite of what I had said on Yom Kippur eve, the president's final words when he bid me good-by were that he wished I could become the rabbi of the congregation. Thanking him profusely, I replied that my interests pointed in other directions.

At the age of twenty-four I was chosen to be the principal of the first Modern Hebrew School and Social Center in the Boyle Heights section of Los Angeles.

The school was situated in an old residential section on the east side of Los Angeles, which had attracted a large migration of Jews from New York. Many had come for their health. The hilly part of the area with its fine climate—there was no smog in those days—drew those afflicted by tuberculosis and other diseases of the city slums. Families followed other families, and within a few years after the First World War, the Jewish population of Boyle Heights grew to about 40,000. The construction of new synagogues, schools, hospitals, and old-age homes, and a cultural and recreational center on Soto and Michigan were an integral part of the building boom which was to make Los Angeles the second-largest Jewish community in the world during the mere space of a quarter century.

Boyle Heights did not only attract the sick. It also attracted the healthy and the hopeful. They came seeking greater opportunities for the expansion of their material and intellectual activities. There was a proportionally high influx of artists, writers, musicians, and a mixture of intellectuals drawn to the humming life of Boyle Heights. Brooklyn Avenue was its main street. Its restaurants, cafés, meeting halls, and the crowded boulevard reflected the vitality of New York's East Broadway. Here, as on the East Side of New York, one could hear Russian, Yiddish, German, Hebrew, Polish, and some English, which quickly and inevitably replaced all other spoken tongues in the Jewish quarters.

In our new cultural community center, English and Hebrew were the predominant languages. However, for the young generation I tried to preserve a knowledge of the Yiddish language and literature by inviting the well-known Jewish playwright, Peretz Hirschbein, to deliver a series of lectures; Noach Nachbush and other noted artists from the Vilna Troupe staged some of its best Yiddish plays. This, and the literary evenings which I initiated, were greatly appreciated by the Yiddish groups. Nonetheless, everyone in the community was aware that I was primarily committed to the building of a Hebrew cultural center with emphasis on the Hebrew language.

Soon after I assumed my post as principal and director of the center and school, I induced four of the best available Hebrew teachers in America to join our staff. They came from all over the United States, from New York, and as far as Seattle, Washington. Together we succeeded in forming an excellent team of teachers, which soon doubled in number. Students flocked to our school from all parts of Los Angeles. The sonorous cadences of the modern Hebrew language reverberated through all the classrooms and corridors of the building. For the first time in the history of California, Hebrew became what Ernst Renan, the French writer, said of it: "A quiver full of steel arrows, a cable with strong coils, a trumpet of brass crashing through the air with two or three sharp notes."

Since my administrative duties were shared by my colleagues, and the assistant social director was in charge of club activities, I was able to devote time to teaching. I conducted a course of study, in English, for young adults on the ancient history, archeology, and civilization of the Jewish people.

Often there was little age difference between my students and myself. This seemed to increase rather than diminish our mutual respect and attachment.

From my readings of the ancient teachers I had learned that peace of mind is often dependent on the amount of solitude at one's disposal. Some people can carry their solitude wherever they are, and if they find themselves in the presence of oppressive or unfeeling company, the inner solitude preserves their equilibrium.

After three unperturbed years, I began to feel some ripples of dissatisfaction with my work. We had an incident involving a teacher whose outspoken, radical views created some gossip, even though he expressed them outside of the school precincts. Some members of the board wanted to take the teacher to task, and for the first time, I was unwittingly drawn into unpleasant discussions and arguments with board members. The incident left me with a sour taste and undermined my enthusiasm.

Somehow, word got around that I was chafing in my present job. Dr. Edgar F. Magnin, a leading Reform rabbi in Los Angeles, had been approached by a film producer who was looking for a historical advisor on a new production. The job would last about a year and a half, said Dr. Magnin when he called me in as a likely candidate. I welcomed the opportunity. The proposed movie was *King of Kings*, which turned out to be the most popular film of all time. Its producer and director was the world-famous Cecil B. DeMille.

IV
HOLLYWOOD

I was interviewed by one of the heads of the studio and then ushered into Mr. DeMille's office. Mr. DeMille seemed a little taken aback to see a young, unscholarly-looking person like myself. Because he was pressed for time, he suggested that I dine with him that evening at his home above Griffith Park.

My conversation with Mr. DeMille worried me. I knew that some of the ablest directors did not achieve their goals, no matter how lavish their productions. This was especially true in the creation of historical films or those about religious personalities.

The filming of the life and teachings of Jesus presented some grave problems. In both my study of the Bible and in the classes I taught, I had included a fair amount of reading from the New Testament. My knowledge, though limited, was augmented by Dr. Joseph Klausner's book, *Jesus the Nazarene*, by the writings of Josephus, and the works of some liberal Christian scholars. In these readings Jesus was not presented from a fundamentalist point of view, certainly not as he appears to most devout Christians. How would I be able to reconcile my views with the literal New Testament scenario?

An even more disturbing problem, however, was how I could possibly participate in making a film that might include some of the prejudices in the New Testament references to Jews, especially the Pharisees. It is true that for me Jesus was one of the great Jewish prophets. His teachings are in the spirit of the noblest writings of our people. Jesus was born, lived, and died a Jew. His doctrines, if accepted and followed, could change the nature of mankind. I had no doubt that bringing them to the attention of people through any medium would be a blessing.

On the other hand, I also knew too well how the teachings of Jesus and his disciples had been distorted to justify the murder of Jewish men, women, and children in vicious pogroms. The inflamed cry of ''Christ killers'' echoed and re-echoed in all the lands of Christendom. It had led to the extermination of whole Jewish communities throughout the world at the hands of the Crusaders.

These were the doubts and troublesome questions I brought with me to Cecil B. DeMille's hilltop mansion, where I was warmly received by Mr. DeMille's graceful and charming wife.

Mr. DeMille was much more relaxed than he had been in the morning. During dinner our conversation focused on some of the Biblical themes closest to my heart. I told Mr. and Mrs. DeMille of the years I had spent in teaching Jeremiah and the other prophets. DeMille asked me questions and urged me to talk frankly and freely. He surprised me with his knowledge of the Bible. He was the first non-Jewish layman I had ever met with a genuine love of the Book that is so little understood. His was the knowledge of an uncompromising believer.

After allowing me to speak candidly of my doubts and reservations, DeMille began by assuaging my fears regarding the possible negative consequences of his magnum opus. He assured me that he knew as well as I how the New Testament had been abused by men without conscience or scruple to instill hatred instead of love. He protested that he knew how my people had suffered throughout the generations from a false and criminal interpretation of the holy words. That was the very reason, he told me, that he embarked on this greatest project of his life. "You know, of course," he said, "that my mother was Jewish." I later learned that she converted to Christianity when she was a young girl.

"Let me assure you," he told me, "that I feel the way you do. That is precisely why I want you to be associated with the making of *King of Kings*." It seems that he needed and expected of me more than the technical help I could give to the department heads. He wanted my help in understanding the deep meaning of the Hebrew Biblical words used to convey the thoughts of Jesus and his disciples. He mentioned that Dr. Magnin had told him I had a thorough grasp of the language in which Jesus and his disciples had prayed, and that I also knew the language they spoke, Aramaic. He wanted to get to the source of the times in which the Savior lived. He said he wanted me by his side all the time to observe everything and make all the helpful suggestions I could. "Even if we disagree," he said, "I feel confident that we will get along."

I believed these were honest words. I was reassured and greatly relieved.

When I appeared the next day on the lot at the DeMille Studios, nearly everyone I met knew that I had had dinner on "The Hill" the previous night. Every actor or assistant director wished for no more than that. For DeMille's associates a private dinner at DeMille's home meant that they had "arrived," that they were needed, not just tolerated. All doors swung open for me.

After being given a chance to familiarize myself with the script and the many preparations, I was consulted on the research, set designing, costume, makeup, casting, and other aspects of the film. "What did the top of a stove look like in the first century?" was one of the questions. "What was the thickness of the loaves of bread?" was another. Because one print of the film was to be made experimentally in color, the hairdresser wanted to know if the

Jews who followed Jesus had red beards. DeMille asked me about the color of the oil that Mary Magdalene used in anointing the feet of Jesus.

My first impulse was to answer in Yiddish "*Zol ich visen fun meine tsores,*" May I not know of my woes. Searching for the answers to some of these questions robbed me of many hours of sleep. A hesitant reply or no reply at all could be the cause of costly delays. DeMille would hold up the shooting of a scene until all sets, costumes, and utensils were historically and archeologically accurate.

Before I came to work on the picture, the chief set designer had ordered an expensive staff for the High Priest. Copying the staff of the Greek Orthodox archbishop, which had a cross on it, he made the staff of the Jewish High Priest with a beautiful, bejewelled Star of David. When I pointed out to DeMille that the Star of David was not used in that way, there was a terrible argument between DeMille and the art department, followed by confusion for a half-hour with all the cameramen, actors, and lighting technicians impatiently waiting to start.

For the making of a good film, imagination is required above knowledge or experience. This is especially true in the making of films depicting great events of the past. I was pleased to learn that it was not really my knowledge of the period in which Jesus lived but my imagination that DeMille was after.

When asked about this or that cloak, beard, set, walk, gesture, parable, or law, I most often answered that "I imagined" it was so and so. How can a scholar be sure about everything that happened 2,000 years ago? Even the most reliable books and chronicles of the period are prone to human error.

Film, which is subjective art at its best, can only use objective facts imaginatively. This was the greatness of D.W. Griffith in *The Birth of a Nation*. He used history as he imagined it to be.

While DeMille was not a D.W. Griffith, he was quick in the use of his imagination. His imagination in providing the masses with films they loved was extended to other areas, such as banking and real estate. In a short time he became a wealthy man.

There were many who were in awe of DeMille and many who were afraid of him. I learned to know his qualities and to understand his weaknesses. He was generous, stubborn, and shrewd. He could be humble with those he loved and respected, and just as arrogant and merciless with those who tried to outsmart him.

DeMille once turned to me and pointed to an assistant director. "You see him and those around him?" he said. "They are men without imagination. Goddamn it, how can I stand them?" he shouted.

DeMille was ruthless toward those who didn't live up to his expectations. One of the men who worked with him for years as a set designer presented a drawing to DeMille that lacked "all imagination." "Is this your final design?" DeMille growled. When the frightened designer answered in the affirmative, DeMille turned to him in fury, saying, "You're Goddamn right, it is your final design. You're fired!"

One day, after a few weeks on the lot, heavily laden with books and scripts, I ran into Julia Faye, who was the closest woman to DeMille, next to his wife. She told me that DeMille had said that he likes me. In Hollywood, to be "liked" was a rare phenomenon. Hollywood was an unusual world, in which scarcely anyone liked anyone else. Nowhere did I see people smile at each other as much as on the sets, locations, or the drugstore on Sunset Boulevard. They always said the most complimentary things to each othere. "You are great, wonderful, terrific. What you did was marvelous, just marvelous!" "Marvelous" was the word used most frequently. Anyone with eyes to see and ears to hear couldn't escape the sad truth that very rarely was there any sincerity in the effusive praise.

Words were used for effect or to hide a total obsession with oneself, one's career, and one's success. Each person was either consciously or unconsciously looked on as a means to advance one's ambitions. It wasn't that the members of that make-believe world couldn't like and love and give of themselves unstintingly, like anyone else. But to do so, people have to be free of pressures, ambitions, harassments, and obsessions.

There were several members of the cast with whom I formed close relationships. The many privileged hours I spent with Rudolph Schildkraut were like spending time in the company of a sage. Schildkraut, who was born in Vienna, was the most acclaimed character actor in Germany before he left for the United States. Then Hollywood discovered him and gave him leading roles in some of the outstanding silent films. DeMille could not have picked a greater actor to play the difficult role of Caiaphus, the High Priest. In the New Testament Caiaphus is portrayed as a bigoted, uncompromising foe of Jesus. Rudolph Schildkraut's son, Joseph, a star of stage and screen, was selected to play the part of Judas Iscariot. Two Jews were chosen for the most heinous roles of the Gospel!

This caused me great concern. Why did Jesus have to be played by a blond, Nordic-looking actor? Why were the Jewish Galilean disciples all gentile-looking actors, while Caiaphus, Judas, and the tax collector were all "Jews"? I shared my anxiety with Rudolph Schildkraut. He thought it was ironic that the casting was done contrary to the letter and spirit of the New Testament, which refers to the founders of Christianity as Jews. Who could have been more Jewish than Jesus, who preached in synagogues, was circumcised in the Temple, and fulfilled the words of the Prophets? No one could have calmed me more than Schildkraut with his philosophic outlook, sagacity, and understanding. He said he had studied the part of Caiaphus as thoroughly as he had studied the character of Shylock, which he had played many times. He felt that what mattered even more than the written words was the interpretation. He consoled me by saying that another actor might have played Caiaphus more viciously than he, though he was aware that no matter how he played Caiaphus, it would not be to the liking of some of our people. He assured me he would do all he could and he believed that DeMille was also making the utmost efforts to mitigate some bad impressions. "But who knows what will happen in the cutting room?" he shrugged.

Catalina Island, where we went on location, was twenty-three miles from the coast of southern California. It was owned by Wrigley of chewing-gum fame. Except for a small hotel used by DeMille's staff, it had only a few insignificant buildings. We all lived in tents close to the ocean, where many of us spent our free time fishing, swimming, and surfing. There was no drinking on location and some of the habitual frivolities of the actors were forbidden. DeMille wanted to observe a purity in keeping with the subject of the film. As additional entertainment for the actors, DeMille had suggested the reading of the Bible. Most of the people hadn't opened a Bible since school days. With this new preoccupation, the actors besieged me for answers to all sorts of questions.

As the second half of the filming of *King of Kings* progressed, the mood of its participants changed. The "Bye-Bye Blackbird" tune, continuously played by a quartet hired by DeMille, seemed to have lost its colorful overtone. Seriousness and gloom replaced the gaiety which had prevailed during the first month of shooting.

"Every ascension must have a descension" is a refrain from one of the Cabbalistic chants. Among some of the reasons for the change was DeMille's unbounded enthusiasm and his projection of vast expenditures, which went way beyond the budget. Never before were there such costly sets as the Praetorium of Jerusalem with its Corinthian columns, or the Holy Temple with the Nicanor gate. The bankers backing the film were alarmed. DeMille's previous film, *The Volga Boatmen*, had been a financial failure and *King of Kings* could not assure them of a successful box office. The backers demanded drastic cuts in all expenditures and threatened to start foreclosure proceedings. Salaries were cut and workdays were extended to the late hours of the night.

In spite of the pressures, DeMille retained his calm. He wouldn't allow anything to daunt his spirit or weaken his resolve to complete the undertaking. Never before had I found DeMille impatient with me, although at times I sensed I was being a nuisance. But now when I begged him to cut a small part in one scene, he was annoyed. "Don't ask me to cut scenes," he snapped, "talk to Jeannie MacPherson about any changes." From past experience I knew that talking to MacPherson, who was writing the script, was like talking to the wall.

I was never as free in her presence as I was in DeMille's, but the matter at hand was crucial and so I went to see her. The scene I wanted her to eliminate was that of Pilate washing his hands free of the guilt of Jesus' crucifixion. Since some of the Gospels omit any mention of Pilate washing his hands, I didn't think it would be difficult for Miss MacPherson to omit it. This was especially important because one of Mr. DeMille's motivations in making the film was to prove that Pilate and the Romans had crucified Jesus. Not the Jews! Without listening to my reasoning, she retorted, "Don't you know that the washing of the hands by Pilate is in the Bible?" "Yes," I repeated, "but it is not in the spirit of the Bible and all historical facts. Here, let me read you what Klausner says about Pilate, and certainly, there is no greater authority than Flavius Josephus, who lived in the first century and who said that Pilate was a cruel 'man of blood.' " I repeated "man of blood, who crucified people at the blink of an eye." Irritated, she turned on me. "You always keep asking me to believe and write the way *your* scholars did," she said, "but I have told you many times that I can only rely on the New Testament and the beliefs of millions of Christians."

There was nothing more I could say. I felt that after the tone and nature of my conversation with MacPherson, I could never work with the woman again. When the day's shooting was at an end, I told DeMille what had happened and asked him to release me from my job. He begged me gently not to be impetuous, to go home, to get a good night's sleep, and then to see him again in the morning.

I didn't have a good night's sleep, nor did I go to teach my late class that evening at the John Kahn Institute. Instead, I went to see Dr. Edgar Magnin and J. J. Lieberman of the B'nai Brith. They were concerned on hearing what I had to say, but after going over all the pros and cons, each one of them asked me to stay on the job for as long as DeMille would tolerate it.

The next morning DeMille asked me to sit down next to his director's chair while preparations for shooting were underway. He repeated some of the assurances he had made before and he promised to meet me part of the way insofar as it was in his power to do so. I believed him. I don't think he wanted to keep me out of calculated shrewdness or because he wished to avoid a scandal, as one of the papers subsequently indicated.

The next few days were devoted to the filming of Jesus and the woman taken in adultery. The role of the adultress was assigned to Viola Louie, a pretty actress with limited talent. She was the niece of Jacob P. Adler, one of the greatest actors on the Yiddish stage. Again, I thought to myself, even for the part of a whore they had to pick a nice, Jewish girl.

Viola had very little experience in acting before the cameras. She was frightened of DeMille, and his old style of directing was no help to her. The more DeMille exerted himself to make the poor girl feel her part, the more paralyzed she became. Hours passed. DeMille used every one of his tricks, including a slap on the face to make her cry, and the results were worse and worse. Looking on Viola as my *landsman* (compatriot), he asked me to talk to her and try to explain what was wanted.

I patted her arm. I told her how much I admired her uncle, how I had watched him act in the Second Avenue Theatre from the second balcony for ten cents. The ten cents brought some light into her eyes. DeMille saw it and asked me to direct the scene. The next day, when we saw the rushes, we were all amazed and delighted by Viola's good performance.

DeMille was not a great director but he was very inventive. He strove for big things. One of his most important contributions to the making of films lay in the creation of atmosphere through lighting. I watched him work for many hours with Pev Marley, the cameraman, to extract the maximal use of light. He played with it endlessly until he obtained the exact effect he wanted. Many museum curators throughout the world are notorious for the poor lighting of their finest treasures. They could have learned a great deal from DeMille. His lighting of the large set for the crucifixion was the only thing that inspired me in this scene. I missed the pathos and depth of the Aramaic words, which I taught H. B. Warner to pronounce when he was all alone on the cross, "Eli, Eli, lama savaktani?" (My God, my God, why hast Thou forsaken me?) I consider these the most stirring words in the martyrdom of the Jewish people. But DeMille did not consult me on the elaborate, extravagant scene, crowded with people who distracted from the drama of the tragic end of a great soul.

In spite of all the denunciations implicit in the roles of the actors, who were accused in the film of having sold their souls for thirty shekels of silver, it was the Jewish actors who gave the most convincing performances. In the end their parts were mercilessly mutilated in the cutting room. The betrayal of Jesus by Judas, played by Joseph Schildkraut, was handled expertly. Like his father, he knew how to ennoble the miserable part assigned to him. Rudolph Schildkraut as Caiaphus was unable to make use of his widsom and artistic skill. While Joseph was successful, Rudolph failed. Only once was he able to rise to greatness when he took upon himself the blame for the death of Jesus. Albert Perry wrote in *The Jewish Tribune* that "Schildkraut's original fair and artistic portrayal was most brazenly crippled and perverted by treacherous camera tricks and by cutting and titling efforts of DeMille's technicians." *The Jewish Tribune* also quoted me as saying:

> Officials reiterated that I would be consulted when the picture was assembled and cut so that objectionable features would be eliminated. But no Jew was involved in the work of assembling, cutting, and titling of the picture.

Geneviève Harris in *The Eagle Magazine* wrote: "J. M. Alkow, an authority on Jewish history, brought the wealth of his technical knowledge of ancient Judea." She did not say, however, how it was used or how much of it was used. Not until the bitter end did I learn how little remained of my contribution.

Of over one million feet of film, there emerged only 1,400 feet in the final print. There were many people who had a final say on what was to be included, among them some fundamentalist ministers and priests. Some lovely scenes of the shore of Galilee and of the Holy City and its Jewish residents disappeared in the cutting room. My contribution to the scenes in the synagogues, where Jesus appeared as a Jewish teacher, was cut and so was a great deal of the everyday life of the Godfearing people of the country. On the other hand, most of the miracles were left untouched by the editors and cutters.

After viewing the completed version, I failed to see much of what I had labored on so assiduously. Yet, somehow I had expected all this, and accepted it philosophically. Nevertheless, I was sorry that many of the scenes of Jewish and historical interest were mutilated.

Gardner W. Gregg's view, appearing in *The Motion Picture Director*, was worlds apart from what I saw and felt:

> The work begun by da Vinci, Raphael, Rembrandt, Rubens is being carried on in the *King of Kings*. We are enabled to get a clear conception of Christ and his teachings untrammeled by creed or dogma.

The *King of Kings* touched on the most sensitive nerve in the Jewish community. Some rabbis and leading laymen raised a roar of protest against what they believed the film had depicted and the injurious effects it would have throughout the world. Rabbi Louis I. Newman of San Francisco's Temple Emanuel led the avalanche of protests and criticism on a nationwide scope. He thundered from his pulpit and the press:

> I accuse Cecil B. DeMille and his minions of having planned and promoted through the educational medium of the motion picture, a work offensive to Christian and Jew alike, misrepresenting the personality and teachings of Jesus and maligning the religion of Judaism and its adherents. I accuse Jeannie MacPherson, the scenario writer, of having deliberately twisted out of character the story of the New Testament.... I accuse those rabbis in and about Los Angeles who aided DeMille in the details of the picture.

Referring to Rudolph and Joseph Schildkraut, he accused them of "having betrayed the honor and safety of the Jewish people." He accused the Anti-Defamation Committee of B'nai Brith, Lodge Number 4, of having failed to take the necessary steps to prevent the filming of *King of Kings*. In listing all the participants, Jewish and gentile, he also included my name, misspelled as Jacob M. Alcow.

This wholesale accusation was countered by Judge Isidore M. Golden, chairman of the Anti-Defamation League of the Pacific Coast, who wrote:

> Rabbi Newman's articles, 'I accuse,' are well captioned. He does, indeed, with wholesale abandon accuse everyone, eliminating himself, of course, and one or two others from his blanket indictment. He accuses DeMille, MacPherson, the Schildkrauts, Rabbi Edgar F. Magnin, Henry Radlin, Ernest Trattner, Jacob M. Alkow, and others in and about Los Angeles and numerous Christian ministers (also unnamed) who are alleged to have made anti-Jewish capital out of the picture. Whatever may be our opinion concerning the spectacle of one rabbi publicly castigating other rabbis and other Jews, we prefer to be silent.

Another noted rabbi from the north, Rudolph J. Coffee, was somewhat milder in his criticism and a little more objective. He said:

> The new DeMille Jesus is such a pathetic figure, so alone among a lot of Jewish hoodlums who could not stand the strain of a gentleman in their midst. Yes, DeMille would have us believe that the blond, Nordic, marcelled and carefully manicured Jesus was the only Jewish gentleman in his era. Every student of history knows that Jesus was born a Jew, lived a genuinely Jewish life, preached reform Jewish doctrines and died a Jew. Yet DeMille carefully keeps such facts from being screened. DeMille Rasputinized Caiaphus into a perfect, dime-novel villain. Never for one moment does he allow anyone to forget that Caiaphus is a Jew. The DeMille Gospel yells prejudice in reel after reel.

Regardless of the merits or demerits of what most vociferous anti-DeMille rabbis claimed, and true as some of their allegations may be, didn't they know what the New Testament has to say? What truth was there in the allegation that "The motion picture is offensive to Christian and Jew alike?" Understandably, the film could be offensive to Jews, who are very sensitive to the repercussions of many of the New Testament references. But it was in no way offensive to the multitude of Christians who accept every word of the New Testament as the word of God.

King of Kings became the most popular film in Christendom. It ran continuously for over fifty years. In an article in *The Los Angeles Times* of March 29, 1969, Dan Thrapp, the religious editor wrote:

> The most popular motion picture of all time is not *Gone with the Wind* or *The Sound of Music* or even *Birth of a Nation*, but a silent film of the career of an unpretentious carpenter made more than 40 years ago. *King of Kings* has been seen by multitudes. Billy Graham estimates their number at two billion. Others say only a mere eight hundred million. Missionaries have screened it for tribes far up the Amazon and in the depths of the Congo. H. B. Warner played Christ so well that one minister told him, "Every time I think of Jesus of Nazareth I see your face."

In all of the fifty years of the showing of *King of Kings* from one end of the world to another, no one has said what would have happened had the film been made by anyone other than Cecil B. DeMille. D. W. Griffith's *Birth of a Nation* was a great artistic triumph, yet Oswald Garrison Villard of *the Nation* said, "*Birth of a Nation* is a deliberate attempt to humiliate ten million American citizens." Griffith's film was the direct cause of race riots in Boston and other abolitionist cities. Both blacks and whites attacked it. A storm of protest spread throughout the south.

In spite of the dire warnings of the rabbis, nothing of this sort happened as a result of the showing of *King of Kings*. With all of its faults from an artistic and historical viewpoint, it has proven itself to be quite inoffensive as far as Jews are concerned. The Jews in the film were regarded by some viewers as simply the "bad guys" like the "bad guys and good guys" in a Western film.

With all my respect for the greatest part of the New Testament, most especially that of the Sermon on the Mount, there are some parts of the New Testament that are more damaging than those included in its pictorial version. Having lived with all of it for two thousand years, we Jews were slowly approaching a new era, a new promise of a better understanding. The church, with its ecumenical councils and pronouncements of brotherly love, has made great strides in eliminating the collective blame that the Jews killed the "Messiah." The sermons broadcast over the radio and television by Graham and a multitude of preachers nearly all stress the noble teachings of Jesus and his exemplary Jewish life, rather than the other aspects which had so disturbed me.

V
DECISION

A year's hard labor had ended. Before I could draw up a balance sheet of my achievements and failures, I was invited to return to my former post as principal and director of the Modern Center in Boyle Heights. I was also allowed to continue as director of the John Kahn Institute for Adult Studies.

Although this work was most gratifying, it wasn't quite as rewarding as it had been before I joined DeMille. Some of my former brilliant students had moved to the west side of the city, joining the mini-migration that occurred at the time. Transportation was a problem. Moreover there was a serious rift between the two best teachers in the school, which affected their work. While both were good friends and honorable men, the lovely, childless wife of the older teacher had fallen in love with the younger teacher.

At this time my youthful dreams of the Holy Land returned in full force. Ironically, it was *King of Kings* that rekindled my Zionist zeal. Pondering over the reconstruction of life in Palestine two thousand years ago, I felt a yearning to be a part of twentieth-century Palestine. I decided that now was my chance to make the break and become a pioneer in the Land.

In the early spring of 1929 I resigned from all my jobs. The greatest part of what I had earned throughout the years was invested in stocks and bonds, but I had also funneled a large amount of savings into my art collection.

I had chosen a fortunate time to collect paintings. At the end of World War I, a new breed of immigrant introduced art objects to the American market, which was more affluent than the one in Europe. With my passion for art, born the day I first entered the Metropolitan Museum, I began to buy works that caught my eye and which I could afford.

When an opportunity arose for the purchase of a painting of the Archangel Michael by an unknown seventeenth-century Italian painter, possibly Giordano Lucca, I reduced my total savings from $1,300 to $200. I had to postpone a vacation I was planning, but it didn't matter. With my earnings from the DeMille Studios, I bought a few Impressionist works as well as some American paintings. I also acquired my first Chinese porcelain, which set me on a new course in art.

An absorption in art can overcome self-absorption. With the walls of my one-bedroom apartment covered with pictures, and with my books at my side, I never felt lonely. Throughout my life I agreed with George Bernard Shaw, who said: "Without art the crudeness of reality would make the world unbearable." Art soothed and comforted me during many trying years.

Sailing for Palestine posed the question of where and with whom I could leave my paintings and books. The San Diego Museum agreed to accept the Archangel Michael on a two-year loan. Finally I decided to place the other paintings and books in the spare room of my parents' house. My father knew their value and I could find no better guardian.

Two years earlier my parents had decided to join their children and had bought a house in Los Angeles. The plum, peach, and fig garden in their backyard added to their peaceful life, which was further enriched by my father's interest in history and frequent family visits. My brother Harry and I—the only ones still unmarried—always joined our parents for the Sabbath meal on Friday nights.

No one close to me seemed to approve of my decision to leave Los Angeles for the remote shores of *Eretz Yisrael*. My oldest brother, Sam, who was a scholar and a rabbi without a pulpit, was visibly upset by my throwing up a "beautiful career" for adventures in the "barren wasteland of Palestine." When he argued that a rolling stone gathers no moss, I reminded him of what the rabbis said of "evven she'ain la hofchin," i.e., a stone that no one bothers to turn over. Sam and I had very little in common. I liked him and thought him a good man, but I was not very receptive to his solicitations. He would phone me early in the morning to remind me to take vitamin pills and breathe deeply.

My younger brother, Harry, who was an unsuccessful lawyer, was not unduly upset about my leaving. What worried him was finding a new source for loans.

My sister Sarah was very sad. I had grown up with Sarah, and when I was a child she helped me and understood me more than anyone else.

"Why do you want to go?" she asked. "Why not get married? Whatever can you find in that unpopulated country?" As a settled sister with two children, she couldn't seem to understand the motivations of my restless soul.

There was only one person who enthusiastically supported me in my resolve to go to Palestine. That was my sister Libby. She and I were the only Zionists in the family.

My mother knew that I did what I did because I had to, and that it was best for me; for my father, my escapades were a reflection of the vagaries of his own life.

Cutting myself off from a beloved city proved more difficult than I had anticipated. My ties to Los Angeles had grown with the years. I was a founder of the Hebrew Cultural Society and on the inner committee of the Hollywood

Art League. At our meetings, happily without minutes or points of order, we listened to lectures and reports on all aspects of literature, theatre, art, and dance.

When I took leave of my city of eight years, which had grown so rapidly and powerfully, I had no idea that the Great Depression would change it so disastrously in less than a year.

On my arrival in New York I was met by my brother Izzie, and his wife, Minnie. By Izzie's standards, Minnie was an educated woman because she had a high school diploma. After work his main passion centered on the ballroom floor. Our house was filled with his dance hall trophies, for which I had very little esteem. Not until many years later did I discover the great pleasure in social dancing.

In spite of our different outlooks, he was the only one capable of diverting me from my studies. He did it with his pure white Anderson convertible, which was the sensation of our block. Though I was six years younger than Izzie, I used to join him and his friends on trips to the Catskill Mountains. He never finished school, but took courses at night in the city's adult education program. He said he wasn't worried about my going away. "Nothing will hold you back from the U.S.A.!" he confidently assured me, wrapping his big arm around my shoulders.

On the night of my departure Izzie, Minnie, and her jolly brother-in-law, Abe Funt, a successful builder, accompanied me to my stateroom on the *Berengaria*. It was scheduled to sail at midnight for England, my first stop on the long trek to Palestine.

The *Berengaria*'s hoarse whistle blew a blast to wake the dead. The boat pulled out from the pier. Standing on the deck against the rail, I waved good-bye to Izzie, Minnie, and Abe Funt. In my mind I was eagerly looking forward, not backward, to my new life ahead.

VI
ON THE WAY TO PALESTINE

In London I was met by Uncle Berel, my mother's youngest brother. He had been en route to America when he was barely seventeen and had managed to get as far as London, where he took a job to raise the money for a steamship ticket to New York. Within a short time he began to prosper. He married, raised a family of eight children, and never left England. Uncle Berel was an attractive, cultured, self-educated gentleman, who wore a beard resembling that of his esteemed sovereign, King George V, and he was a dedicated Zionist.

I spent more time in London than I had planned. Therefore, I made very few stopovers on the way to Brindisi at the southernmost tip of Italy, where I was to take the boat for Palestine. Within two days after my arrival at the small, primitive port, I found accommodation on an Italian vessel in a second-class cabin for two. The day before we sailed I met my roommate on the dock.

He was a medical student in Rome, on his way home to visit his parents in Tel Aviv, and he turned my wait for the boat into a pleasant experience. His native Hebrew, pronounced in an Oriental, Sephardic accent, regaled my ears. For years I had yearned to hear the authentic inflections and rhythms of the language that was closest to the ancient speech of rabbinic sages. I would always awake before my friend, and when I said to him, "*Tsafra tova,*" good morning, in my Ashkenazic accent, he came to life in a burst of laughter.

There was a large group of young men and women from Poland, Lithuania, and Rumania, who, like myself, waited in the port two days for the arrival of the ship which was to take them to the Promised Land. The Hebrew they spoke was very poor, and their pronunciation was even worse. Though I would ask them to talk to me in Yiddish, they never complied. They were on their way to a new land, a new life, and a new destiny. Their native Polish or Yiddish gave way to the language of their future.

For the *halutzim*, the pioneers, as well as for people like myself who were deeply affected by the miracle of the rebirth of a language dormant for 2,000 years, Hebrew was not a means to an end. It was not a means to reach the God of the Patriarchs. Hebrew was an end in itself. Chaim Bialik once said that Hebrew warms the heart for the disparate elements of Jewry and leads to the redemption of its soul. The Chief Rabbi of Palestine, Abraham Isaac Kook, aroused the ire of the extreme orthodox, who felt that Hebrew is desecrated through everyday use and should remain a language of prayer and study, when he observed that "Conversation in the sacred tongue is bound to satisfy the soul of the speaker."

Throughout the diaspora, said the noted Zionist writer Chaim Greenberg, the Jew walked through a world of darkness carrying a lantern in his hand; the Jew was the greatest spiritual adventurer and antifetishist in human history. But now the *galut* Jew was living with a lantern whose light had dimmed. Hence the crisis of self-alienation, the uprootedness, and the search for roots.

Looking at a young *halutz*, I saw the same age-old lantern in his hand. More than many of the youths of the diaspora, he was ready and able to fulfill the yearning for roots. I saw the dedication and overpowering will for redemption. It was a kind of mystique that I had only seen before in the printed word of the Bible. From these young people I began to learn anew the Jewish longing for self-realization. It was personal, national, and universal. Later on, in their hard struggles on the barren soil of their homeland, it also became economic, cultural, and spiritual.

"Ah, well it is," said the Hebrew poet Uri Zvi Greenberg, "that we have forsaken Europe and all the splendors and have become comrades to all the barefoot, who burn in fever and whisper love to the sands and stones of Canaan."

Resisting the fleshpots as well as the pleas, the tears, and the inertia of their parents, they turned their backs on Europe and directed their gaze toward the bright sun of the east.

I often exchanged books with my young fellow travelers. One of the books was by a late Hebrew writer whom I had not read. His name was Brenner and he had been murdered by Arabs outside of Jaffa. "Only those whose foundations of life are in their hands," wrote Brenner, "are the salt of the earth. They are the ones who make our people an *am segulah*, a chosen people." For Brenner, Martin Buber, and the young pioneers, the concept of *am segulah* did not denote a sense of superiority but a people with a sense of destiny.

Unlike the parents they left behind, these young immigrants paid little stock to the oft-repeated prayer of "Thou hast chosen us." No one, they believed in their rebellious mood, can choose anyone. It is up to you to choose yourself for a cause you deem worthy.

"If," says Martin Buber, "you boast of being chosen instead of living up to it, if you turn the chosenness into a static object instead of obeying it as a commandment, you will forfeit it."

My young friends knew very little of the philosophy of Judaism, but none was imbued with its spirit more than they.

I was carried away by a new kind of religious frenzy. It was without psalms or prayers but I felt that its components had withstood the fire of the ages. We formed circles and swayed and danced to tunes that I heard for the first time.

Our behavior may have seemed incomprehensible to the older people aboard who were going to the Holy Land with altogether different expectations, fulfilling a lifelong wish to be buried in the sacred soil of their faith.

On the eve of the Sabbath, I joined the old men in their prayers. Many years had passed since I had attended a strictly Orthodox service, but here on deck, as the sun set into the sea, accompanied by the roar of the waves, welcoming the Sabbath bride produced an ambience of exaltation. A rabbi once said that in prayer we "shift the center of living from self-consciousness to self-surrender." I surrendered myself completely.

With the rise of the sun on the Sabbath, I did not say good morning to my companion. I arose before he could ask where I was going so early. I climbed up to the corner of the deck, where I could already hear the old men's voices chanting, "How goodly are thy tents, Jacob, and thy dwelling places, O Israel."

After the services, as I stood on the lower deck, something made me look up toward the deck of the first-class passengers. There stood a young lady with a gentleman, staring at me. When our eyes met, the young lady called to me and asked if I, too, was a pioneer. I answered that I hoped to be one and she laughed. She said it was difficult to carry on a conversation from such a long distance and invited me to come up to the first-class compartments.

Nellie was a dancer from New Jersey. She and her brother-in-law were on the way to meet her sister in Jerusalem. We spoke about some of the people from New York we both knew. One of these was Louis Lipsky, president of the Zionist Organization of America, who had received me in his office when I was not yet quite sixteen and encouraged me to be the "Zionist boy orator" on the street corners of the East Side and Williamsburgh.

While we were standing alongside the rail, an elegant gentleman approached us. He had seen Nellie practicing on the upper deck and he asked her brother-in-law if Nellie would dance at the evening program. Nellie agreed and invited me to be present. I asked her if my roommate, Yechiel, could come too, and she graciously extended the invitation to both of us.

Before parting for dinner, Nellie filled a valise with fruit, cheese, salami, white bread, and a bottle of wine. She had collected it during the day for my friends in steerage. Her gifts of food continued for the balance of the trip to Haifa.

I returned to third class and enthusiastically told Yechiel of Nellie's invitation. To my surprise, Yechiel did not want to join me. He thought it demeaning to seek acceptance by the privileged class. I told him angrily that it was unworthy of him to be so sensitive and susceptible to meaningless, social trivialities. That seemed to convince him. He softened up and jumped three stairs at a time until he reached the top deck ahead of me.

Nellie was talking to the elegant British gentleman when we found her. As she introduced Keith Roach to Yechiel, I felt his body stiffen.

"Do you know who this man is?" Yechiel asked me under his breath.

"Yes," I answered, "I heard he was the British governor of Jerusalem."

"You are right," he said, "this man is the bloody governor of Jerusalem. He is like the Roman Pontius Pilate, whom you told me about." I said nothing, and we watched Nellie dance beautifully before an appreciative audience.

Nellie asked if she might join us on the next day's excursion. The boat was docking in Piraeus and we would spend the day in Greece.

During our trip from Piraeus to Athens I related to my friends how, like Judea, the treasures of Greece were scattered throughout the world. The Winged Victory of Samothrace graces the steps of the main entrance hall of the Louvre; the Lacoon Group is in the Vatican Museum; even the Metropolitan and Boston Museums have preserved the classical heritage of the Greeks. The British ambassador, Lord Elgin, who removed twelve marble statues and over a hundred friezes from the Acropolis in 1800, took them to the British Museum. There, they would be safer than in Athens, he claimed. While Lord Elgin's motives may have been sincere, the treasures remain "safe" to this day in British hands. For a hundred years the Greek people have been demanding the return of the beautiful Elgin Marbles.

"That's just like the British," was Yechiel's comment. "What they take they never return."

"This is true of the British Empire," I added, "but it is not true of the British people. From my visit in England I found the English to be the opposite of their Imperial government."

We visited the Acropolis Museum and then the Athens Museum. Yechiel and Nellie learned of the great cultural influences of Greek thought and art on Judea. I told them of Philo, the Jewish philosopher who drew his inspiration from Plato, and how Maimonides and many sages for generations after were influenced by Aristotle.

When we returned to the boat, exhausted from sightseeing, Nellie retired to her cabin while Yechiel and I remained to talk with the young *halutzim*. One of them asked us to describe what we saw. Yechiel answered, "How can I describe it when there are no words to describe it?" I smiled my assent.

On the last night at sea a bishop and some priests, who were in first class, kept an all-night vigil with chants that came from old Hebraic sources. The priests, like both the old men and my young friends, were waiting for the first glow of light to appear over the Holy Land. From the first class to the steerage we were united in an outpouring of emotion for a land dear to us all.

With the earliest streak of dawn over the Carmel, my friends and I joined in a dance and sang *Anu banu artza*—welcome to the land, to build and be rebuilt.

VII
TEL AVIV

We left in a truck bound for Tel Aviv with stopovers in different settlements. I was immediately struck by the color of the land, the bright skies, and the clear atmosphere. In spite of long stretches of sand dunes and wasteland, my heart rejoiced. Like some of my fellow travelers I felt that the words of Isaiah would come to pass: "The wilderness and the dry land shall be glad, the desert shall rejoice and blossom like a crocus." Ezekiel prophesied: "And the land that was desolate shall be tilled, instead of being the desolation that it was in the sight of all who passed by."

Palestine had been neglected and abused by both its conquerors and settlers. Until the Jews returned to the land, travelers saw nothing other than the holy places and the desolation.

It was in Zichron Yaakov, our first stopover, with its suntanned workers and children, its fertile, green fields, its grapes and wine cellars, that I saw the true beginnings of the new Palestine. I saw the plowers and the planters, and it was as Ben-Amitai said, "If thou hast sown a seed, or planted a tree, have faith. It will not die. Each clod is a rock of strength to us, and every foot of soil an ageless shield."

In Zichron we ate the luscious grapes, which had just been harvested, and we drank the milk of the cows and ate fresh cheese that had never tasted better. As we drove along we saw the old Arab settlers, whose work in the fields was the same as it had been for thousands of years. I saw the young maidens, as described in the Book of Samuel, who were "coming out to draw water."

After a circuitous three-hour route, we arrived in the small, charming city of Tel Aviv. Founded about twenty-two years before on sand dunes outside the city of Jaffa, it was the first civilized oasis that delighted the eye. In its twenty-two years it had grown to a population of 40,000 people. It was bustling with life. It had four theatres, a music hall, synagogues, hotels, and a dance casino on the shore of the Mediterranean with an orchestra that played popular American and European music.

I had accepted Yechiel's invitation to stay at his home for the first two days. Busy and excited by the arrival of her only son, Yechiel's hospitable mother cooked all of his favorite dishes. Except for what we had eaten at Zichron Yaakov, we had had no food since the previous day. After lunch we adjourned for a few hours sleep.

Refreshed by the nap and the meal, I left Yechiel and his mother and set out to see the first all-Jewish metropolis of modern Palestine. I started with the Gymnasium, the high school on Herzl Street, and came in time to audit a session on Hebrew literature. When the lesson was over I introduced myself to the teacher as an American colleague. He was delighted. I was the first American-trained Hebrew teacher he had met. He invited me at once to come with him to his home for a glass of tea. On our arrival at his light and airy two-bedroom apartment, he announced to his wife that he had brought a very dear guest from America who "speaks better Hebrew than we do." His wife shared her husband's pleasure in entertaining what she called "an interesting guest." She prepared tea with some freshly baked cakes, and preserves ordinarily reserved for special occasions. An hour and a half's conversation passed too quickly. I had been invited by Yechiel's family to join them for an eight o'clock supper. Promising to return to their home for dinner, I parted from the charming couple. Little did I know at that time that three long months would pass before I would see them again.

At Yechiel's house I met his father, who was a physician and a well-read gentleman. Yechiel's only sister and her husband had come from their kibbutz to welcome him back. Another fine and festive dinner was served, and we drank a bottle of Palestine wine accompanied by hearty, lively conversation in a flowing, correct Hebrew punctuated with outbursts of laughter. Only one day in the country and I felt more at home than in my own city. Much of it had to do with the language that we shared freely. I. L. Peretz said that "For Jews, Hebrew is the only glue which holds together our scattered bones, just as it holds together the rings in the chain of time." At midnight Yechiel's mother, who knew we hadn't slept the previous night, insisted that we go to bed.

The next morning, after a breakfast of freshly baked bread and home-made yoghurt, Yechiel and I went out to see the sights and meet his friends. We went from one house to another, and in each one I saw embraces, kisses, and laughter.

We walked along Bialik Street, which was named after the living poet whose house stood on one side of the tree-shaded block, and then on to another street named after an ailing writer who was regarded as the cultural and spiritual guide of Zionism: Achad Ha'am. The month before Achad Ha'am passed away, the police had cordoned off the street so that no vehicle traffic would disturb him. It was a manifestation of love and affection not for a prince or political hero, but for a writer, theorist, and philosopher.

Continuing our walk past stores and markets and people, people of all lands and all backgrounds, we reached the large expanse of the Mediterranean, which washes the shores of Palestine. The sea is for Tel Aviv what the hills are for Jerusalem. They open the heart and the mind to distant vistas.

Finally I left Yechiel and his friends and went on alone, walking slowly. A city is like a painting. To be seen in depth it should be seen alone.

In the evening, Yechiel and I went to see a performance of the satirical theatre *Matateh*, The Broom. The first act was hilarious and I laughed all through it. As we rose to go to the lobby during the intermission, a young man approached Yechiel and greeted him warmly. They were former classmates and he asked us to join him for a few words outside.

When we reached the sidewalk, Yechiel's friend told us in a hushed voice that serious trouble was expected the next morning in Jerusalem. Could we arrange to join a caravan within one hour? Both Yechiel and I tried to explain that we had just arrived and that I had special duties as a correspondent of a paper—but it was no use. The representative of the Haganah kept repeating, "Believe me, if it were not so urgent I wouldn't ask you, but we're desperate and in need of every available man."

We returned to Yechiel's home and, when he told his mother, she cried out, "They can't do this. You just came. Tell them you'll go a week later." But even as she spoke the words, she realized that it was of no use. I packed a few summer belongings in my valise and left my winter clothes and books in Yechiel's room.

When we reached the embarkation point we found several trucks waiting. One, with benches on either side, was nearly full. The Haganah representative told me to take the seat nearest the end. Yechiel was ordered to go to another truck. We said good-bye to one another and promised to meet in Jerusalem.

The bus took off, and from where I was sitting I could see some distant houses and the hills on both sides of our poorly paved road. The clear, moonlit night brought me no relief as I listened attentively to the instructions and answered all the questions asked by our commander. I was one of the few who had little experience with firearms. My knowledge of how to handle a gun was limited to a short course I was once compelled to take at the officer's training school at college. We were told to expect planned attacks by the Arabs on Jewish areas in and around Jerusalem. The British were without military reinforcements and could not be counted on to protect Jewish lives and property.

I had never in my life been involved in any brawls or physical fights. I detested brute force and had always been upset by any kind of cruelty on the part of people or even animals. I was told that this was exactly what I would have to learn to live with for a week or two "or more."

After we covered the first part of the distance to Jerusalem as far as the Shaar Heguy, we were warned not to make any noise whatsoever, not even a whisper. A little after midnight we were brought to the old headquarters of the Keren Kayemet building in Jerusalem. We were given some food and told to stretch out on the floor in our clothes for a three- to four-hour sleep. Our suitcases were stored in one of the rooms.

Altogether our group had about forty men and women and there was barely an inch of empty space in the main hall of the building. Three young people, one of whom was a girl, and I were asked to go into a small side room for some training in how to use a gun. I didn't do badly and after an hour I was permitted to join the others on the bare floor. I had never felt a floor with so many bumps in it. Nevertheless I managed to sleep for about two hours.

At four-thirty we were awakened for bread, jam, and tea. Assignments were made. I was placed in a group with three men, one of whom was a Yemenite and a native of Jerusalem. I had never met a Yemenite before. We got along very well and he became my main source of inspiration. When I listened to him talk Hebrew in a rapid Arabic pronunciation, I was somewhat cheered and began to overcome my discomfort and distress.

My Yemenite friend was a well-trained Haganah fighter. He assured me that I had nothing to worry about—all I had to do was carry out his orders and teach him some English. He brought us to a remote place outside of a garage, where we monitored the movements of some Arabs who were coming from a distance. They had guns and knives and came from a nearby village which harbored some reckless cutthroats. Hidden from view, we allowed them to pass. As soon as we saw their backs we all fired in the air. Frightened and panicky, the Arabs scattered in all directions. One dropped his gun, another lost his knife. It was my baptism of fire.

It was on a Friday. The Arabs were incited to come to Jerusalem, ostensibly to visit the mosque. Their leaders had given them orders to bring knives, hatchets, and guns with which to kill the Jews. The ringleaders knew that the police force in Jerusalem was ineffective and that nearly one-third of the high-ranking officers were on vacation. The High Commissioner was in London, and many leaders of the Jewish community were attending the Zionist Congress in Zurich.

Thus, Friday, August 23rd was the fatal day. The area we were assigned to guard was relatively isolated, and we didn't know what was going on in the rest of the city. Later we learned that two brothers returning from their work in Bethlehem had been slaughtered. A journalist was killed. A family of four in the religious section was murdered. By nightfall there were seventeen dead and hundreds of men, women, and children were wounded. The police were helpless and the Jewish self-defense units didn't have enough men to cover the city. We attended brief Friday night services, but the joy of the coming Sabbath was more like the mood at a funeral. Worse was yet to come.

The small police force lacked reinforcements. One of the most important sections was Talpiot, a beleaguered neighborhood, where our volunteer forces helped to save a large part of the population. Every able-bodied man was taken into the defense forces, including twenty-eight Christian students of the Theology Seminary of Oxford, who willingly joined in the defense.

In 1924, 600 Jews lived in Hebron and there were 150 students in the yeshivah. Hebron had been King David's capital before he conquered Jerusalem. According to tradition, it was the home of the Jewish patriarchs and matriarchs who were buried there in the Machpela Cave. Like Jerusalem, Hebron was never without Jews throughout its history. Jews lived there and Jews came there on pilgrimages. At the end of the last century more than ten percent of its population was Jewish.

The Haganah was worried. Yet the Jewish leaders in Hebron felt that their anxiety was unwarranted. They were on the best terms, they claimed, with their Arab neighbors. The mayor assured the Jews there was no danger of attack.

On Saturday we received the news that a mob of infuriated Arabs had broken into a building and, with knives and axes, butchered forty-five defenseless young students and wounded countless women, old men, and children. Other Arabs had risked their lives defending the Jews and some of them were also murdered. These atrocities started a wave of further pogroms throughout the land.

As one who could be more readily dispensed with, I was asked to help with the conveyance of the dead and wounded. The cries and eulogies were heartrending.

After a number of trying, tense days with little sleep and less food, I was assigned to work with Mrs. Ben-Zvi, the wife of the man who later became the second president of the State of Israel. My job was to convey messages from Mrs. Ben-Zvi and others in the Jerusalem Haganah to the British authorities.

When I went to the storeroom where I had left my valise, I found that the building had been ransacked during the first week of the riot. My valise and all my clothes were gone. Except for a shirt and underwear which I had in a paper bag, I had nothing to wear.

VIII
JERUSALEM

Jerusalem has the longest continuous history of any city. It goes back over 5,000 years. Many ruled over Jerusalem before and after Abraham's victory over the "kings of the east." The Jews were, however, the first to proclaim it a holy city. One thousand years later it also became the holy city of the Christians, and still later of the Moslems. Since the time of King David Jerusalem was never without some Jewish inhabitants. In 1880, when the Jews began to return to Jerusalem, its population had dropped to only 31,000, of whom 17,000 were Jews and no more than 11,000 were Arabs.

The British conquered Palestine from the Turks in 1917 and received a mandate from the League of Nations to rule over Jerusalem and all of Palestine. At the head of the administration was a high commissioner. The first high commissioner was a Jew, Sir Herbert Samuel, a cousin of DeMille's mother. When the Mandatory Government began to waver in its pledge to help the Jews establish a homeland in their ancestral country, the strong ties forged between the Jewish community of Palestine and the British steadily worsened.

Seventy times Jerusalem was conquered and reconquered by Babylonians, Romans, Turks, and finally the British. For Jews it had always been more than a landmark or an economic or political asset. It was the reflection of their soul. Every day, every Saturday, every holiday, the Jew prayed for its rebuilding. It was a prayer that united Jews of all lands, of all generations.

Walking along the historic streets, I couldn't stop thinking of how much Jerusalem had suffered and bled. Before coming to the Holy Land, my credo of a new Jerusalem was the same as Herzl's who envisioned a Jerusalem and Palestine where "we will honor the rights of the non-Jewish population and set an example for the whole world."

Many unemployed Arabs from neighboring lands came streaming into Palestine. The more Jews, the more development, the more Arabs. The neglected, ravaged soil, which had suffered so greatly from thoughtless exploitation, began to respond to the needs of all.

After 1920 there were opportunities which, if rightly used, might have brought us closer to the Palestinians of those days. The Arabs then were not as politically sophisticated or fanatical as they are today. Even Jewish labor, with its socialist slogans, missed these opportunities. In theory, it advocated the establishment of a just society, which could tolerate neither unorganized labor nor the exploitation of non-Jewish workers. What followed was, in some ways, inevitable. Arab workers were not accepted in certain Jewish factories. The failure of Jewish organized labor to mix Jews and Arabs in factories and fields in an intelligent and broadminded way led to bitterness among Arabs. The Jewish leaders of labor and government, who espoused the ideal of *avodah ivrit*, or Hebrew labor, discriminated unwittingly against the poor Arab peasants who were ready to flood the labor market. Jews took the necessary means to protect their own workers by excluding Arabs, a natural blunder for which we paid dearly. Much of man's sufferings has been the result of innocent mistakes, of ideals which, in their implementation, created unanticipated social ills.

At the time we had opportunities to enter into a dialogue of some kind, even with those not fully prepared for dialogue. There were even opportunities for shifting and rearranging populations without detriment to either Jew or Arab.

For those who complained that it was impossible to forge a dialogue with an intransigent opponent, Buber remarked, "In a genuine dialogue each of the parties, even when he starts in opposition to the other, hears, affirms, and confirms his opponent as an existing other." This is what was and still is required in Israel, a confirmation that the opponent is an "existing other."

"There can be no social justice in society," Kaplan once said, "unless each individual lives up to the awareness that he is accountable for the way he uses his own powers."

The British brought reinforcements to Jerusalem from Egypt and the city resumed its usual life....

I stood before the sacred stones of the holiest shrine of the Jewish people at twilight, but there was just enough light for me to see the only remains of the former splendor of the Temple.

I had studied every reference to the Temple for years, and in 1927 I was asked to share my knowledge with Rabbi Ernest Trattner of Los Angeles, who was working on a research project on the Temple. Three months after I completed my work with Rabbi Trattner, I was surprised to find it among other papers in the research department of the DeMille Studios. They were placed on my desk for consideration in connection with the building of the Temple in *King of Kings*.

In ancient Jerusalem, according to the Talmud, there were 480 synagogues in addition to the Temple. Near each one was a school and a house of study. In 1929 there were still 58 historic synagogues in Jerusalem. Most of them were in the Jewish Quarter of the Old City, which Jordan destroyed in 1948.

I went to visit the places I had studied about since childhood. I listened to tales and legends and was shown a high window ledge, on which there was a pitcher of pure oil and a *shofar*, a ram's horn, which no mortal hand was allowed to touch. Both were waiting for the hand of the Messiah, "who will use the pitcher to rekindle the eternal light in the Holy Temple, and the *shofar* for the sounding of the liberation." The synagogue was among those burned to the ground in 1949 by the Arab Legion.

On the thirtieth day after the massacre in Hebron, there were commemorative services in synagogues and yeshivoth. I chose to go to a Lithuanian yeshivah. A young man came over and sat down by me. He said he remembered seeing me around the wounded and the dead. He was a yeshivah student with a beard, skullcap, and black coat, whose youth was spent within the walls of the building. After the services, I studied with him. He did the kindest thing possible by accepting me as a fellow student. He was not in the least surprised that a man, totally different from himself in appearance and in thought, could follow him so closely in his dissertation.

Then one of the elder students, holding a Talmud Tractate, clapped his hand on the stand. Everyone stood up. The headmaster of the yeshivah entered to deliver his lesson. It was a clear, logical exposition of a Talmudic text. I was very moved when he related his subject to the martyred Talmudic students of the Hebron massacre. Everyone rose, tears in all eyes, to participate in saying *kaddish*, normally recited by mourners and those who lead in the prayers.

I went up to the rabbi, and when I told him where I was born and who my grandfather was, he brightened. Reb Elijah, the *dayan* from Gur! Of course, he knew him. He had studied in the same yeshivah as my grandfather many years before.

After the warm reception by the rabbi, a yeshivah student invited me to come to his father-in-law's home for the Sabbath meal after the prayer. I accepted gladly. When I came, I found I was not the only guest at the table of his wife's father. There were two other guests—simple, pious, poor, uneducated men.

The following day, I went to see Professor Klausner at the Hebrew University. Established only four years before, the Hebrew University was small. It had only a few classes in the liberal arts program, but these were very advanced. They were slanted toward students who had already acquired their preliminary learning elsewhere. The teachers of these classes were men who were attracted to the University for reasons other than material advantage. They were men with ideals, for whom the opportunity to teach in the first Hebrew university in the history of the Jewish people was a gift of God. Situated on Mt. Scopus and dedicated by two men, Lord Balfour, the author of the Balfour

Declaration, and Chaim Weizmann, a great scientist and Zionist leader, the University soon became a magnet for many of the qualified Jewish teachers in the world.

Professor Klausner was an expert in the history of Hebrew literature. I had used his books and essays in the classes I had taught. I had read and reread his book, *Jesus of Nazareth*. Jeannie MacPherson, the scriptwriter on *King of Kings*, disliked him more than any other Jewish writer in the world. He was the primary cause of many of our arguments.

When I learned to know Dr. Klausner intimately, I told him the stories about *King of Kings*. To my surprise he laughed heartily. Though he was a religious, observant Jew, he wholeheartedly approved of my work on *King of Kings*. He had read about it and had known the use I had made of his book. I could never have imagined that the relatively insignificant work I contributed to the film, and for which I was unduly criticized, would reach the attention of a man like Dr. Klausner.

One afternoon in my rented room on the second floor of a modest pension near the King David Hotel, I read in the morning papers that Yechiel had been murdered by Arabs in the vicinity of a settlement near the Syrian border. There were a number of other casualties. I read the words over and over until I grasped what they meant, and in a state of shock couldn't venture out of my room until two days later when a Haganah representative came to see me. He told me the British were looking for me. Somehow they had found out about my Haganah activities and had a warrant for my arrest.

The Haganah men seemed to have a solution for everything. There was a military camp of the British Army at Sarafand, near Ramleh. He suggested I hide out there.

"Are you crazy?" I asked.

"No one will look for you there," he answered, "they need a Hebrew–English translator. You will live in the officers' quarters and the food will be good. Furthermore, you may be of use to us in that position."

The next morning I set out to apply for the job of translator for the British Army in the military camp at Sarafand, which was to be my hideout for almost a month.

IX
GALILEE

Sarafand was situated near Ramleh which, at that time, was an all-Arab town. Jews avoided passing through Ramleh at night and would only enter the city in the daytime if they were fully armed, but I was told nothing of this. The officers, who talked and laughed a great deal in the evenings, were tight-lipped on serious matters in the morning.

One day I was sent to Ramleh in the company of a sergeant and a Jewish civilian driver. The sergeant didn't speak Hebrew and the driver didn't speak English, but he knew a little Arabic. I went along to translate. Our mission was to pick up some bread in Rishon leZion for the camp kitchen and buy some gallon cans of gasoline in Ramleh. The sergeant and I got in the back of the open half-ton truck and proceeded to the bakery.

It was a beautiful mid-Eastern day. The sun was shining, little clouds flecked the sky, and the weather was cool and dry. With the bread in the truck we set out for Ramleh, which was about fifteen minutes drive from Sarafand. When we reached the heart of Ramleh we were stymied. We didn't know where to find the gasoline depot. A man was passing and we hailed him. The driver asked directions in halting Arabic. The Arab was fat and wore a black and white *keffiya*. When he pointed out the way and told us to follow him, we thanked him and drove slowly while he walked ahead.

Our driver became very nervous. The helpful Arab had led us into a road which dead-ended in a high wall. He was trying to convince the sergeant in sign-language to leave the truck and follow him farther to pick up the gasoline. "Don't separate," said the driver. Mumbling in Yiddish that I shouldn't allow the sergeant to leave the truck, he ended up wailing, "This will be our end."

I turned to the sergeant, but before I could explain all this he had grasped the situation. We looked around the blind alley and saw that a ragged crowd of Arab youths was gathering and had almost surrounded our truck. Some of them had trachoma and infected matter was running from their eyes. They were shouting in Arabic. The sergeant and I didn't understand the words, but we saw their mouths contorted in hatred and their eyes glowering in anger. We sensed they must have weapons.

I realized the gravity of our position. I took an armful of the loaves of bread and tossed them to the crowd. The Arabs jeered when they caught the bread, but the tension was not dispelled. On the contrary, they started yelling wildly. At this point the driver broke down and began weeping for his poor children about to be orphaned.

I turned back to the crowd and saw that the Arab boys had drawn their knives. The blades were rusty and seemed to be twitching in their hands. I saw their boodshot eyes. I didn't want to be killed by a rusty knife and I felt sick in the pit of my stomach.

The sergeant was very pale but controlled. The driver and I were unarmed. The sergeant turned to me and in a low voice said, "Take my revolver from the holster and shoot into the air when I do." He directed me to tell the driver to put the shift in reverse. As we fired, the driver came down hard on the gas pedal and the truck lurched back crazily, momentarily out of control. Some of the people standing behind us were knocked down and started to scream. The screams were taken up from all sides.

The fear we felt seemed to pass from us to them. We fired again and again. The mob panicked. We kept on firing. The driver managed to turn the car around and we gathered speed. The mob scattered, and by the time we reached the main road it had melted away.

We returned to Camp Sarafand, and I was summoned before the major to corroborate the sergeant's report of the incident. The major was furious that a lieutenant had sent us on a dangerous mission with only one sergeant instead of a full complement of three soldiers.

Eventually, I grew restless in Sarafand and longed for something more interesting than just translation. I thought it was time for me to leave my genial British hosts. I hitched a ride on an army lorry which was going to Nazareth, and there I was once more in the world of the past. Though it was my first visit to Nazareth, history made it seem familiar to me.

From Nazareth I hitched a ride to Deganiah, the oldest kibbutz in Palestine, situated on the southwestern shore of the Sea of Galilee. The poet Levi Amitai lived in this settlement, which was surrounded by fields, greenery, and vegetation different from any I had seen before.

I was told by a representative of the Haganah to stay in Deganiah and mark time until I might be needed. Never in my life was I more willing to oblige. For two days I walked around the fields like "one who is drunk with wine." The charm and beauty of nature, which I knew in my youth in Shumsk, was like the balm of Gilead for my troubled soul.

However, one of the things I didn't particularly enjoy was the indoctrination. I don't mind buying anything that is genuine, but I never like to be "sold," be it antiques, religion, or socialism.

We were sitting at the table in the dining hall when the enthusiastic secretary of the kibbutz began with, "We are opposed to private ownership and individualistic interests." I interrupted him politely by asking him to pass the bread. Having broken the spell of the secretary's intended lecture on socialism, I asked him to tell me something of the kibbutz movement. I had read about the movement, I said, but hearing about the events from those who had experienced them would be more vivid.

"The first collective settlement," he said, "was the result of ideas that had their origin in eastern Europe."

"I know that," I interrupted again. Then he smiled and went on to tell me what I wanted to hear, his own story, free of platitudes:

"When we came on the parched soil of our land, we had ideas but no experience of how to implement them. The results of many of our first experiments broke our hearts. We planted trees that had grown so well in our old countries of Europe, but here in the hot climate of the Jordan Valley they withered and died. Then we tried to follow the agricultural methods of the *fellahin* and our results were no more productive than theirs. The soil did not give us enough to sustain body and soul. But after some years our bad luck began to change. The answer to our main problems was irrigation. It revolutionized our way of life." I learned how they had established their first pumping plant and how they had built an aqueduct to bring water from the Jordan, which gave new life to their fertile fields.

It was in the open space of the dining room that I began to appreciate my brother Izzie's obsession with dancing. There seemed to be nothing more therapeutic than the nightly folk dancing. All the tensions, worries, and fears of the bloody days miraculously disappeared. Physically exhausted from the strenuous activity, I never slept better.

In my desire to bear a part of the work load, I volunteered to work in the fields. After a very pleasant, though hard day's labor, I was told by the secretary that I would be of greater help in filling in for a sick teacher. I started my class enthusiastically with the older children and was startled when they giggled at my Ashkenazic pronunciation. For me, this development was totally unforeseen. How could I teach children who laughed at me? The next day I switched with a teacher of six-year-olds. With them I was a terrific success. Both the little ones and their parents were very pleased and I won my way to their hearts. After class, many of them used to tag alongside of me as I walked to my kibbutz home. It was through one of my little pupils that I met a gentleman who nearly changed my life.

David was the grand-uncle of the six-year-old who introduced us. He had come to Deganiah to spend the Sabbath with his niece. A publisher of literary works, David was interested in expanding his business to include art books and books for children. Because of our common interests, I made an agreement to call on him at his home in Haifa on my return from Galilee.

The children took up about four hours of time during the day. This whetted, rather than diminished, my desire to learn more about their life. I had always been a believer in the traditional relationships between mothers and children. I thought there was only one viable family structure—that the private kitchen and all housework were an inseparable part of normal family life. My stay in the kibbutz changed those views radically.

While the communal kitchen was not always an easy place to work, it was a great improvement over the drudgery of a private kitchen. With the rotations and the help of the men, it was a relief from an endless, boring burden. The communal dining room also brought about great changes for many who suffered from lack of social contact. Here they were able to eat with people, converse, and exchange ideas. In Deganiah I saw for the first time the new role women could play.

Never until 1929 had I heard of women conscripted into military service. In Deganiah every girl was a member of the self-defense organization. Their relationship to society was the same as that of the men. The stress placed on the values of the group extended to the whole of the society of Palestine. Their return to nature, to the land of Israel, its soil, water, sky, was the most important means by which they could serve their people and hasten its redemption.

The exemplary relation of the kibbutzniks to society in no way interfered with their attachment to their families. I found theirs to be the healthiest relationship among those who toil for their bread. In the crowded tenements of New York, exhausted fathers returned to their apartments after work without the energy or will to communicate with their children. Sometimes the father had just enough strength to eat and go to bed. Other times he returned home after working overtime to find his children already asleep. Father and children wouldn't see each other for days. Unlike the urban proletariat, in the kibbutz, parents did not regard the child as a burden.

Freed from the care of the child's daily needs, a kibbutz mother returned home after work filled with expectancy and joy. Together with her husband she saw the healthy, well-fed children in the best possible light. The children responded in kind. They spent the Sabbath day with their parents, playing, chatting, or walking, all in an atmosphere of wholesomeness. Holidays like Passover, Shavuoth, and Succoth, enacted in a natural, historical background, had far greater significance for the children.

On one of my last days in Deganiah I was asked to transport some urgently needed small weapons to a beleaguered outlying kibbutz. I was given a light coat, such as the priests wore, and told to cover my body with the small arms. The pistols were belted around my stomach. They advised me to wear the hard straw hat which I had not worn since Jerusalem. I asked hesitantly about the danger of such an expedition.

"Don't worry," the Haganah man said, "you don't look Jewish and in this outfit they'll think you're a priest." The Arabs were known to permit the clergy freedom to come and go without restriction. A cart would take me part of the way and drop me at a point where I could make my own way on foot to the designated settlement.

It was during the heat of the day when I descended from the cart. I walked, according to the directions, for about thirty minutes and came within sight of the settlement. Three Arabs with guns at the ready were patrolling the road. One approached me and pointed his rifle at my stomach. I looked him straight in the eye. Neither of us said a word. He studied me carefully and paid special attention to my foreign straw hat. Those few seconds seemed like hours, but the straw hat saved me. After studying it intently, he removed the gun from my stomach and waved to his comrades. It was my *laissez passer*.

I continued walking toward the settlement in measured steps, hardly daring to breathe, waiting for something to happen. It took all my courage not to run or turn. I knew that if I made one wrong move a bullet would be in my back. I kept walking, walking, until the fork in the road where I was to turn left toward the kibbutz. Nothing happened. I was on my way.

When I reached the kibbutz I was sorry to give them the coat. I would have liked to keep it as a memento, but others would have to use it as a disguise, just as I had. The atmosphere was of high tension. All my joy in Deganiah turned into gloom. The sleepless nights when I was on guard duty were filled with horror.

A few days later the British police wound their way up to the kibbutz. At first sight of the police convoy ascending the hill, all members hurriedly hid their military weapons, but this time the British didn't search for illegal weapons. The police were heartily received by the whole kibbutz and were offered whatever refreshment there was. The British captain assured us that all the troublemakers would be removed and that the kibbutz could peacefully continue its work in the fields.

When I told the captain that I had served at Camp Sarafand, he looked at me curiously but asked no questions and cheerfully agreed to take me to Haifa in his special car.

In Haifa I found the situation different from any other part of Palestine. The Jewish self-defense was excellently organized, and instead of maintaining a hopeless, defensive position, it took a strong, offensive stance. It tolerated no nonsense from any quarter of the Arab population.

In Haifa I was the guest of David, the publisher whom I had met in Deganiah. He told me a great deal about his publishing house, located in Tel Aviv. In spite of the pervasive turmoil and depression in Palestine, people did not stop working, planning, and expanding. There was an urgency and a sense of greater determination to build and grow and strengthen all that had been achieved. Their eyes were on the future.

My host told me that the sale of books had dropped considerably, but he wasn't worried. A month or two would pass, he said, and all the books that were now accumulating dust on the shelves would be sold.

David had been making inquiries about me and, in the process, had met my cousin in Tel Aviv who owned a bakery. I had only seen my cousin for a ten-minute visit and had promised to return the next day. But when the next day came I was whisked away to Jerusalem by the Haganah.

Without many preliminaries David offered me a partnership in his firm. He was frank, and informed me that although my editorial talents would be put to good use, the company also needed cash. From my cousin and some friends, he gathered that if I were interested in his offer, I could provide the necessary capital of nearly $15,000.

He didn't ask me to commit myself right away, but he did ask me to go into the office in Tel Aviv, meet with the people in charge, and study the books they were publishing. He also provided me with a long list of original works and translations of world literature which his firm hoped to publish. We parted as good friends and made an appointment to meet in Tel Aviv four days later. I spent two more days in Haifa and then went south to Tel Aviv.

The first evening I went to pay my respects and condolences to Yechiel's parents. Yechiel's mother had aged so much in those three months that I barely recognized her. When I unexpectedly entered their apartment, we looked at each other and started crying.

"You have changed a great deal," Yechiel's mother said falteringly, "you look much more serious." When she went into the kitchen to bring us something to drink, Yechiel's father told me about Yechiel's childhood. Yechiel had told him that I was one of the best friends he had. I remained for dinner, but I could hardly eat as I listened to Yechiel's parents; I realized how much Yechiel had meant to me. They offered to let me stay in Yechiel's room, but I felt I couldn't.

The next day I went to meet David at the publishing house. I was very excited over the opportunity to participate in an activity close to my heart. For the first time in months I considered my financial situation, mentally counting my assets, which consisted mainly of securities. I never regarded my paintings as part of them. I figured that my gross assets amounted to $30,000. Of this I owed $12,000 (on margin) on the stock I had bought. With an investment of $15,000 I would be left with approximately $3,000.

I was still not in a position to commit myself to David. I wanted to consult different people, talk to a lawyer (who was a distant relative), and study the nature of the business more thoroughly. I had a room in a hotel on Allenby Road facing the Mediterranean. It was expensive, but to me it was worth more than the money I paid. I spent a great deal of time looking out of the window and thinking things through.

In the mornings I wrote my articles for the Anglo-Jewish Press and visited different galleries. Afternoons were dedicated to spending time at the sea and visiting friends. Evenings were dedicated to the theatre.

During my first six days of city life I realized how, in spite of my love for the country, I was addicted to the city. The exciting, bustling life of Tel Aviv overshadowed Kibbutz Deganiah.

On my eighth day in the city I was badly shaken by a headline in the morning paper. GREATEST CRASH IN THE HISTORY OF WALL STREET screamed out from the page. "Fortunes were lost in the worst panic of the century," the article continued.

I waited a day before telegraphing my broker to find out about my securities. The cabled reply upset me. To save whatever equity I had, they needed $4,000. All I had with me amounted to a little more than $500, which would just cover the cost of a suit of clothes and a ticket to New York with a stopover in Paris.

I rang David to tell him I had to leave Palestine unexpectedly; I rushed to the steamship office to book passage. I hurried to Yechiel's parents to say good-bye, pick up my coat, my good pair of shoes, and my books. The next day I went back to Haifa to meet the boat that would take me to Marseilles.

When I left Palestine it was as though I were parting from my dearest family.

X

PARIS

If it weren't for the *London Times* and the *Financial News* of November 1st and 2nd, which I found on board, I might have enjoyed my voyage. The graphic account of Black Thursday, October 24th, and Tragic Tuesday, October 29th, was most depressing. The description of the confusion and hysteria on Wall Street, the suicides that followed, the hundreds of thousands of people who lost everything, made me sick at heart. It was little consolation to me that I was no different from the millions of other innocent people who were shorn of all their possessions.

In search of some explanation I read everything I could about the unsound economy, the unequal and unjust distribution of wealth in the land. Five percent, they wrote, received thirty percent of all the income in America up to the big crash of 1929. Much of what happened, I read, was a result of economic and social blunders, as well as greed on the part of the bankers and moneyed classes.

Why, I asked myself, didn't I know of all this? Where were my eyes? Why had everything looked so sound, so solid, so perfectly geared for everyone in this so-called world of plenty? How could I have allowed my special interests to divert my mind from the bitter reality which dawned on me so suddenly? These tormenting questions kept rising in my thoughts. Little did I know that the new-found reality had eluded everyone. Tens of millions of bewildered people asked the same questions from one end of the country to the other.

The prospect of returning penniless to my home where, according to the headlines, TERROR HAS SEIZED THE NATION, made me tremble. A fear I hadn't experienced in the bloodiest days in Palestine possessed me. There was nothing I could do to shake it off.

I was feeling the same seasickness that drove most of the people to their cabins. Nevertheless, I was determined to remain on deck and fight the wild sea in my own way. I allowed the salty foam of the beating waves to wash every part of me. I breathed deeply and walked as firmly as I could, holding on to the rail. As the hours passed I felt more and more refreshed. On becoming completely soaked I went to my cabin, changed my clothes, and walked unsteadily up to the dining room, hurrying to reach it before it closed. No liquids could be served because of the pitching and rolling of the boat, but the solid meal brought back my strength.

A sudden change came over me. Both my fight against the elements and the substantial meal paved the way to a healthy transition. I was lifted out of my deep despair. The pressures and anxieties over my hopeless financial condition eased up, and I started to feel almost carefree. It was as though I were suddenly liberated from a dungeon. With very few people on deck, the boat was mine and I returned to my brisk walk. I was now able to forego the support of the rail, but couldn't afford to get wet again. I didn't own any more dry clothes. I remained on deck well past midnight. Forgetting my woes and woes of the world as well, I began to plan for my short visit to Paris. My father's oldest brother's son lived in Paris. I sent my cousin a cable announcing my arrival.

The boat train from Marseilles reached Paris in the evening. I was surprised to see my cousin, Lyova Alkovitsky, waiting for me at the station. Lyova embraced me warmly and for the first time I moved my cheeks, French fashion, from side to side.

Lyova, tall and elegantly dressed, with the rosette of the Légion d'Honneur in the buttonhole of his beautifully tailored jacket, resembled my uncle from Vilna. In a mixture of Yiddish and Hebrew he related all the nice things he remembered about my father. He told me how happy he was to be reunited with a close member of the family. Then he suddenly said, "Vladimir Jabotinsky is waiting for you to report on the latest events in Palestine."

This was a great surprise. Jabotinsky waiting to see me! I recalled talking to a journalist in Tel Aviv who was one of Jabotinsky's devoted followers. When I mentioned I was going to Paris, he said he hoped I would have a chance to meet Jabotinsky. I told him how deeply I had been moved by Jabotinsky's lectures on Bialik, which I had attended in New York.

Lyova took my bags to his new and expensive car and then drove to a café. The sight of the people strolling along the wide boulevards was too great a competition for my cousin's endless questions.

When I entered the café I spotted Jabotinsky at once. He was sitting at a corner table. My heart began beating strongly. Though I was no acolyte of his Zionist political line, I knew, instinctively, that I stood before a great man. On the first day of my stay in France I was unexpectedly privileged to spend three hours with a man, the likes of whom I had never met before.

Jabotinsky's greatness was not in his political philosophy which my cousin espoused. It was perhaps not even in his great gifts as a poet, a dramatist, or his marvelous talents as a Hebrew translator from Italian, Russian, and English. I was sixteen years of age when I first read Poe's words in Hebrew, "*Leolam lo*" instead of "Nevermore." He moved me deeply as an orator; he lifted my soul as a visionary; he inspired me as a poet. He was truly a universal man.

Ever since I read his marvelous Hebrew translation of Edgar Allen Poe's *The Raven*, his *leolam lo* had the opposite meaning for me. Instead of depressing me with the poem, Jabotinsky elated me with his translation. For me, he was an affirmative, *leolam ken*—evermore, and not *leolam lo*.

I was politically naive and greatly influenced by the leaders of the World Zionist Organization. They strongly disapproved of Jabotinsky's adventurous behavior as a politician; thus my attitude toward Jabotinsky was ambivalent. However, no one moved and inspired me more than he. No Zionist leader envisioned the new Jewish state in brighter colors. He foresaw a Jewish state which would banish all poverty, inequality, and the enslavement of man by man. In this vision he included the Arabs, with whom the Jews would live peacefully. The state would supply everyone with a minimum of food, lodging, education, clothes, and medical services.

Utopian as it sounds, Jabotinsky seemed to be realistic and convincing. "Poverty," he said, "debilitates and diminishes every society in which it prevails. The proper distribution of the wealth of society strengthens and enriches it in proportion to the equal share enjoyed by its members." The cost of giving every citizen full participation in the wealth of the country, said Jabotinsky, is less than the cost of maintaining an army. If the large states had smaller armies and happier, fully cared for citizens, there would be less need for the military.

Our national redemption, said Jabotinsky, "must be based on the redemption of the individual from fear of poverty and inequality." He must be able to use "his talents for an unlimited *aliya*," ascension and growth.

I recounted to Jabotinsky what happened in Palestine from the day I arrived until the day I left. Then we discussed the theatre and art and neglect of the beaches, which we considered one of the great assets of Palestine. Before I left, Jabotinsky told me he was very pleased that his journalist friend in Palestine suggested he see me, and that my cousin, who was the head of his political organization in Paris, had brought me to him.

On the way home Lyova told me all about his wife and two children and the success he had achieved as an inventor and manufacturer of pens. It was for his contribution to French industry that he was made a member of the Légion d' Honneur.

One of the blessings of humanity is the existence of a kind, closely knit, warm family. "No matter how many communes mankind invents," says Margaret Mead, "the family always creeps back." Even though it was quite late, Lyova's children, who had been told about their new cousin, refused to go to bed before we arrived. Bernard, who was eight, and Jacqueline, who was four, helped me unpack my meager belongings.

Lyova had already heard the story of how I had lost my clothes. He stood aside, eyeing the poor trousers and cheaply made jacket which I had bought in Palestine. I placed them carefully in the Louis XV bureau. When I finished unpacking Lyova said, "The first thing tomorrow morning we will go to the Louvre." I was delighted. Lyova continued, "There we will buy you some clothes." "Clothes in the Louvre?" I questioned. Lyova smiled. "The Louvre is a department store near a museum of the same name." I told him I would prefer to go to the Louvre Museum. He convinced me when he said that the museum would wait, but not my pants and jacket.

From the Louvre Department Store I found myself in front of the one place where I spent the greatest part of my stay in Paris, the Louvre Museum. First I went to see the objects of antiquity. The statues of the early Sumerians, Egyptians, Greeks, and others related a wordless story of humanity's supreme ahievements.

I stood in wonder before a six-foot slab of black basalt. It was the Code of Hammurabi from 1300 B.C. On top of the stone is a vivid carving of Hammurabi receiving the laws from the sun god, Shamash. The word, *shamash*, sun, was used in Mesopotamia in the days of Hammurabi and Abraham, and is to this day the word for sun in Hebrew. The statue commemorates the conquest of Hammurabi, and it contains the earliest code of laws. Like many of the laws of the Bible, the code contains 282 laws relating to the social life of that ancient epoch.

Henry Moore observed, "Art is an expression of the significance of life, a stimulation to great effort in living." I had come to the Louvre in need of stimulation to renew my effort in living, and I found it there.

One night, after I attended a late performance in Montmartre and was walking to my cousin's house, I sensed that I was being followed by two men. Since I had reached a street where there were few people in sight, I increased my pace. The two men increased theirs. I didn't have very much money with me, but it was all I had and I didn't want to part with it. I began to run as fast as I could, and the two men ran after me. I couldn't see clearly, but I thought I glimpsed a knife in one man's hand. Running faster than before, I caught up with two nuns about half a block ahead. I separated them and walked in-between. We didn't say a word. They turned into a courtyard. I went with them there and stayed put for a few mintues after they left me. When I peeked out at the street, it was empty. The two men had disappeared. No one was ever able to explain to me what the two nuns were doing at that time of night in such a deserted quarter. Maybe they were two angels, I mused, the two angels that accompany a Jew on the Sabbath eve.

Cousin Lyova and his wife entertained me royally. What I enjoyed most were the Russian restaurants which, in 1929, still employed counts and princes of Czarist Russia as waiters and doormen. My cousin tipped the musicians generously and they played his favorite Russian songs. One of them was *"Yamschik Ne Gani Leshadai,"* " Driver, do not drive the horses too fast, there is no one waiting for me." The first time I heard this melody with its mournful lyric, my cousin pressed my hand. He detected the sadness in my eyes. He knew all about my loss on Wall Street and the world to which I was returning.

Several days before my departure from Paris I received a letter from my brother Izzie. He tried to console me on the loss of all my money and he wrote that Abe Funt, the brother-in-law who came to see me off, committed suicide by jumping out of a window. The whole family was in great distress. No one had thought that so soon after the crash on Wall Street, Funt would lose all desire to live. Izzie added that he was sure my loss would be easily forgotten. He wrote that he knew I placed no great importance on material things. Nevertheless, he enclosed a $200 bank check. Little did he know how badly I needed it. All I had left after buying my ticket third-class to New York was $60. I didn't tell Lyova how little money I had, especially after he had spent so much money for my wardrobe.

My cousin, Lyova, had a well-developed sense of world politics. The only trouble was that he based it on a logical order of things, just as I and millions of others had predicated our faith on the logical order of the American economy. Lyova didn't foresee in the following years that the world would be governed by the wild impulses of ruthless, fanatical men. Though not blind to reality, he had too great an admiration for the noted statesmen of his beloved France to doubt their vision and competence. With the breakdown of the American economy, he reasoned, France would remain the only bastion in the democratic world and the safest place for a Jew to live.

When I engaged Lyova in a serious conversation on Jabotinsky's nationalist views, I saw that he was baffled. He was a good Zionist and believed that Palestine would become the Jewish national homeland, but on the other hand he thought that if the next world war would break out as a result of the American economic decline, the Jews of Palestine would be the first victims. In spite of his strong Zionist views, he told me that France would remain his home and the home of his children; Lyova was convinced that France was the safest place in the world for Jews.

Twelve years later my cousin Lyova, his wife, her parents, and all their cousins died in Hitler's gas chambers. When the Nazi police came to my cousin's home to round up the Jews, Jacqueline was sick in the hospital. She, alone, survived.

XI
AMERICA—1929

My brother Izzie was waiting on the dock as the boat neared the pier. On the way home he told me some of the gruesome aftermath of the Wall Street crash.

"Everyone is affected," he said. "Banks throughout the country are being taken over by receivers, and depositors are losing their life savings." He related the terrible circumstances that led to his brother-in-law's suicide.

Izzie must have sensed my discomfort and switched to an optimistic note. "I know America," he said, "and in spite of what the bums have done to her, she will pull through!" I smiled. His homespun philosophy dispelled the gloom I brought with me from the boat.

It had not been a good trip. There hadn't been much space in the overcrowded third class, and I was forced to share a cabin with three Slovenian immigrants with whom I had no common language.

A stream of relatives and friends came to welcome me back, and I was cheered and revived by their questions and good humor. In their conversation there was not a trace of the troubles plaguing the country. When they came to my brother's house they seemed to have left their problems behind.

On Monday I went to see Meyer Weisgal, the editor of *New Palestine*, and secretary of the Zionist Organization of America. I had known Meyer for several years and had written him about my return to New York. Meyer Weisgal was a true friend; he couldn't be anything else. He was also one of the more colorful personalities in public life. Quick, sharp, witty, even brilliant, he knew how to be on equal terms with the greatest. There were two men to whom he was attached with the strongest devotion: Louis Lipsky, President of the Zionist Organization of America, and Chaim Weizmann, who was to become the first president of the State of Israel.

When I entered Weisgal's office I heard his familiar greeting, "Hey, you bastard, why didn't you come to me sooner?" No one ever took offense at Weisgal's greetings.

I answered him in the same spirit, and without a "hello" said "I came too soon as it is."

Weisgal grinned, went to my side, and put his arm around my shoulder saying, "Good to see you, goddamn it. You don't look half as bad as you appeared in your damn articles."

"So how in hell do you feel?" he asked, and without waiting for an answer he continued, "Do you need a job?"

"Yes," I said. "I feel fine and I need a job."

"All right," he rejoined. "I have a job for you for three months. I want you to go on a speaking tour through the country. We are having a membership campaign for the Zionist Organization. Of course there is very little money in it—$100 a week plus all expenses."

Before the last words left his mouth, I said, "Okay, I'll take it. When do I start?"

"In ten days, but I need your pictures and biography right away. Wait a minute, I have a photographer in the building. He'll get me the pictures quicker than you." This was characteristic of Meyer Weisgal's genius. He knew how to deal with a multitude of details with the fewest words in the quickest time.

"Here is a note for $250 in advance. That's all I have," said Weisgal.

"That's fine," I said. "It's more than I have."

"I know, I know," he commented, "you lost all your goddamned money. That's why I'm giving you the job. The chief told me this morning he wants to see you." For forty-five years Weisgal referred to Louis Lipsky as "chief." He picked up the telephone and spoke to Mr. Lipsky's secretary. "Your appointment is for eleven A.M. tomorrow. Call me right away after you see him." Just as there was no hello, there was no good-bye. I left on this note.

Louis Lipsky combined the traits of a leader with those of a bohemian. Tall, attractive, with finely shaped features, he never sought to be a leader. Leadership was forced on him by the Zionists in the same way that Elijah forced the power of prophecy on Elisha.

Lipsky had begun his career as a theatre critic. For him the world was a stage with people playing varied parts. Each night at eleven o'clock, winter and summer, one could find Lipsky at the head of a large table in the Tip Toe Inn on Broadway, where his friends could come, sit down, and talk to him. This was his catharsis. His escape from the oppression of the office regime.

At age fifteen I had been Lipsky's office boy for a year and a half. Through Zionism and the theatre I was to remain close to Lipsky for the next forty years. When Lipsky was nearly eighty, he and others formed an independent Zionist organization. He asked me to be its secretary. Though I had many business affairs going at that time, I couldn't refuse the chief.

When I entered Lipsky's office, the first thing I noticed was the five-cent cigar; he smoked cheap cigars continuously. After asking about my personal experiences in Palestine, he suddenly came out with "Why did Jabotinsky want to see you?" I was surprised that anyone other than my cousin, Lyova, knew about it. It seems there is always a listening ear at the side of every public figure. Lipsky had a high regard for Jabotinsky, although he considered Jabotinsky's political maneuvers naive.

After I reported to Lipsky on my conversation with the great man and what I thought of him, Lipsky agreed that Jabotinsky had a complex personality of "strength and imagination . . . a man who marched forward alone believing that the legions would follow him." Lipsky then suggested that we go for some sandwiches. There, in the modest coffee shop, he asked me all about the plays I had seen in Tel Aviv, about the talent of the actors, the skill of the directors, and a great many technical details. With all the conversation we had, Lipsky never mentioned a word about what he expected me to do in the next three months. He left that to Meyer Weisgal.

I had ten days to myself before starting out on my speaking tour covering cities and towns throughout the country. Before leaving New York I took advantage of the time by revisiting my old schools and my friends. In the evenings I went to the theatre and caught up on the plays I had missed during my eight-month absence.

Broadway was not the same. The theatres were half-empty. The gloom that was to hang over the the street for four years was already in evidence. Actors, musicians, writers, and artists are always the first to feel the impact of a serious depression.

During the next three months on my speaking tour, I learned to know America. I found not one America, but many Americas, all different yet all the same. It was the differences of the towns and cities which excited my interest, while the sameness of their Main Streets bored me.

For a while I was inspired by my audiences, but as the weeks passed my work lost its glamour. The same elderly people and lonely widows congregated in the same chilly, provincial halls in each town. I knew how hungry they were for some cheering words, words to remind them of their youth, their dreams, and hopes. I tried my best to reach out to them. At times my audiences were responsive and appreciative. After the lecture people came up to me thanking me profusely, invited me to their homes for tea, and showered me with endless questions. At such times I found great satisfaction in my work and considered it my mission. At other times, no matter how hard I tried, I seemed to be unable to communicate. The reports reaching New York were varied.

At the end of my speaking tour I arrived in Los Angeles to find that the tentacles of the depresson had already reached the members of my family. One after another, my sister's apartment houses were in line for foreclosure by the banks. In 1929 nearly every mortgage on rental apartments was for two to three years. Today they are for a twenty- to twenty-five year period. In normal times the mortgages were automatically renewed, but with countless vacancies and the growth of unemployment, there were now no renewals and the full amounts of the bank loans were called in. With values dropping as much as fifty percent in many instances, nearly all equity of property owners was wiped out. All within the space of ten to twelve months.

I came at a period when my sister Lizzie was unable to offer me a free apartment in one of her buildings. It was just when I needed it most. I didn't want to spend the money I had earned from the lecture tour before I was able to find work.

My sister Sarah insisted that I move into her apartment until I could get back on my feet again. The apartment consisted of two small bedrooms shared by Aaron (the Aaron who had traveled with me to Vilna to buy a watermelon for Rosh Hashanah) and Sarah, and their two little daughters, Eleanor and Rita.

Aaron and Sarah placed a folding bed in the living room. That folding bed was the only place I enjoyed any privacy during the first two months of my return to Los Angeles. But in spite of our crowded quarters, I enjoyed my stay with my sister and the children. I was reminded of words in the Talmud: "Where there is love, two people can live on the point of a needle."

For four years, the center and the school which I had built up in Boyle Heights had been the pride of the Jewish cultural community. Now it was on the verge of shutting down. The teachers, who had not been paid for several months, deserted the school one by one. Only the janitor remained. When he saw me coming up the stairs of the building, he burst into tears. I had no words to console him.

Now I knew there was no turning back. I had to begin my life over again from scratch. I was in a benumbed frame of mind and I didn't want to call any of my close friends either in the Hollywood Art League or the John Kahn Institute. I had always been diffident about asking for help.

In my second week in Los Angeles the art column in the *Times* announced a dance recital by Carmelita Maracci. Impulsively, I picked up the telephone and called Carmelita. She was overjoyed. Why hadn't I written? Why hadn't anyone heard from me? She took my telephone number. During the rest of the morning I received calls that moved me deeply.

One was from my black friend, Clarence Muse. Billie, his wife, was preparing a dinner for a few friends. Carmelita would be there, and he said I must come without fail. Moreover, he declared he would buy the best bottle of wine there was to celebrate our reunion. The evening was just what Clarence promised it would be and much more. Before it was over, Clarence told me that he was working on a film and that he would talk to the producer about getting me a job. It was ironic that with all my Jewish connections and years of self-sacrificing work in the community, it was a black man who was the first to stretch out his hand in true brotherhood.

I didn't have long to wait. At ten the next morning, Clarence Muse called to say he had found two months' work for me in the research department of the studio where he was doing a picture. Would I like the job? "Times are bad," he added, "and they will only pay $125 a week." When I hung up the receiver I never ran for a job faster.

When the pleasant two months at the studio ended, and there was no other employment to be found, I accepted an offer from a former rabbi to work with him jointly selling annuities and life insurance. With the Talmudic maxim that no labor is demeaning, I began my new job at a most inopportune time.

People lacked the money to pay the rent or even to buy groceries. Life insurance and savings for their children's education was one of the last things they could think of. Nevertheless, I did what I was advised to do. I selected thirty names of people who knew who I was, and wrote them short, personal letters. Within a week I received two encouraging replies. I was on my way.

With my first month's earnings of about $300 I was able to rent a magnificent apartment in North Vermont Avenue overlooking Hollywood Hills. It cost $35 a month. A year before it had rented for $125.

The insurance business did not take much of my time, so I returned to the work I loved. The Hollywood Art League arranged a series of lectures for me in one of the abandoned studios. At the end of my second session I met a young lady who had a Marxist outlook on art. In the society we lived in, it was difficult for her to accept the view of "art for art's sake," which was, more or less, my view. She was a beautiful woman with sad eyes. I was enchanted by her exquisite hands. Impulsively I took them in mine and told her that only Durer could paint such hands. She blushed and I realized she was shy and reserved.

Within a week I learned to know Vera quite well. She told me, blushing again, that she couldn't explain what made her come over to talk to me. It was Vera's diffidence and sincerity that eventually won my heart.

I was aware that in my poor financial state I couldn't think of marriage, and yet precisely at such a time, my greatest dream was to have a home, a wife, and children. For that I needed "a woman of virtue," a woman with the qualities that would give me added strength. Vera appeared to be the one I was looking for.

With her glowing, beautiful face and the gentlest hands that I had ever seen, she was honest and truthful. I told her that in Russian, *vera* means truth, and the name fitted her very well. Vera was the name her father had chosen for her. She adored her father and I felt I was lucky that she found her father image in me.

Vera came from a poor, working-class family in Boston. All she remembered of the first seven years of her life was poverty and sickness. Her father had been an idealist and a radical. He was a gifted violinist but unable to provide for his wife and children. Her mother went out and did housework to help support the family. When her father died, it was rumored he committed suicide, but Vera didn't know if this was true. She only knew that he died when she was seven. The shock was too great for Vera's mother, who suffered a mental collapse and was taken to an institution, where she spent the remaining days of her life.

Vera was cared for by her mother's sister, who took Vera into her home in a basement apartment. Vera's uncle was a presser of men's vests, and besides herself, five other children lived in a dark, two-room apartment. Vera's four-year-old brother was adopted by an orthodox Jewish family, who didn't want him to know that he had other parents. Not having had any children of their own, they wanted him to consider himself their son, who will say *kaddish* for them after their death. Vera was not allowed to enter their home, and she had no personal contact with her brother for nine years.

At the age of twelve, Vera and her cousin, Roe, would hurry to the schoolhouse to watch her brother Tommy run around in the playground. At that time Vera and Roe had only one pair of good shoes between them. When one went to a party, the other stayed home. After school they would play a little and then go home for the meager food Vera's aunt was able to provide for her children. In the afternoon Vera, Roe, and another cousin, Anne, would run to their neighborhood library and stay there until it closed. It was their only refuge.

At sixteen Vera got a job in a five-and-ten-cent store. She earned enough to buy her clothes and put some money in the bank for her education. Supplementing her savings by part-time work as a waitress, she got herself through college.

In Boston College she found friends among a radical group of students, to whom the structure of our society was anathema. From that group she was drawn into the Communist Party, where she became a fiery and devoted member. With her independent mind, she was soon discouraged by the irrational, emotional approach of her young comrades and later abandoned the party and her old friends. Then she turned to music, attending Fiedler's Pop Concerts, and later, when she graduated from college, Koussevitsky's magnificent concerts.

For a change of atmosphere she came to Los Angeles on a vacation to visit her mother's first cousin. She fell in love with the climate and the open spaces of the city, and a friend helped her find a job. Her cousin offered her a room and she stayed.

At about the time I met Vera, I received a call from a man whom I knew by reputation for many years. His name was Nahum Zemach. He was the founder of the Habimah Theatre. Before he explained the nature of his call, I told him of the many things I had heard about him in Palestine. He listened patiently and then said that it was through a former colleague that he had learned about me.

Nahum Zemach was the first visitor who came to see me in my new apartment. I had already hung my paintings and brought over my books, which had been stored at my father's house. Now the apartment was home to me.

I wanted to ask Vera to join us, but she didn't know Hebrew and Zemach didn't know English. The first thing Zemach did on entering the apartment was to examine my library and my paintings. "This," he said to me, "makes me feel at home." No one who ever visited my home and looked at my paintings has given me the same feeling of pleasure and understanding of art as Nahum Zemach.

I told Zemach about some of his friends in the Habimah and how badly Hannah Rovena, the leading Habimah actress, felt when Zemach severed his connection with the troupe. But I could see that the subject was painful to him, so I asked him to tell me what he had come to talk to me about. He wondered if I would be his assistant in the direction of *The Dybbuk* in English. The management of the Pasadena Playhouse, the best repertory theatre on the coast in 1930, had invited Zemach to come from New York to direct the play. More than any other work, *The Dybbuk* had made his original Habimah troupe famous throughout Europe.

The Dybbuk by S. Ansky, originally written in Yiddish and translated into Hebrew by Chaim Bialik, became a classic of the Hebrew theatre. Now it was to be presented for the first time in English with a cast of prominent actors of the stage and screen. Because he had no mastery of the English language—in fact, no knowledge of it—Zemach felt that I could be of great help to him. Since he would be very well compensated for the six weeks' work, he was sure that the Pasadena Playhouse would be glad to pay me at least the union-scale salary.

Nahum Zemach founded the first Hebrew dramatic group in Russia when he was twenty-five years of age. In 1917 he founded the Habimah Theatre in Moscow with the help of Stanislawski and Vachtangov, both great Russian directors. For nine years the theatre flourished and the plays awakened a deep interest in the spoken Hebrew language as well as the literature.

After a triumphant reception in the United States in 1926, a bitter quarrel arose within the troupe. This is not unusual in the life of the theatre, but the quarrel that began on account of Zemach was very like a Greek tragedy. Zemach's wife, who played the leading role of Leah in *The Dybbuk* when she was twenty, still insisted on playing the same role when she was past thirty. The ensemble was fed up with her intransigence. Zemach sided with his wife; he loved her and was ready to make any sacrifice to please her. The episode ended in a rift which left Zemach and his wife in New York in 1926, abandoned by those he had brought into the Habimah, while the rest of the troupe went on to Tel Aviv.

Zemach was a gentle, sensitive person, who possessed the perceptive, intelligent qualities of a good director. He never shouted or ordered anyone about. My task was to translate all the preliminary explanations so that the parts would be well organized. After that, it was principally to convey what the actors wanted to say rather than what the director wanted them to do. By a soft word, a movement of the hand, a smile, or the raising of an eyebrow, Zemach was able to communicate with the actors without an intermediary.

There was generous public applause and praise from the press for Zemach's *Dybbuk* in English. It was a pity that it hadn't been staged ten years earlier. Fate had placed him in the wrong slot at the wrong time. During the days of silent pictures, Zemach would have found an honored niche among the successful directors of Hollywood. Now, in the throes of the Depression and with a scant knowledge of English, his production at the Pasadena Playhouse was his swan song.

During the next two years he struggled to find work. Here and there, he found scraps of work in one man's show or the direction of an amateur Yiddish production. I tried to help by maintaining Zemach's morale. The saddest memory I have of our friendship is when, at the depth of the Depression in the fall of 1931, I went with Zemach to buy old, stale bread at half price. Proud as always, he refused to accept the things I wanted to give him. He knew that like everyone else, I, too, had to be careful of my expenditures.

A cruel fate dogged his heels. Zemach left Hollywood and moved to New York, where his wife became a drama teacher. A year later she divorced hm. He died in 1939 at the age of 52.

When my long series of art lectures ended, I felt the need to become more involved in the serious problems of the day. Once, after I had addressed a group of schoolteachers, I was sounded out on whether I would run in the coming elections for the city Board of Education. I didn't want to become involved in a campaign against a political machine with vested interests. It was no job for an amateur. I declined to accept the challenge, but didn't shut the door completely.

After discussing the matter with my friends, they convinced me that even if I failed, the effort would serve a good purpose. My family was against it. They said, "Who, in these crazy days, needs any more headaches?" I did not follow the advice of my family.

Within two weeks an impressive list of prominent liberal leaders of the community was drawn up. It included several clergymen, a rabbi, and an outstanding political leader, Mendel Silverberg. Most of the supporters contributed to the campaign. I was not called upon to put in any money of my own.

As soon as my candidacy was announced, our campaign committees began to receive support from different sectors of the community. Attorney Barry Sullivan, who was politically active, was among the first to endorse me. He was followed by L.G. Sherer, a secretary of the state's Association of California Architects. On May 20, 1931, the bulletin of the Municipal League of Los Angeles wrote: "Of Mr. Alkow we spoke and speak again in the highest terms, a man of vigorous intellect, high ideals, and broad culture." The Scripps

Canfield newspaper, *The Record* published a strong editorial "in support of J.M. Alkow, brilliant young educator, for the Board of Education."

My strongest support came from the black community. In numerous articles on the Board of Education elections, Fay Jackson of *The Eagle* described the Citizens' School Committee, the group opposing me, as being dominated by real estate brokers, school-supply men, and furniture dealers, who barred anyone from the Board of Education "who does not pledge himself to their immediate interests. . . . It is time to become alert. There is one man running for the Board of Education who will carry on the fight. . . . That man is J.M. Alkow, a progressive educator. This is neither a racial nor a purely personal fight. It is a fight for progressive measures on behalf of education in Los Angeles."

In another article, L.B. Granger wrote: "J.M. Alkow is an intelligent student of social conditions, whose background and experience equip him to regard the problem of our colored group with a sympathetic eye."

My campaign turned into a crusade. Numerous organizations, including the Los Angeles Council and the United Veterans of the Republic, jumped on the bandwagon. The inner committee of my campaign consisted of friends: Louis Babior, a city attorney; Isidore Lindenbaum, who fifteen years later was my partner in the Filmtone Studios; Clarence Muse; Vera, and several others. They met daily from six to ten in the evening to plan strategy on a citywide basis. There were evenings when I appeared three to four times before different groups that were evaluating candidates for councilman, judgeships, and the Board of Education. There were also numerous appearances during the day. I didn't get much of my own work done.

To raise funds for literature and advertising, the committee organized parties and picnics. At that time this was a novel tactic in political campaigns, which were usually sluggish, tense, and boring. We fostered hilarity and festivity, with banjo players and musicians of all sorts. Little wonder that the *Los Angeles Times* frowned on the company that surrounded me.

While I didn't think the Hollywood Art League should be involved in a political effort, my friends disagreed. Against my best advice the Art League joined in with a special concert to raise funds. The noted artists, George Liebling, pianist, Maria Caselotti, opera singer, and Clarence Muse filled the auditorium in the Council House on Loma Drive to capacity.

The more we got into the campaign, the more we realized the difficulties we faced. Though we made a lot of noise, our opponents took no chance on losing their control of the Board of Education and its vast expenditures. One evening I was confronted with some good news. A small truck delivered cartons filled with placards, bumper strips, all urging people to vote for J.M. Alkow. No one knew where they came from or who had printed them, or even who had ordered this large, expensive, badly needed supply of publicity. When some of the neighborhood volunteers came to pick up the material for distribution, we were jubilant.

Suddenly one woman shrieked with alarm, "There is no *bug* on any of it." Without the *bug*, or union lable, such printed matter would have alienated every working man. Who would stoop so low as to send us this gift? There was only one answer.

My opponent was a harmless, frightened little old man named Lucius C. Dale. He was the candidate of the Prohibition Party and was endorsed by the Citizen's League. A bachelor, he lived with his sister and earned his livelihood by soliciting subscriptions for a small Prohibition paper, which depended largely on county legal advertising for its income. He knew next to nothing about education.

I met Dale on two occasions and I laughed when he told me on each of them, very timidly, "May the best man win." I joked with him and said that regardless of the outcome, I hoped we would be good friends. "I hope so," he replied in his quavering voice. I later repeated this to an audience and asked, "How can I possibly fight such a nice, little man?" My listeneres howled appreciatively.

One afternoon I appeared before the Los Angeles Women's Republican Club. Lucius Dale was also scheduled to appear and we were both supposed to respond to questions from the floor. Dale didn't appear. I was not surprised. They never allowed him to speak before a large audience. When the meeting started, the frigid audience gave me a smattering of applause.

I was asked only one question. Where was I born? I told the interested lady that I was born in Shumsk and I didn't elaborate. Then the chairlady apologized for Dr. Dale's absence and read a letter purportedly written by him, asking the ladies to vote for him. Now there was a thunderous outburst of applause.

As I walked toward the door one well-dressed, Republican lady ran after me. In a voice almost choked by tears, she kept repeating "I am ashamed, ashamed of what happened. I hope you are not hurt. God bless you!"

The night of the primaries a sizable crowd gathered in our headquarters to listen to election returns on the radio. As the vote count progressed, more and more of my supporters went home dejected. Only five or six of us remained until midnight to hear how much I was trailing behind Lucius Dale. When Vera began to cry, I shut off the radio and we all went home.

Next morning I awoke to find myself in the headlines of the *Los Angeles Times*. After the support I received in the black areas was counted, I was nominated as a runoff candidate with Lucius Dale, who had failed to get the majority vote. Every radio station had announced this news just after midnight.

The agony of electioneering was prolonged for another month. We went through the same activities. We gained more support then we thought we would, but as we all knew, it's hard to beat a powerful well-geared, political machine representing certain interests. Lucius Dale was elected.

During the three months of the campaign my mind had been somewhat distracted from the cancerous economic situation, which was spreading unabated. I personally had been able to manage quite well, even though I neglected my own work while running for office. But I was saddened by the conditions in which I found my friends and my family. My inability to help them made me unhappy and frustrated. Even with strangers I was depressed at not being able to do anything.

During the summer months, we dispelled a good deal of our depression with excursions to the magnificent mountains of California, and with symphonic concerts at the Hollywood Bowl. The Bowl is one of Southern California's main attractions. Set in a natural amphitheatre, it was designed by a friend of mine from the Hollywood Art League. Zarah Witkin was by profession an architectural engineer. His second love was art films, and we often used to go to see foreign films together. Once we saw a Russian film and Zarah was enchanted by the leading actress. When he first told me he was in love with her, I laughed, but I never laughed at him again.

Zarah became so infatuated with the actress that he went to watch her movies again and again. For a while this satisfied him, but finally he set out for Russia to see her personally. The story that followed was that Zarah reached Moscow and actually met the actress. He fell in love with her reality as much as he had with her screen image. Then he dropped out of sight. Zarah didn't write, and our letters were returned with an "Address Unknown" stamp. He vanished completely.

Vera lost her job. Her employer had gone bankrupt. She desperately canvassed from one agency to another, but found no success and became despondent.

Then Vera's cousin called from Boston to tell her there was a vacancy in the place where she had worked formerly. There was no choice. Vera had to return. On the way to the train both Vera and I were very tense. Our highly charged emotions prevented us from saying much to each other, except for a few awkward, unfinished phrases. But I knew what Vera wanted to convey. Without asking me to make her any promise, she looked at me deeply and mournfully.

I had to turn my head aside to avoid an inevitable break in our controlled behavior. Without words, I, too, conveyed to her my strong feelings that before long I would ask her to come back. As she mounted the steps to the train, her eyes filled with tears. Her parting words were, "Please, please call me as soon as you can."

XII
SAN BERNARDINO

Two Los Angeles rabbis changed the course of my life. One led me to Hollywood, the other to San Bernardino. Both changes were for the good.

Rabbi Isadore Isaacson of Temple Israel in Hollywood telephoned one day to ask how soon I could come to see him. Rabbi Isaacson's warmth and love of humanity had created a large following among both Jews and gentiles. His services attracted actors, actresses, directors, and producers. I don't believe it probable that anyone else could have brought these people to a religious service.

When I entered his study, he began by saying, "On account of you I broke one of the rules of my congregation—not to discuss politics in the temple. I told my people to vote for you."

"I know," I said, "and that's why I'm here. I also want to thank you for the $20 you sent anonymously." He laughed.

"Now that I owe you so much, how can I repay you?" I asked.

He smiled and came to the core of the matter. He had been to San Bernardino a few days ago and met with members of the local temple. The community of San Bernardino was one of the two oldest Jewish communities in California and it was without a rabbi.

"No community I know of has been harder hit by the depression," he said. "It has the largest rate of unemployment and the Jewish community cannot afford a full-time rabbi. Would you agree to conduct their High Holiday service?"

"Why me?" I asked. "There are more unemployed Reform rabbis in Los Angeles than anywhere else, and they are more qualified than I am."

"I know, I know," he said. "First, I do not agree that they are more qualified, but most important is that I want you to take the post because no one I know can lift their spirits better than you can." Rabbi Isaacson's last words were not meant to flatter me. They did the opposite and I grew very serious. The frivolity with which we began our conversation turned into a challenge which made me humble. I told Rabbi Isaacson that religiously I was a follower of Rabbi Kaplan and I was not overly fond of the Reform prayer book.

"I don't care whom you follow," he said, "or whatever prayer book you want to use. You are the kind of man who would not use any accepted prayer book. Will you take the job?"

"Yes," I said, "I will, but only because you ask me." When I left Isadore's study I wondered whether I had accepted his offer of going to a remote, small community because he had asked me or because I had an inner urge to do so.

San Bernardino is sixty miles southeast of Los Angeles. It lies at the foot of the snow-capped mountains of the same name. The County of San Bernardino is the largest county in the United States and one of the richest in minerals and agriculture. In 1851 there was a large migration of Mormons and some Jewish families. In 1881, a Jew named Louis Cara donated the lumber for the first Catholic church in the city, and Yedis Jacobs was the first president of the oldest bank of San Bernardino. Joseph Rich, who was court reporter for fifty years, and whose mother was the first Jewess to be married in Los Angeles, recalls: "My father and mother settled in San Bernardino because my father was convinced that San Bernardino would become the metropolis of California, not San Francisco or Los Angeles."

It was to this dreamed-of metropolis that I drove one day in August to prepare the arrangements for the High Holiday services. With me was a young, Jewish, unemployed opera singer, who was recommended by Clarence Muse. He was to assist in the musical part of the service.

On our arrival at the two-story Colonial building which housed the temple, I was impressed by the choir and the charming Catholic lady who was the organist. In a few hours of coordinated effort, we completed our preliminary work. My hardest job was with the opera singer. He couldn't read Hebrew. I provided him with a transliteration of the Hebrew words written in English letters. I brought him some cantorial records and went over every word so there would be no flaws in his pronunciation.

On the eve of the Jewish New Year all regular seats were fully occupied. The congregation put in extra chairs in the aisles and in the rear of the temple, and they, too, were filled. The service began dramatically by the choir and organ. It set the mood.

I chose a text from the book of Isaiah which I believed was appropriate: "Watchman, what of the night?" With the night of the Depression engulfing them, my mere mention of these words brought a wave of emotion to many of my listeners. I tried to avoid the clichés of the usual High Holiday sermons. I didn't dwell on the values of Judaism or the holiness of the festivals. I spoke of simple, everyday happenings, of the joys and sorrows of our life.

I began by telling the congregation that on my first approach to San Bernardino, I saw nothing but barren mountains behind it, but when I left the valley and progressed into the heights of the mountains, I saw a new world. I saw the mighty, ageless trees reaching into heaven. I saw both the light and the shadows. I saw the beauty of God's handiwork, which I had been unable to see from the valley. Without quoting from Scriptures or the Talmud, I concluded with the words of Thomas Wolfe:

> I think the true discovery of America is before us. I think the true fulfillment of the spirit of our people, of our mighty and immortal land, is yet to come.... Our America is here, is now.... It is not our living hope but our dream to be accomplished.

When the services ended there were few who hurried off. With bright faces and a feeling of gladness, people were loathe to leave the place where their spirits had been lifted, just as Isadore had predicted. After the sermon there were two people who came up to me: an old lady who thanked me for the comforting words, and the secretary of the Chamber of Commerce, who was one of the gentile friends traditionally invited to the services. He characterized my sermon as "the best patriotic speech" he had ever heard. It was a good beginning.

For the next morning's services I prepared the opera singer to give a faithful rendition of the traditional prayer, *Hineni Heani Mima'as*, Here am I, the poorest of the poor. I explained the meaning of the words to the congregation and what it meant to me when I heard it in Kenna at the age of eleven. Most of the members were hearing it for the first time, and when they saw how I wept, they wept with me.

Generally, on the second day of the new year no more than fifteen or twenty older people came to services. This time the temple was nearly full. My other sermon dwelt on what I had experienced in Jerusalem, Athens, London, Paris, and in Ramleh, where I confronted the drawn, rusty knives of the Arabs. I layed stress on what we could learn from these experiences. By Yom Kippur the congregation was ready and receptive to an interpretation of the teachings of the Prophets and the Talmud.

On the morning after Yom Kippur, while I was packing for my departure, a committee of three elders came to the hotel room. They brought me a check and asked if I would be willing to return the following week for the Succoth festival. If I agreed, they would call a meeting of the Board and decide on a fair compensation for my services. I agreed, because the holiday services meant as much to me as it did to them.

Two days after my return from San Bernardino, Isadore Isaacson called to tell me that he had heard from the leaders of Temple Immanuel of San Bernardino. He asked if I would drop in again and tell him of my experiences there.

"You know," he said, "that I have a special interest in that community." He told me that the temple was "most anxious" to engage my services on a basis that would not occupy all my time. Since there are no Sabbath morning services—90% of the male congregation were merchants—all that would be required of me would be to conduct Friday evening services and supervise the Sabbath school. He also told me that the president of the San Bernardino Junior College heard me speak in the temple and wanted me to give a lecture course at the college.

"If you accept," he said, "I will induct you into your post at the temple in an official capacity and with all due ceremony."

The San Bernardino Junior College obtained my license for secondary education and I started my two major jobs at one and the same time. Rabbi Isadore Isaacson and one of his colleagues led an impressive induction service. Among the large audience attending, there were many prominent civic leaders.

My work at the temple progressed satisfactorily. That, and my lectures at various service clubs and classes at the college filled my schedule.

But with one-third of the population out of work and with storekeepers struggling to keep their doors open, it seemed to me that teaching the lessons of the Prophets without implementing them was not my destiny in San Bernardino. I began to tackle some of the chronic problems of the city and was elected chairman of the Unemployment Relief Commission. This, plus my other duties, required some arrangement of my life. I needed Vera's love and her company.

After school closed and the activities in the temple were ended until the fall, I decided to visit Vera in Boston. I told her that I had saved a little, not very much, but almost enough to set up a home. We would have to wait a little bit longer. The Santa Fe Railroad, whose headquarters were in San Bernardino, unwittingly encouraged romance when they granted me a free pass to travel on their line.

I have talked a great deal about the agony of the little men and women whom the Depression struck mercilessly. I did that first because they were the majority. They were the most innocent of all, in whose lives the light of American prosperity penetrated very feebly.

There was a much smaller class of fortunate people, born with silver spoons in their mouths, spoons that were never removed either in good times or bad. In hard economic times, most had remained rich; depressions had come and gone, but their wealth usually increased.

However, this was not the case in 1929. The Great Depression hit both rich and poor. One such casualty was the leading merchant of the entire area. He was unmarried, a Jew who paid little attention to the formal ways of religion. He had lived in San Bernardino nearly all his life, but he seldom walked into the temple before I arrived.

His name was Herman Harris and he was born in Germany. In 1905, Herman and his two brothers came to San Bernardino and established a modest store. The store prospered and expanded into two department stores, the largest in San Bernardino and Redlands. Herman was the genius of the family. It was he who built the fortunes for all his kin. He was satisfied to live in a spacious, rented room, to which he invited me frequently. We often dined together. My own rented room was very small, just big enough for my books, a little table, and a bed, thus I was unable to reciprocate.

Once when we sat over a cup of coffee, talking about Herman's busy life, he turned to me directly and said; "It's our loneliness that drives us to ceaseless activities." Throughout the years, when I engaged in many unrelated activities, I always remembered what I heard from Herman in a shabby little San Bernardino café.

Herman was very busy with charitable activities. He was active in the Y.M.C.A., the Salvation Army, Boy Scouts, and numerous other organizations. His first true appreciation of Judaism came to him, he once told me, from the Friday night services and my lectures at the college, which he attended occasionally. He was my severest critic and frequently reminded me not to be too emotional.

"You can do better with your mind than with your heart," he said.

Herman loved books and he had a passion for music. It was he who helped divert my attention from the all-consuming concern with community affairs and teaching to the soothing strains of music.

His new department store, considered the architectural gem of the city, was threatened with foreclosure by the financial institutions which controlled the mortgages. He was often forlorn and despondent, and I always sensed when he felt that way. It was mostly on Friday evenings when he gave up some other activity to come to the temple. I was sorry when he left before the end of services. I wanted to sit and talk with him. I, too, was terribly lonely.

Herman's scholarship grew out of his involvement in vast business enterprises. I, however, entered into complicated business from the world of scholarship. Somewhere, by accident, we came together. In our long discussions we covered literature, music, and ourselves. He had an attentive ear and had rarely talked about himself before, but now he told me about his youth in Germany. His family had left Germany about 1870 and came to the United States just after the Civil War. They quickly became Americanized, so much so that they wanted to forget their past. But with me, a Jew, foreign-born, and also an immigrant, he could open up, and we both exchanged stories about our early youth in the old countries.

On March 20, 1933, Herman Harris died. His family wanted to invite one of the leading rabbis of the country to officiate at the funeral. His nephew knew how close I was to Herman and convinced them all that I should deliver the main eulogy. A judge of the Supreme Court was to join me. *The Sun*, a leading San Bernardino newspaper wrote: 3,000 ATTEND SERVICES FOR HERMAN HARRIS. ALL CITY PAYS LAST TRIBUTE. Business houses closed in his honor. All city offices were closed.

I visited Los Angeles after an absence of many weeks and learned that my sister Lizzie had lost all her properties. They had been worth hundreds of thousands of dollars. Fortunately, she retained a small plant for the manufacture of liquors. It was operated by Lizzie and Sarah's husband, Aaron. They also owned the Tux Ginger Ale and Liquor Company and both businesses supported two families and about twenty employees.

When I told Aaron that I was planning to go east to see Vera, he suggested I make a little extra money on the way by selling some of the Tux liquor products to distributors in the south. I happily agreed, and two sample cases of fruit brandies were neatly arranged for my trip to Boston via New Orleans and New York.

My first and most important stopover was New Orleans. While waiting for an appointment with the largest distributor of liquor in the south, I spent two delightful days in the company of one of the Hebrew poets, E.E. Lisitzky, whose poems on the Indians and Blacks are classics to this day. I was sorry that I was called back so soon to attend to business.

When I arrived at the offices of the large warehouse of Goodman and Beer, I found six people waiting for my samples. Three were professional tasters and the others were executives of the firm. My different samples filled many glasses and the testing and tasting commenced in my presence. I was then asked to go to another room. They gave me a number of magazines, and told me to wait for an hour or so until they called me.

When the hour was up the vice-president of the firm came in and informed me they had decided to order a carload of mixed liquors. It took me a while to grasp the size of the order. After repeating my questions and seeing the figures in writing, I wanted to dance with joy. Within less than an hour I had the written order in my hand and I was given a room with a telephone for my calls to Los Angeles and Boston.

When I reached Los Angeles I spoke to Aaron. He couldn't believe what I told him. Three times he asked me, "A car load? Are you sure you're reading it right?" He put my sister on the phone and after I read the contract to her, she wanted the company to cable the contents at once and send a copy of the contract by registered mail. They still couldn't believe it.

I asked how much commission I was entitled to. She said $1,400. I repeated my question three times. On the third time she said, "It may be a little more."

I then called Vera and the first thing I said to her was "We can get married!" Startled, she also asked me the same question three times. When we are accustomed to hearing uninterrupted bad news, good news penetrates the mind very slowly.

Before reaching Boston I had to stop in New York, where two companies kept me waiting for four days before they could decide what to do. Finally they decided not to do anything. Luck does not strike twice at one time. I didn't care. I had more than I hoped for. I spent the four days in a beautiful room at the Waldorf Astoria Hotel, paying the exorbitant rate of six dollars a day.

My young cousin, Irving Marantz, who was a "starving artist," moved in and stayed with me. We spent all our time in museums and galleries. When the New York liquor distributors decided not to place any orders, I took back all the samples. Irving and I went down to the delicatessen and bought a big salami, a corned beef, dozens of pickles, three loaves of bread, and anything else that captured our eye. Then he called three of his friends from the Art Students League to come to our party. The five of us probably had one of the most enthusiastic feasts in the history of the Waldorf Astoria. They all stayed overnight, sleeping on the floor of the most luxurious hotel in New York.

The next morning I was on my way to Boston. While there, I got a trial order, which brought me in another $200 in commissions. Vera took her vacation that week, and together we saw the picturesque sights of New England. I was happier than I had been for three years.

Because of my long absence from San Bernardino, my pressing work on the relief commission, and the approaching holidays, we set our wedding for October. During the week of the festival of Succoth we were married in San Bernardino by my dear friend, Rabbi Isadore Isaacson.

On January 22, 1935, our first child was born. We gave her the Hebrew name of Hedvah, the meaning of which is inner joy. Many people thought that the name was Scandinavian. Perhaps they were thinking of Hedda Gabler. Our Hedvah brought her full share of joy and light into the home.

Soon after the wedding I bought a two-bedroom house with a library in the hilly part of town for only $2,800 with $1,000 in cash. Five years before it had been $10,000. Such were the effects of the Depression on real-estate values all over the country.

With the advent of President Roosevelt's New Deal, the country gradually began to recover from shock. We were able to see the distant rays of light in the economic and social life of the nation. This was reflected in San Bernardino and Riverside Counties, where a vast number of the population suffered from unemployment. There were still many months ahead when orange growers would invite people to help themselves to the ripe oranges before they rotted on the trees. Large melons were selling for one cent apiece and gasoline was eight cents a gallon, but things were picking up.

One day, when I was visiting the home of a family on our relief rolls, my eyes wandered to the wall, where I saw a picture of a saint, a picture of the President of the United States, and a newspaper clipping. The year was 1933, the depth of the Depression. The clipping showed a quilt made by the people for whom we helped obtain jobs. The reason for the news photo was a ceremony in which the quilt was turned over to me. I had been charged to deliver it to the head of the W.P.A., the Works Progress Administration, who would present the quilt to President and Mrs. Roosevelt in the name of the workers. The W.P.A. was a federally funded organization that assisted writers, painters, sculptors, and other artists to engage in their respective callings through federal grants. The W.P.A. also ran large city-works projects.

The Depression assumed many faces in San Bernardino. One manifestation of it was the thousands of old jalopies that poured into the San Bernardino area. They were filled with refugees from the dust bowls of Oklahoma, hungry people looking for bread and jobs. Forty million acres of their arable soil had been totally destroyed, and over a hundred million more acres of topsoil were carried off by the worst windstorms of our era. With no food from the fields and none in the home, the "Okies" abandoned their dried-up farms, and with the whirling dirt filling their throats, they set out for the promised land of California. San Bernardino was their main stopover after they came through the Cajon Pass. These unwelcome arrivals were called a "dirty, ignorant lot." We had difficulties explaining to our frightened residents that behind the rags and grime and the drawn faces of the newcomers were human beings, who deserved the same care we extended to our own needy.

At about this time the elderly lady whom we had engaged to take care of Hedvah decided to return to her daughter in Minnesota. We needed a maid, and we went to one of the camps the invading army of Okies had set up. There was no difficulty finding a strong, healthy girl. She was twenty years old and her name was Opal.

Opal's vocabulary was very limited. Her formal education was obtained in a one-room schoolhouse of sixteen children ranging in age from 6 to 15. Opal completed second or third grade. We bought her some new clothes and provided facilities for her to shower and wash her hair. When she came out of the bathroom, hair combed, face and skin glowing from the scrubbing she gave herself, I hardly recognized her.

Along with gainful employment, Opal wanted to attend night classes and learn to read English "different from the way Ma and Pa talk." She did not care "nohow" to talk the way they did, especially after the way they had deserted her. They never told her where they were going and never bothered to discover her whereabouts.

Everything went well with Opal. She learned fast and she took good care of Hedvah. We had one problem with her during the nighttime. Opal slept in Hedvah's room. Hedvah was about six months old and would occasionally wake up at night crying. Opal slept very soundly and didn't always hear the baby. Either Vera or I would rush in. In the hot summer months it was embarrassing. Opal had never heard of pajamas and when we bought her some, she thanked us very much and didn't wear them. In her sleep she would toss off her sheet. After that Vera would always go in when Hedvah cried.

One day I got a call from the warden of our local jail. He had a girl locked up, he said, "for having walked out of a store with a coat she hadn't bothered to pay for." I told Vera where Opal was spending her day off and that I was going to pay her a visit. When I entered Opal's cell, she began weeping. I asked her if it was true that she stole the coat. She raised her head with a frightened, bewildered look.

Fortunately I knew the judge, who was a fellow Rotarian. I asked if he could give Opal an early trial and if there was anything I could do to help her. "Yes," he said, "you can help her if you guarantee to keep her in your care for at least one year." He agreed to suspend her sentence and put her in my custody. I was also told to talk with her before she went out to make large purchases. This proved unnecessary because the Baptist minister took care of that. He was grateful to me for having increased the poor attendance at his church with another soul. Opal, on the other hand, was glad I had introduced her to the minister because she met a "nice boy" in the church. She told Vera that she liked the church because they could meet there, pray together, and then go out for ice cream.

The federal projects opened new sources of employment, and the mood of the country brightened. My burdens also eased up and I could devote more time to my family, my studies, and my interests.

I was always careful to avoid any involvement in controversial issues, but there are times when one's sense of duty calls for a stand that may ruffle the feathers of the powers that be. After Sinclair Lewis's novel *It Can't Happen Here* appeared, I was asked by the San Bernardino Literary Group to review the book for its membership. This group was known for its liberal views and was strongly disliked by the American Legion. Without my prior knowledge the organizers of the lecture rented a large hall and gave the planned review a great deal of publicity. This aroused the ire of the conservative groups who, without having read the book, regarded it as un-American.

Representatives of the Legion and the Chamber of Commerce requested some of our Jewish leaders to ask me to cancel my appearance. Many worrisome meetings followed, I explained to everyone that regardless of the way in which my review would be given, I could not, in good conscience, cancel my appearance.

I discussed the matter with some of my Christian colleagues. The Episcopalian and Congregational ministers and nearly all the teachers at the college supported my position. To avoid any possibility of an unfortunate confrontation, I told a committee of the American Legion that they should send a representative group to the lecture hall, and if anything I said was un-American they should rise as a group and I would terminate my address.

The Legion representatives, some of whom had heard me speak many times, consented. They considered the suggestion fair. When I entered the hall, which was rapidly filling up, I saw five Legionnaires standing in the rear. They seemed poised for action. When they saw that three distinguished clergymen, the president of the college, and other well-known citizens entered the hall and took front seats, the Legionnaires sat down shamefacedly.

I spoke for sixty minutes and concluded with an emotional appeal for tolerance and love for democracy. The papers played up the incident and many books were sold. Requests for my lecture from other clubs and organizations largely enhanced my side income.

In the summer of 1934 demands on my time piled up. I was invited to address a session at the convention of the Zionist Organization of America. I was also invited to attend a conference on social work. I was still president of the County Council of Social Agencies at that time. These engagements and visits to my relatives in New York necessitated my being away from home for about five weeks and worked some hardship on my family.

A new spirit, especially noticeable in the younger generation, became very evident during the following years of my life in San Bernardino. It was as though the community had risen from its deep slumber. However, for my fellow Jews and myself, it was unfortunately not the same. Sinister, dark clouds began to hover over our lives. Finished with the greatest economic depression, we began to face the deepest tragedy of our people in modern times, the advent to power of Adolph Hitler.

Two years before Hitler's rise to power, I had been elected a member of the San Bernardino Rotary Club. At the time I was the only Jewish member in our club. Nevertheless, I never felt more comfortable or more at home in any organization. The club utilized my services freely. Smaller clubs often called on us for assistance when they needed a speaker for meetings. I was one of the few who gladly obliged. Little did I think that the bread I cast upon the waters would return to me.

With the imminent danger to Jewry posed by the anti-Semitism emanating from Germany, I felt duty-bound to change the nature of my activities. I began to devote a great deal of my time to our struggle against Nazism so as to prevent its spread to the American shore.

The Rotary Club is strictly non-political and avoids any issues that are not universally accepted by all Rotarians. Some slight exceptions were made by the officials of the Rotary in connection with my addresses against Nazism. Not only was I not restrained in what I said, but I was encouraged to arouse public opinion against this "menace to humanity." The Rotary of San Bernardino, in affiliation with five other Rotary clubs, was the first one in America to place itself on record in an open struggle aganist Nazism.

The increased demands on my time cut into my work in the Unemployed Emergency Council. But since the economic life of the community had improved, I believed that my resignation as the president of the Council would be justified. When I announced my resignation I was deeply moved by the appreciation of the community for my services. I was the subject of the following editorial in *The Orange Belt News*:

> Too much praise cannot be given the work of the retiring head of the city's relief group. Such effort, such sympathy and understanding, plus the technical knowledge for handling welfare work on a large scale make him one of the most valuable adjuncts to the city's official life.

Free from responsibilities on the relief commission, I had more time to devote to my classes at the college. One on Biblical Archaeology was my favorite class; the other, attended by some ministers and a unique group of fundamentalist Christians, was on the Hebrew language. There were thirty-four students in the language class. One was a Jew, our closest friend, Dorothy Neumann. Twenty-two belonged to the fundamentalist group, which believed that every letter of the Hebrew alphabet was sacred. I do not remember what they called themselves; I only remember that they were a young, intelligent, dedicated, fanatically religious group. They tried to emulate the life of Jesus and engaged in manual trades. The three leading members were carpenters. When I was in an inspired mood and explained the meaning of a Hebrew word in depth, they were in ecstasy. They loved to listen to references from the Cabbalah, whose mysticism fulfilled their yearnings.

They were insatiable for the amounts of homework I assigned them. I told them they would have to correct their assignments through their own collective efforts. They were most respectful and did all they could not to burden me with extra work. I never realized how devoted they were to me until I announced my departure from San Bernardino. They gave me a farewell party and brought simple, handmade gifts. One was a marvel. It was Noah's Ark, carved and assembled from the finest wood.

Freed also from my communal activities, I found time to make trips to Los Angeles and renew my interest in art. The most important personal development during my last two years in San Bernardino was my increased knowledge and appreciation of Chinese art. During one of my lectures on art, a gentleman came up to me after the speech and introduced himself as Roger Williams, art collector and long-time resident of China.

He invited me to his home to see his remarkable collection of Chinese paintings, porcelains, and statuary. He appreciated people who understood and loved the art he had collected over the last thirty years. He invited me again and again to come whenever I was free. In our many conversations about the paintings, porcelains, and bronzes, he told me interesting things about the great culture of China. This encouraged me to explore a field remote from my traditional interest. What I saw and read was reflected in my Friday night addresses. In this new Eastern source I found material to freshen some of my tired talks.

In the summer of 1936 I was asked to join a study mission to eastern Europe, in the light of developments in Germany. I was also given an opportunity to earn some money during the summer by writing a series of articles for the Anglo-Jewish press on eastern Europe and Germany.

Until then, I had been so deeply involved in depression relief that I had not felt the need to venture beyond San Bernardino. Now I needed air to breathe. I craved the big libraries, the museums, the theatres, and the concert halls which had always been part of my life.

Vera stayed at home with Hedvah. I jumped at the chance to go to Europe, Palestine, and Egypt.

In New York I met with the study mission and arranged to meet them again in Bucharest. I then proceeded alone to Palestine via Egypt. Seven long and good years had passed since the time of the great crash on Wall Street, when my savings had been wiped out and I had been forced to abandon plans to establish myself in business in Palestine. In spite of my total immersion in American life, not one week passed without nostalgia for the little, ancient land so dear to every Jewish heart.

One of the regrets I carried with me from 1929 was that I had to forego my chance to visit Egypt. I had planned to do so before embarking on my proposed publishing career, but the Wall Street crash had put an end to both projects. With the approval of the *Jewish Community Press*, which agreed to publish my articles, I now set out for Egypt in 1936.

Max Weber (standing) speaking of his last work with Alfredo Valente and Jacob Alkow at the Valente Gallery.

XIII
EGYPT AND PALESTINE 1936

"To travel is to live history," said Dr. Logan Clendening. In 1936 the usual approach to Egypt was through the city established in 331 B.C. by Alexander the Great. Alexandria's harbor marks the end of the winding Nile River, which fructifies a long desert strip with its rich deposits.

When I first glimpsed the city through the portholes of my cabin, it was six o'clock in the morning. Two things fascinated me: the European skyline in back of the harbor, and the large fleet of British warships moored in its port. It was a period when the British Navy was at the zenith of its power and, in view of Hitler's preparations for war, it gave us a false sense of security.

As we were preparing to land, a Baptist minister stood beside me at the rail of our French boat. We were both gazing at the city. "For years I have wanted to see this city," he said, "because this is where the Hebrew scriptures were first translated into Greek. That was in the third century B.C. The Septuagint means a great deal to us Christians."

"I can understand that," I said, and proceeded to tell him what Alexandria meant to me. "It was here that we had the largest synagogue in the diaspora. Thirty percent of the population was Jewish, and it was from this harbor that all the imports of Roman grain were carried in ships owned by Jews. It was also here in Alexandria that two Jewish brothers were the principal generals of Cleopatra's army."

Although I was fascinated by the Greco-Roman Museum and its breathtaking sculptures, it was another, unknown aspect of Cleopatra that impressed me most. I had read in Plutarch that the greatest grief of Cleopatra's life occurred when half of her library was lost during the struggle to retain her throne. When Marc Anthony offered this noblest of all queens in history whichever Roman colony she might desire, she chose the smallest and poorest, Pergames, because it had the finest collection of manuscripts. They were later transferred to Alexandria's library.

I had been waiting a long time to see four places in Cairo: the museum, the Sphinx, the pyramids, and the Ibn Ezra Synagogue. Two of my four days in Cairo I browsed among the historical and archeological treasures in the museum.

On the third day I went to see the Sphinx, the pyramids, and the oldest house of Jewish worship outside of Jerusalem. The sexton of the Ibn Ezra Synagogue informed me proudly that the present structure was rebuilt in the ninth century and stood on the very spot where Aaron and Moses had worshipped. When he also claimed that the prophet Jeremiah had worshipped there, I believed him. Jeremiah propshesied from Tachpanches in the delta of the Nile, which is in the vicinity of Cairo. In this ancient synagogue the greatest Jewish religious teacher in the last 1600 years, Maimonides, also worshipped. The most interesting feature of the synagogue was its *genizah*, or the "hidden place" where thousands of parchments and books were stored; under Jewish law, sacred books no longer in use may not be destroyed.

Late in the last century two young girls who studied at Cambridge University were on tour through Egypt. In Cairo they bought some trinkets at a curio shop, and the dealer persuaded them to purchase two small pieces of old parchment with writing on them. Neither the dealer nor the girls could identify the script. The girls thought it was probably a Semitic language, and upon their return to Cambridge, they showed the parchments to the professor of Semitic languages, Dr. Solomon Schechter.

When Dr. Schechter saw the parchments he became very excited. "Where did you find these pieces?" he asked. The girls described the curio shop. Dr. Schechter hurried to the steamship office and took the first available boat for Cairo. He was sure these parchment pieces were the most important Biblical discovery of the century. They were fragments of the original Hebrew book of Ben Sira, of the Apocryphal literature. Until then, the book was known only through its Greek translation. The original Hebrew version had been lost.

The professor found the curio dealer and learned that the parchment had reached him through a worker who had been hired to clean the Ibn Ezra Synagogue. He must have discovered some way of reaching into the hidden, enclosed *genizah*, and pulled out a few pieces.

With the help of the authorities and requests from Cambridge University, Professor Schechter obtained permission to open the *genizah* which contained the greatest treasures of old Hebraic writings. The whole scholarly world was aroused. Among the many parchments deposited hundreds of years ago was the lost Hebrew book of Ben Sira. Portions of the Talmud and the Mishna, hitherto unknown, were revealed. For years scholars have been working diligently to bring to light all that was found in this Cairo Synagogue. When I stood before the *genizah* and peered at it in the shadows of the synagogue, I asked myself how many other secrets still lay there, waiting to be deciphered by a scholarly hand. "The enhancement of knowledge is the joy of the heart," said the ancient rabbis.

A bayonet fixed to an overworked rifle was the first sight that greeted me on my return to the Holy Land. In Haifa I could not walk through the streets of the mixed Jewish-Arab population without being accompanied by a fatigued, young British Tommy. His concern was as much for his own life as it was for mine. His eyes shifted rapidly from side to side, scrutinizing the movement of suspicious-looking Arabs who were as frightened as he was.

There was a general strike of the Arabs, and much killing and wanton destruction by bands of Arabs. It was so similar to 1929, and so familiar to me, that I could not believe the years had passed. I had always hoped that what happened in 1929 would never be repeated.

On the way from Haifa to Tel Aviv I kept shaking my head in disbelief when I saw the fires set by the Arab incendiaries to consume Jewish fields. Our train was stopped twice, and when it did proceed, it dragged along very slowly. Two bridges had been blown up by terrorists, and until the tracks were laid again, the train was held up. In the eyes and the speech of those who defended the Jewish position, I saw the same resolve and determination not to allow the frenzied Arabs to get the upper hand.

After several days in Tel Aviv, it was not easy for me to reach Jerusalem. Our bus had to join a caravan of four cars. The convoy was led and followed by open trucks with rapidly revolving machine guns. Near each machine gun were two soldiers ready to fire into the hostile hills on either side of the road.

When I arrived in the city, which was more beautiful than ever, and which I love more any any other city in the world, there was a temporary curfew. After the bustle in Tel Aviv, the curfew in Jerusalem put me in a bad mood. To be confined to one's room and bear the silence of a large, empty hotel was a new and unpleasant experience. Even my life on the kibbutz near Deganiah in 1929 with the continuous shooting outside had been more tolerable. There it involved activity; in Jerusalem in involved confinement.

Next morning there was a most beautiful sunrise from behind the surrounding hills, and it changed my mood. After breakfast I went into the busy daytime streets, crowded with people of all ages, races, and religions. The sadness and anxiety of the previous night disappeared. I was filled with enthusiasm and eager to go everywhere and see everything.

My first trip was to the Hebrew University to see my old friend, Professor Joseph Klausner. He was delighted and straightaway invited me to have dinner with him. The campus of the university was filled with students despite the summer vacation. This same campus was now many times the size it had been when I first saw it seven years earlier.

With the large migration of Jews who escaped from Germany, Jerusalem had become a new center for music. For its size, it was the most music-loving city in the world. In spite of the troubles in the land, there was not an evening without a concert. Wherever I turned I was intrigued by familiar sights. I was again like the man of whom Rabbi Kook said "he was one great question mark—all his answers are nothing but questions."

I went to the Wailing Wall. I would not see it for another twenty-two years. I then left Jerusalem to continue my trip.

As I stood on the deck of the *S.S. Polonia* en route from Haifa to Constantza, and watched the disappearing Palestine skyline, I was filled with regret. I had never left the Holy Land less sure of what the blurred future would be. I was trying to collect my thoughts and assess the picture objectively. The result was one of doubt and uncertainty. For the first time my faith was shaken. In the face of distrust and bitter opposition of the Arabs, coupled with a betrayal by the British Empire, I could not see how the Jews could achieve their goals of building a homeland.

For a clear, reassuring answer to the questions and doubts that surfaced in me for the first time, I had to wait until I reached Rumanian soil. In Mamaya, Constantza, Kishinev, Bucharest, in Rumanian trains and wretched Jewish villages, I found the answer, the justification for the sacrifices and martyrdoms made to ensure the unabated Jewish settlement of Palestine. Whichever way I turned, I found an undisputed determination to persist in the Zionist venture, against all odds.

When I arrived in Tigenia, the last Rumanian city before we crossed the border to Russia, I finally got a full picture of the Jewish tragedy. The news of my arrival had quickly circulated through the town and crowds of young men and women, boys and girls, filled the street in front of my dilapidated boarding house. They came to hear about Palestine. They were hungry for news. The impoverished Yiddish newspaper printed in Rumania did not satisfy them. They were nearly all Zionists in Tigenia, and what worried them most was the fear that Jewish immigration to Palestine would be curbed as a result of the disturbances. They asked me all the details.

I talked to people on every aspect of the Palestinian question, trying to give a fair picture, but even the derogatory things I had to tell them did not dampen their enthusiasm and loyalty to their homeland. None of my descriptions of the horrors I had seen, none of my stories about the young workers who were killed, none of my portrayals of the hardships arising from the antagonism of the Arabs, none of my accounts of the natural difficulties in developing a poor country—none of these had the slightest effect on the young people's determination to go and live in Palestine at any cost.

"We will carry on," they said, "we will break through and smash the wall with our heads. We cannot retreat, because Palestine, alone, is the land that remains for the Jews of Rumania. It is our only hope. Without Palestine there is nothing to live for." This was three years before the Second World War. Their desperation was evident long before the survivors of the extermination camps found a haven in Palestine.

When I met the study mission in Bucharest, I told them of my experiences in Palestine and in the towns and cities of Rumania. I feared we had no time to lose. We had to do everything possible to bring a few hundred thousand Jews from eastern Europe into Palestine at once. Not only would we save the Jews of Rumania and Poland from their state of desperation, but we would safeguard our bridgehead in Palestine.

I was now headed for Russia to continue writing my articles and reports. On the Russian train from Bucharest to Odessa, I met a group of Jewish workers who were on their way home from a vacation on the Black Sea near the Rumanian border. We entered into a lively conversation in Yiddish. They asked endless questions about Palestine and America, but what interested them most were my shoes and my jacket. "Not since the revolution in 1917," said an older worker, "have I seen such beautiful shoes and such a finely styled jacket."

When I told them how much my shoes cost, they translated it into rubles. When they arrived at the equivalent value, they couldn't believe the price. I compared the number of days I had to work to earn enough money to buy my shoes with the number of weeks they had to work for an inferior pair. Then when I told them I was a teacher and not a capitalist, I added to their amazement.

One of their group was a science teacher and he was the only one who knew Hebrew. I began to speak to him in Hebrew, thinking we might strike up a better relationship, but he looked around and withdrew from the group. I never saw him again.

"*No Hebraish,*" one older lady said. "In our Soviet Union it is forbidden." I later discovered that when a foreigner approached a group of Russian citizens, there was usually a secret agent present who listened to every word. When we were leaving the train, a man pressed my hand warmly and whispered, "Please be careful. Shalom."

XIV
RUSSIA

The roots of the modern Hebrew renaissance arose in Odessa. Among those who lived and worked there prior to the Russian revolution were Chaim Bialik, the poet; Mendele Mocher Sforim, master of the new literary form of Hebrew writing; Achad Ha'am, founder of cultural Zionism; Dr. Joseph Klausner, Biblical scholar; and Vladimir Jabotinsky, the versatile literary and political figure.

Odessa was the youngest of the large cities of Europe. It was built about 1800 on the ruins of the ancient Greek city of Odessos, which had been destroyed by the Goths in the third century. Jews were among those who had rebuilt the city. In 1936, when I first saw its famous steps, there were about 600,000 inhabitants. Fully one-third were Jewish. Before the Russian revolution nearly 60% of the stores were owned by Jews, who also controlled 80% of the exports going through the harbor of Odessa. Now I found barely a trace of the rich cultural and spiritual life which had spread its wings over the Jewish countryside of Russia. The Bolsheviks had killed the Jewish soul of Odessa. Eight years after my 1936 visit, the Nazis finished the task by exterminating nearly two-thirds of the Jewish population.

In Odessa and elsewhere in Russia, I was accepted most graciously, owing to my wife's former connections with the Boston Intourist Office, a bureau that made arrangements for tourists visiting Russia. Vera had worked as secretary in the Boston Intourist Office. Before our marriage she personally disavowed her connection with anything pertaining to the office. Nevertheless, her former employer gave me a letter to Russian Intourist, which helped open many doors in the securely bolted offices of Stalin's regime. In Odessa I was assigned to a small group of English-speaking professors and writers for the guided tours, and I was given special privileges in my hotel and traveling accommodations. Having been introduced as a journalist, I rated a special guide during the hours I escaped from the members of my group.

A young lady named Tania was our guide through Odessa and Kiev. She was also my personal guide in the evenings and procured all the tickets for us. It was a pleasure for which I ask my wife to forgive me. Tania was a university graduate with special training in the guiding of VIPs through sensitive Russian areas. At that time there were very few important persons who required the particular guidance Tania was trained to offer. I benefited greatly from this situation, as I had Tania at my side any time I needed her.

She was a beautiful girl with reddish hair and a glowing complexion. In addition to Russian, she spoke four languages. She knew German better than English, which enabled me to practice the German which I would have to use later on. She also helped me with Russian, which I had spoken in my childhood and had almost forgotten. Much of it began to return. I was particularly pleased when I grasped the lyrical, musical poems of Lermontov. As a rule she was not supposed to devote her time and talents to the reading of Russian poetry. I tried to justify it by telling her how much better I was able to write when inspired by literature or art. She laughed and then turned serious, saying, "I hope my superiors can accept what you say." Tania was very businesslike and correct. She called me comrade and I called her comrade.

On two occasions after Tania explained the projected five-year plan in the most positive authoritative manner to our group, I questioned her privately. Was there a possibility that it might not all materialize? She looked at me, frightened, and all she said was "Please."

That evening I tried to speak with Tania more freely about herself, her husband, and her work. She didn't want to talk about her work. When I pressed her and asked if she was unhappy in her job, she squeezed my hand and said, "It's not that. You wouldn't understand it. It's torturous." The German word "torturous," which I heard for the first time, was later to become a most familiar term. Immediately after the performance, we parted in the lobby abruptly, as on previous occasions.

I derived as much personal, physical pleasure in the cities of Russia as I did in the cities of the United States. My hotel accommodations were the finest and the food, though heavy at times, was delicious. For breakfast in Odessa, Kiev, Moscow, and Leningrad, there was a large silver bowl of iced, black caviar. The waiter would ask whether I wanted a *malinkaya* (small) omelet or a large one. What was the difference? The small one was made from four eggs, the large one from six eggs. And then the thin, thin pancakes, cheeses, jams, and fresh black bread! For dinner, if I wanted chicken there was a whole, young, broiled chicken in an elegant silver serving tray, probably stolen from the home of some prince. Along with a ten-course dinner after the theatre, there was vodka and a bottle of fine wine. With dinner there was classical music, and after dinner there was dance music.

All this when the majority of people outside the hotel queued up in long lines to buy a loaf of bread, a little milk, or cheese. But nothing was too good for the very few that the regime might need. The same luxuries offered to the select group of visitors were also offered to the commissars and their wives. Generally I dined with some member of the group, but since I was unable to warm up to any one of them, I preferred to dine alone. Both in Kiev and in Moscow, commissars or politicos, who had imbibed more vodka than water, asked me to dance with their wives. For the first time in five years, I realized that there was a good deal of fun in dancing, even with the commissars' usually corpulent wives. The first one in Kiev didn't mind how many times I stepped on her toes. She kept pulling me back to the floor. Her husband was hilarious. This entertainment lasted till three in the morning.

On the afternoon of our arrival in Kiev, Tania reappeared. We had all been sure we were going to get a new guide. She tried to be aloof when she informed me that she would be able to see me and take me sightseeing the next afternoon. Free of any scheduled hours, I was able to walk around by myself through the crowded streets of the third-largest city of the Soviet Union. In 1936 Kiev had a population of 1,800,000 people. About twenty percent were Jewish.

The Jews of Kiev were the most suspicious people I met. They avoided my presence in any public place. Never was I treated so discourteously. Whenever I approached someone and asked in Yiddish about how things were going, I was answered by a dead silence and a blank expression. I finally found a clue as to why this was happening. My American clothes were the cause of it all. Stalin's secret-service agents were busily engaged in checking all foreigners and rounding up Jewish intellectuals. Anyone who spoke Hebrew was sure to be among the victims who were packed off to Siberia for hard labor.

I obtained this information from a few old women, whom I usually approached for the same thing—a glass of water. The old women were the only fearless people I met, except for Tania. When an Intourist guide asked me how I enjoyed my walk through the city and the Kiev Museum, my least truthful answers assured me the possibility of seeing Tania again. "Yes," said the patriotic Intourist guide, "Kiev, thanks to Stalin, has progressed more than any other Russian city. Wait till you see our industrial establishments and our new university. They will open your eyes."

He could not have known how much my eyes were already opened by those who had kept their mouths shut. The following day Tania took me to the birthplace of the Jewish Mark Twain. In America, Sholem Aleichem is known mainly for the story of *Fiddler on the Roof*. But in the Soviet Union he is regarded as a proletarian writer and the only one of the great galaxy of the old classical Jewish writers who was *persona grata*. Another writer in Yiddish, A. Fefer, was conveniently tolerated until Stalin liquidated him together with Bergelson and many others soon after the war.

Years later, during the war, I met Fefer in Los Angeles. I drove him around and showed him the sights of southern California. He had come to America on a mission for the Soviet Union to gain support for the joint war effort against Hitler. We agreed on many things, but we disagreed on our attitudes toward Stalin and the Hebrew language. He was for the first and against the second; I was bitterly against the first, needless to say, all for the second. Neither of us convinced the other but we parted good friends. I promised Fefer to visit his city, Kiev, again some day in the future. Stalin's criminal acts in brutally killing writers who had dedicated their lives in the service of the Soviet Union actually released me of all desire to see Kiev again.

However, thanks to Tania, I was able to see much that was good, beautiful, and constructive in Kiev. It was in the schools filled with bright students, in the symphony hall, and in the museum of Ukrainian folklore. In the forests where no one followed us, I was free of Stalin's insane suppression of the human spirit.

The following day we visited the most publicized revolutionary project of the Soviet Union, the *kolkhoz* or communal agricultural settlements. In their anxiety to surpass the development of the Western countries "within ten years," the Communists laid stress on heavy industry, which I saw in Kiev, and the collectivization of the peasants, whose settlements I visited in the countryside. I was deeply impressed by both phenomenal developments. In spite of my personal feelings about Stalin as a human being, I could not but marvel at what he had achieved through his autocratic methods. My so-called objective reports on the progress of the Russian economy, of which I wrote in my articles, were not well received by my readers. Some in San Bernardino thought I was too soft and that I had been taken in by Russian propaganda. My first article, which I mailed the second day in Kiev, dealt with the suppression of free speech and the expulsion of the Zionist intellectuals. It never reached the editorial rooms. Russian censorship had made sure that no unfavorable views would leave Russia.

In 1936, and until this day, Americans wanted to hear only derogatory things about Russia, Cuba, or any country whose political philosophy runs counter to our own. It is therefore doubly essential for anyone with an open mind to go to these countries and sift through fact and fiction. I admit this is a difficult task. I myself had difficulties. Together with some of my group, I questioned what I was told. Those who believed they were revealing the truth were unaware that they were half-truths.

More fortunate than the other members of our professorial group, I was able to fall back on the old Yiddish women and on the Jews whom I met. While some of their stories were slanted, I was able to piece together a reasonably objective picture of the complete life of the country. The one who enlightened me most was Tania.

Tania was born and bred in the heart of communism. Her father, a high school teacher, had been a Communist years before the revolution. Tania did not know any other regime and it was difficult for her to understand the society I lived in. The idea of working for personal gain rather than for the well-being of the state was incomprehensible to her. Yet it was Tania who, in our private talks in Kiev, made me aware of the shortcomings of the Communist experiments in Russia.

Tania arranged to show me a project near the thick forests that surrounded Kiev. We saw little of the project and a great deal of the forest, where we spent a full afternoon. It was the first time Tania was free to unburden herself. She sensed a sympathetic ear and poured out her agony as a Communist who was betrayed by the "ruthless, ignorant men who were in control." A few of her Jewish friends were frightened as a result of what happened during the last few weeks when the Jewish doctors were arrested. She, herself, was uneasy and worried. Every step she took was scrutinized.

I tried to cheer up Tania and told her how beautiful she was when she was not subjected to the strain of her job. "Yes," she said, "you think my job is always like the one I have with you and your friends. There are times when it is insufferable."

Once she had had to accompany a minister from a friendly country. He wanted to sleep with her and she refused. He insisted that her superiors assured him she would comply. Then he threatened to tell her bosses that she was an enemy of the state. She was furious and adamant. She threatened to tell her superiors that she would make a capital case out of it. The matter was dropped.

When we sat and ate the lunch we had taken with us, she implied that, if possible, she would be most happy to join me wherever I went. I said that would be out of the question because we were both married. She laughed and said, it was not being married that was the real obstacle as far as she was concerned, it was the secret police. A guide who slept with a man she loved without the permission of her superior ended up sleeping in jail. That was our last afternoon together. The next morning I was on my way to Moscow. Tania was officially asked to see me off. All she said was "Good-bye."

Sitting comfortably in a first-class coach, I allowed my mind to wander over all that had happened during my first week in Russia. I saw the good and I saw the bad. Overall, I perceived the tolerable and the meaningful as well as the intolerable and inhuman phases of life in Russia. Above everything I saw Tania. I saw the disappointment and despair when our ideals are betrayed by the people in whom we place our trust. I remembered how she said that when she was a member of the Comsomol, the Communist Youth Movement, Stalin was a god to her. "Now . . . ," and she never finished the sentence. I remembered how Shelley expressed her sentiments when he wrote of Napoleon:

> In honored poverty thy voice did weave
>   Songs consecrate to truth and liberty
> Deserting these thou leavest me to grieve
>   Thus having been, that thou shouldst cease to be.

I heard this refrain in different words from the lips of many disillusioned people.

I love America. I loved her from the day the German boat brought my family to her free shores. I love America's way of life, her people, her institutions, those who turn their backs on her materialism, and those who in innocence espouse her materialism. I love her cities and I love her countryside. I love Israel. I love her ancient history. I love her beautiful seashores. I love her people, the good, the bad, and the confused. I love her language, her literature, and every one of her ancient stones. Not until I arrived in Moscow, and breathed her air and saw her people, did I realize that I also loved Russia.

It was my first country, where as a child I had listened to her sad songs. It was there my teachers taught me to read by using excerpts from Tolstoy, Dostoyevsky, and Turgenev. The Russian reading alternated with the Hebrew of Bialik, Mendele, Mapu, and Tchernikowsky. In the years I was involved with America, the memory of my youthful life in Russia waned. Then I would hear the plaintive, melodious songs in some Russian restaurant in New York or Paris, and the memory was briefly reawakened.

Over the next few days I was, in spite of Stalin, able to find a part of the soul of Russia. Russia is more than a regime. It is more than one or many tyrants. Russia is the people I saw and talked to. They were kind, good, honest people who, aside from ideology, strove to be free and true. Different people, speaking different languages, wearing different clothes, eating different food, all tolerated each other. Not all were free of prejudice, of racism, or anti-Semitism, but where in the world are all people free of the plagues of society?

In Moscow I was able to rid myself of the prejudice I had had against Russia, a bias engendered by the horror stories of the Jewish people in Kiev. I was hurt when I learned of the sufferings of my comrades who spoke Hebrew and yearned to go to the land of their fathers. I vowed never to return to Kiev, even though the vast population was innocent. Here in Moscow I was able to forget much of what was perpetrated against those who were close to me. I only remembered the good and the best of all that was in Kiev—Tania.

I stayed at the Metropole. In Czarist times the hotel was occupied by foreign dignitaries, and my room was an excellent setting for the old world of Russia which Tolstoy had described so richly. I was still enamored with the bowls of black caviar and the string orchestras I heard every night after the theatre.

The days were filled with sightseeing. Nevertheless I had ample time to browse in the large library and in the museums. Bizzare as it may seem, in spite of the ban against the use of Hebrew, I found many rare Hebrew books, which consumed a good deal of my free time. The Intourist office in Moscow, busy with a large influx of summer tourists, was less rigid than the Kiev and Odessa branches. I was provided with addresses and a driver. At the Moscow University and other scholarly institutions, I was free to audit any courses or classes given in the languages I understood.

In my meanderings around Moscow, I found that art was one of the victims of the revolution. In the Communist paradise, it had withered. This was not the case with the theatre and the ballet; in the Broadway of Moscow there were many theatres, one alongside another. On some evenings I would attend several performances in one night. Notwithstanding my insufficient grasp of Russian, I would see one or two acts in one theatre and the last act in another. And it was all free!

The pleasantest surprise of all was the ballet. Unlike the fettered literature and painting, which were languishing under the heels of the Communist regime, the ballet was free of any interference. Like the Chinese art I discovered in Los Angeles the previous year, I discovered ballet at the Bolshoi Theatre and found in it an expression of the human spirit. Some years later I read that the stranglehold on the creative forces in the Soviet Union was strengthened to include the theatre and the ballet. They suffered the same fate as the writers and the great musicians, Prokofieff and Shostakovitch. This lasted until the death of Stalin in 1953.

Leningrad looks altogether different from any other city in the Soviet Union. It is thoroughly Westernized and is distinguished by having had more spontaneous uprisings than any other Russian city. The repercussions even reached the peaceful county seat of my birth. As a child, I remembered hearing people talk about the bloody revolution of 1905.

Of the many theatres and museums I visited in this second largest city of Russia, the Hermitage fascinated me most. It was originally a palace of the Czars and is now one of the three largest and most important museums of the world. It had twice as many paintings as the National Gallery of London and the Metropolitan Museum of New York combined. Later, in the 1930s, some of its finest art was sold to the National Museum in Washington through the Mellon Foundation. When I was there in 1936 there were 34 Rembrandts, 3 Leonardo da Vincis, 21 Picassos, 38 Matisses, 19 Cézannes, 29 Gauguins, 19 Rubens, and many hundreds of others which filled a large part of the 1,050 rooms of the Hermitage. In addition, it had a distinguished collection of Chinese, Greco-Roman, and primitive art and archeology. There was enough great art in the Hermitage to fill ten museums the size of the Los Angeles Museum.

One of the most interesting rooms was dedicated to the life and work of Russia's poet, Pushkin, and this room attracted more visitors than any other room in the vast building. What impressed me almost as much as the art was the crowds of workers and peasants who filled the rooms and the corridors of the Hermitage every day.

I left Leningrad, and on the train bound for Vilna, I pondered this question: why did I see relatively few workers and peasants in any of the museums in the Western countries, whereas they crowded the Hermitage? I believe the answer is that the workers and peasants were made to feel that the Hermitage belonged to them. It was their national possession, which had been denied them by the Czars from the time of Peter the Great and Catherine. The Czars robbed the bread from the people to acquire their great wealth. now it belonged to the people again. So went the Communist propaganda. Whatever the motives may be of the present ruling class in making the people feel this way, the fact remains that the wealth of the country, including its great art, does belong to the people.

The train chugged along. At the second station after we crossed the Russian-Polish border, I saw a young woman with a group of ten children on the station platform. She waited down below until they climbed up into a third-class carriage next to my second-class car. For a moment our eyes met through the window. In her bright holiday dress and large hat, she looked as though she belonged to the upper class Polish gentry, and it startled me when I heard her talking to the children half in Hebrew and half in Yiddish. I heard the Hebrew word, "*Alu*" (go up) and I called out to her, "Shalom." She looked up, smiled, and answered "Shalom." Before the train pulled out I moved into her third-class carriage. Abigail introduced herself to me. She understood my excitement in finding someone to whom I could talk in the language I was forbidden to use in Russia. Abigail was a part-time Hebrew teacher and she was taking the children to Bialistok. She, herself, would continue with the train until it reached Vilna. During the hour-and-a-half journey I learned all about Abigail's life and studies and plans for her forthcoming wedding, which had been arranged by her parents. She was on the way to Vilna to buy her trousseau. She inadvertently told me toward the end of our first conversation that this would be her last free visit to the city which she loved more than any other city in what was then Poland. She had studied at the Hebrew teachers' school in Vilna, hoping to pursue a career in education, but her family had other plans. Abigail had yielded to her parents, who had chosen a very suitable and respectable match for her.

There was no diner on the train and I had had no food during the greater part of the day. After turning her children over to the elderly gentlemen who came to get them in Bialistok, Abigail took me into the neat, bright dining room of the station and ordered for me. She was not hungry and only drank a cup of coffee, but I ate delicious dairy dishes, pancakes, eggs, and sour milk. I don't know whether it was the food or the delightful company that made the Bialistok meal the most memorable of the entire journey. When she asked me in German "*Shmekt es dir?*" (does it taste good?) I didn't grasp the meaning of the word *shmekt*. In Yiddish it would be translated as "Does it smell good?" When I told this to Abigail she laughed, displaying her perfect teeth

After the train left Bialistok, Abigail moved into my second-class compartment, where we weren't so crowded as before. In addition to unfolding a world I only knew from books, Abigail arranged everything that made my stay in Vilna the opposite of what it could have been. When we arrived we found that the few good hotels were booked full. Except for Berlin, I had no reservations in any hotel in eastern Europe. Abigail had connections, and when she advised the manager of the finest hotel in the city that I was an important American correspondent, he considered me entitled to luxurious accommodations. He settled me in a vast room with large, high windows which, before the revolution, had been reserved for members of the nobility and the ministers of the Russian government. Old world hotel rooms invariably bring back much of an era that has passed. The feeling I had in the Vilna hotel recurred in the Raffles in Singapore, in the Hotel des Indes in Batavia, and the Georges V in Paris.

Abigail was tireless, and it was difficult for me to keep up with her as she led me through every part of the city. Only in Jerusalem did I ever walk so much and so enthusiastically. Detailed descriptions followed one upon another like the waves and cadences of a Beethoven symphony. When her Hebrew vocabulary failed to convey her feelings, she used Polish, German, Russian, and Yiddish words to enlarge and embellish what she wanted to express. And what she wanted to express was what her youth had absorbed; she sought someone who could understand and embrace it in the same way she did.

She made a desperate effort to confide all the things she would never again be able to tell anyone, all her longings and passions. Happy and enthusiastic in one hour, she would be sad, vague, and defeated the next hour. It was not that Abigail was a more complex person than any other well-bred, intelligent, young woman; her tragic plight was that she was out of place in the society in which she lived. She was a big city girl who belonged in Paris, New York, and Shanghai, and not in a middle-class, conservative Jewish town in Poland.

When I arrived at the station in Vilna and beheld the coachmen and horses, the cobbled streets, the unchanged railway station, it was as though I had never left. I promised to pay the coachman an extra fee if he would drive slowly through the streets that were so familiar to me when I was eleven years old. I saw the bakery where my mother used to buy me sweet-smelling cakes. I saw the big apothecary where my parents filled their prescriptions, and I saw the same, little old ladies selling apples. They hadn't aged a bit in the twenty-five years since I last heard their cries of, "*Eppelech, eppelech, zise eppelech,*" apples, apples, sweet little apples. I had to remain in Vilna the first few days to write an article on its cultural institutions. The leading Yiddish daily paper carried a story about the return to Vilna of one of her native sons. The newspaper reached Kenna in the late afternoon, and in that town, which consisted largely of members of my family, the news spread like wildfire. In the evening, on my return to the hotel, I found my cousin Beile and her husband in the lobby. She recognized me sooner than I recognized her and Beile's tears were the first that made my cheeks wet. Very late at night Beile went back to Kenna to tell my two aunts, uncle and cousins that I would arrive the next morning.

Through the window in the train to Kenna I again saw the familiar fields and houses, exactly as I saw them on the trips with my parents. No one in Kenna traveled in second class any more. When the train stopped and I came out on the platform of the second-class carriage, I didn't see any of my family. But down the platform where the third-class carriages stopped, it looked as if half the town was waiting. One of my little cousins saw me from a distance struggling with my two valises and shouted out, "There he is!" Everyone started running towards me. They were mostly the children of my cousins who were born after I left Russia.

My uncle, his ailing wife, Frume Neche, and my favorite aunt, Maryosha, the widow of my father's brother, waited for me in their homes. My rich uncle's home was closest to the station. As I approached it I saw my aunt Maryosha leaning against the wooden rail of her house up the street. It was the same rail that surrounded her house twenty-five years ago. On impulse I bypassed my rich uncle's house and went directly to the aunt who was the devoted wife of my father's brother.

When I embraced and kissed her warmly, she was unable to stop crying. I was the only male member left of her family. Her husband and son had been killed by robbers several years previously while traveling to Vilna. I spent a half hour with my aunt before she told me, "Now you must go to see your uncle."

The house of my rich uncle, who was once the King of the Tarf, was still the same, but had none of the opulence I remembered during the year my brother and I stayed there. My uncle had aged greatly and had mellowed with the years. He was gentler and warmer than he used to be. When he embraced me, he told me that I did the right thing in first visiting my aunt. "Your father," he said, "was her husband's closest brother and friend." He then took me into the sickroom of his wife. Hers was the last face I saw when she stood crying on the station platform as the moving train bore us away from Russia twenty-five years before. Now she was very ill and it took her a while to realize that I was the little boy she wrapped in blankets and took to the station. She kept repeating my name, "Yankele," over and over again. Tears flowed from her eyes and my eyes responded. By the time I returned to Aunt Maryosha the house was full with first and second cousins.

The next day was Friday and the women were busy preparing for the

Sabbath. The husband of my oldest cousin took me to the same bath house my father used when he came to Kenna, to bring me back to Shumsk. I climbed to the highest bench in the steam room, on which my father loved to warm his tired bones, but I couldn't stay long in that altitude. In the evening I went to the synagogue for the Sabbath prayers. Many of my relatives sat in the same places they had occupied when I was a child. The rabbi accepted me warmly and asked me to speak to the congregation on the afternoon of the Sabbath day. I was given my father's seat, which faced the congregation on the left side of the Holy Ark. I knew I was at home.

After the evening services fifteen of my closest relatives came to the festive Sabbath dinner at the house of Aunt Maryosha. The house overflowed with the kind of singing and chanting I yearned to hear. This was followed by endless questions about my parents, my brothers and sisters, my wife, and my little daughter. When I told them my daughter's name was Hedvah, they all laughed. No one in the family had ever been called Hedvah. Hedvah, said the most learned husband of my oldest cousin, is not a name, it is a word for joy that is used under the canopy. When I told the family that while I was in Palestine, I had heard of several Hedvahs, they approved of the name since it was accepted in Palestine. Aside from questions about relatives, asked by those who remembered them, the younger people wanted to know all about Palestine.

When I asked them on what subject I should speak the next day, nearly all responded in kind: Palestine. Not a single one was interested in Russia. Some were deeply concerned with the black clouds of Hitlerism, but it was about Palestine they wanted to hear.

On Sabbath afternoon the synagogue was filled to capacity. I had spent many hours the previous night in a search for the right Yiddish idioms to convey the strong points of my talk. I started my address hesitatingly, groping at first for the words I wanted, but like an athlete who holds back at the beginning, I quickly achieved full control of my speech and it flowed freely. The audience was with me continuously from the first moment. When they began to wipe their tears, I, too, choked up a little. I didn't want to make them cry, but some of the material on eastern Europe and the difficulty of reaching Palestine could not be omitted. On the whole, I dwelt on the age-old faith and hope of our people and our determination to achieve a new life. I ended with the familiar lines of the prophetic reading from Isaiah: "Comfort ye, Comfort ye, my people."

The next day two of my cousins and I walked to Shumsk. I refused their offers of a ride by horse and carriage. I wanted to walk along the roads and paths that my father and I had used on the Sabbath days a quarter of a century ago. My cousins, a girl of seventeen and a boy of fifteen, were perfect companions. Neither said a word to distract my full attention from every hill and tree. It was Sunday, and word was passed to some of the peasants around the village of

Shumsk that I would visit my first home today. Two old peasants, dressed in their best holiday clothes, waited for me near the courthouse, which was the first building we came to on the higher plateau of Shumsk. They removed their hats and bent to kiss my hand. They had been my father's closest employees; one of them had worked for him over twenty years. They spoke in a simple Polish dialect, similar to the Russian used by peasants. I understood all they said when they asked about Zaruch and Zaruchova, my father and mother. With the help of my relatives I answered all their questions. The two peasants followed me to my old home. They attracted many others who remembered the Jew who was a "good employer and a good neighbor."

The current owner of the old house showed me around. It looked much smaller than the house I remembered. The stable and the two-story storage room that my father built a year before we left looked exactly the same as I had pictured them. After enjoying some *kvas*, cakes, cheese, and tea, which the owner's wife offered us, we continued our walk to the forest, the stream, the meadows—all the places that were so much a part of my childhood.

The next morning I parted from my aunt, uncle, and cousins, who came to the railroad station to say good-bye. I had an inexplicable feeling that this would be the last time I would see them, these people with whom I forged such strong links. How could I have known that six years later the stronger men would be forced to dig a large ditch and all men, women, children, all the Jewish inhabitants of Kenna, would be assembled by Nazi soldiers and forced to stand near the ditch as they were machine-gunned to death? One of my second cousins, a student of medicine, had the presence of mind to throw himself into the pit alive. He was the only survivor; his name is Abe Gordon and he is now a physician in Chicago.

On the eve of my departure from Vilna, I met with Abigail, who had already bought her trousseau, visited her family, and seen all her old friends. We had dinner together and then I took her to the train to see her off. I was deeply touched when she said that I had enlarged her final hours of freedom. She made me promise not to turn around or to gaze at her when the train left the station. I kept my promise, although in my mind's eye I could see the bitter tears she wanted to keep hidden.

The following morning I left Vilna for Warsaw. There I met some writers and people who were active in the educational and cultural life of the city. Warsaw had several Yiddish and Hebrew newspapers and a fine Yiddish theatre.

One writer, whose wonderful children's stories I knew through their Hebrew and English translations, was called the Father of the Orphans. His name was Janus Korchak and he was a physician, pedagogue, writer, and professor from Warsaw University. In 1936 he was the head of a unique orphanage.

In American educational circles, Janus Korchak was well known for his revolutionary approach to the education of the child. Through warmth and love, the child was allowed to find ways for his self-expression and his self-love. His books carried such titles as *How to Love Children, People Are Good, Childhood of Honor*. Educators were deeply impressed with the methods he employed in the three-story orphanage, where he remained until 1940 when they were all moved to the Warsaw Ghetto.

In the institution I visited in 1936, I was touched by the self-discipline of the homeless children. A little boy who committed a transgression was brought to trial before three boys who were judges. He was accused and defended by two other boys, and the verdict was posted a day or two later on the bulletin board.

I was moved by the services conducted each morning for the children. Janus Korchak, an assimilated Jew, who saw a synagogue for the first time when he was ten years old, attended these services regularly. At the end he would rise and say *kaddish*, the prayer for the dead, for the parents of the orphans who were in his loving care. I saw the children happy and fully oblivious to the deteriorating economic, social, and political life of the Jews. Their singing and their dancing was every bit as spirited as the singing and dancing of the children of Palestine.

A noted writer, G. Plekanov, once said, "It has long been observed that great talents appear everywhere, whenever the social conditions favorable to their development exist. This means that every man of talent who becomes a social force is the product of social relations." The social climate in Warsaw in the 1930s was such that it elicited Korchak's magnanimity and genius. These conditions brought out his humanity and also led him to the gas chamber. The social conditions created by the Poles and the Nazis enabled Korchak to develop his talents as a writer, doctor, teacher, humanitarian, and subsequently led to his martyrdom. In tribute to the great Polish writer, UNESCO proclaimed the year 1978 as "Korchak Year."

Poland in 1936 was one of the poorest countries I visited. Nearly half of the population had no purchasing power. The people relied on their own crude, homespun articles, and this was reflected in Warsaw, where the number of unemployed industrial workers was more than double that in any other Western city. The Jewish population suffered most. All stores had difficulties meeting expenses, even the bookstores.

I went into one of the oldest bookstores in Warsaw and selected a few books. The proprietor, a woman, showed me one of the latest issues of the *Hatkufah*, a compilation of contemporary Hebrew literature. It had just appeared. I opened the 500-page volume at random and the first thing I saw was a poem entitled "Santa Barbara the Beautiful," by Simeon Halkin. Fifteen years previously, when I lived with my sister Lizzie in Alhambra, California, Simeon Halkin had come to stay with us for a week. He was the brother of my classmate, Abraham Halkin, who was later to become a professor in the Jewish Theological Seminary. Simeon Halkin was a delightful companion. Many years later, my new friend occupied the chair in Hebrew Literature which was formerly held by my old friend, Professor Klausner. We used to take trips together all around California.

When we went to Santa Barbara, 90 miles north of Los Angeles, Simeon was fascinated by the hills and by the ocean which surrounded the city. One morning, as we were sitting on one of the hills overlooking the ocean, I was preparing some work and Simeon was writing. After I finished I waited for quite a while, till Simeon said that he had finished writing a poem about beautiful Santa Barbara, and would I want to listen to it right away. I had long forgotten this incident, which came back to life in a narrow store crowded with books in Warsaw. I showed the poem to the erudite lady and asked her to add this book to the others that she was to send to my home in San Bernardino.

This was my last contact with the rich, cultural life of Poland and Lithuania. Never again would I be able to see it and find it in the guise in which my ancestors had known it for generations.

XV
BERLIN

Berlin looked like Disneyland. The railroad station and all the leading streets to the hotel were gaily decorated with flags, banners, emblems, and large welcome signs to the Olympic Games. All cafés and restaurants were filled with festive crowds of Germans and foreigners in anticipation of the great event. This time, in the summer of 1936, it was Berlin that was host to all athletes from all parts of the world. Berlin was a tremendous contrast to the drab, colorless, eastern European cities I had just left.

Before anyone scrutinized my passport and my Hebraic name, I was treated cordially by taxi drivers, waiters, and porters. To strangers I seldom look Jewish. When I reached the reception desk of the Bristol Hotel and presented my letter of confirmation, the clerk looked at my passport, hesitated, consulted another clerk, and advised me quietly that there was unfortunately a mistake and that all rooms were occupied.

I said very loudly in English that this was impossible. I attracted the attention of several people who were also registering for rooms. Two were Americans. One walked over to me and looked very sternly at the clerk. The clerk had just assigned him to one of the best rooms. He was an important athlete. "Well," the clerk said, "there is one small room that you may have, but I do not recommend it." He asked another clerk to take me to the room. My American benefactor was even more suspicious than I was. He said to me very loudly: "What room are you getting? I will wait for you." The room I was shown had no window; it was a large closet with a small bed. I came back, and before I had a chance to raise my voice, my American friend raised his. He threatened to move out and to go with me to another hotel. Several of the athletes rushed over to the desk.

The clerk disappeared and the assistant manager came out from behind the wall. He was very polite and apologetic. He told my friend that he was sorry that the stupid clerk confused my reservation with that of someone else. I received a beautiful room, right next to my friend's room. He even came in to inspect the accommodations. When I thanked him profusely, he said I owed him no thanks, that he was only too glad to help a fellow American who was Jewish because, "First, my mother is Jewish and secondly I am an anti-Nazi, but the Germans don't know either of these facts.'' The athlete invited me to have dinner with him and his friends. Appearing with the Americans in one of the best restaurants made my stay quite tolerable. No one annoyed me while I was in Berlin. I was able to go freely about the city and see and talk to all kinds of people.

For four years I had closely followed the developments in Germany and worked in the anti-Nazi movement in California. I spoke in clubs and churches in San Bernardino, Riverside, and Los Angeles against the barbarism of the Nazi regime. When Hitler ordered the bonfire in 1933 and burned all great contemporary books, the congregational minister of San Bernardino and I gathered copies of works by Freud, Thomas Mann, Hemingway, Emil Ludwig, Feuchtwanger, and Upton Sinclair. We displayed them on a platform before a large audience and stressed the Nazi regression to the Middle Ages, when books were burned.

It did not take me long to find full confirmation of all that I knew before I came to Berlin. Away from the center of the hotels, the sports arena, or the tourist attractions, I saw signs and placards posted by the Hitler Youth movement. "Jews are not wanted." "Dogs and Jews are not admitted." "Race proud Volk women will not buy from Jews." A ticket agency posted, "No steamship tickets for trips on the Rhine will be sold to Jews."

One day I decided to get a haircut. I picked a neat, respectable barbershop that wasn't busy. After I sat down in the barber's chair, my eyes wandered toward the mirror and I saw through the glass a sign in back of me HERE WE CUT JEWS' THROATS.

Why I remained in the chair and allowed my hair to be cut, I do not know. Sitting in the chair I was suddenly engulfed by fear. Three times my life had been threatened and miraculously saved. I had seen rusty knives moving towards me and muzzles of guns pressed against me during the riots of Palestine, but I had never experienced fear such as that which seized me in the barber's chair. It was as Job said: "Fear came upon me and trembling." It was not a fear for my own safety; it was a fear born of dread forebodings.

I asked the American athlete to go with me to the barbershop to look at that sign. We went when the barbershop was crowded and he was presumably unable to wait for a haircut. When we walked away, he said to me, "I would not have believed it, it scares the life out of me too."

What had led a whole nation to go down the path of madness so suddenly? How did an unknown, embittered, unemployed man without any background, education, or special skills succeed in controlling the hearts and minds of millions of people? I wanted to know and understand.

I met a disenfranchised, German-Jewish professor of literature from the University of Berlin. He felt he was a German first and a Jew only because the

Nazis reminded him that he was one. Most of his friends and family had managed to leave Germany for Palestine, America, and South America. He alone remained. Where could he go? His home was Berlin; his language was German; and his all-consuming love was German literature. For two years he waited daily for a change. One day he was summarily dismissed, with the simple explanation that no Jew could be allowed to teach Aryans the literature of Germany. He could not believe that the situation would continue to be as bad. Yet the situation day in and day out was getting worse and worse.

One day we walked along the cafés of Kurfurstendamm. No Jews were allowed in any of them. As a smokescreen for foreign visitors, the Nazis had set aside one small, poorly lit café, at the extreme edge of all the bright cafés, and designated it for Jews. Some of the Jews, to whom café life in the summer was a ritual, gathered around the little tables.

For my friend the Professor, Hitler was psychotic and paranoid. He told me that Professor Von Gruber, the leading German anthropologist had said that Hitler had "a face and a skull that reveal racial inferiority." Later I read what Professor Von Gruber had said at length. "The expression of Hitler's face is not that of a man in full possession of his mental faculties but a man insanely excited. At the end of his speech Hitler registered a childlike, happy, self-satisfaction."

Having obtained a partial answer regarding the man who controlled the destiny of humanity, I was more troubled than ever. First of all, how could such a man manipulate people to serve his diabolical ends? I read many descriptions of how Hitler was driven by an evil spirit, and how he projected his sense of personal deprivation onto the German people after the war. He had no home, no property, no standing, till he joined the band of the first Nazis. He hated the Jews because he saw their homes in Vienna; he saw their possessions and all they achieved and amassed through their efforts. He had achieved and amassed nothing. This was the beginning of his hate. His main speech at the Olympic Games showed me that he was an orator and a spellbinder.

"No one has set me above the people, I have remained in the people and to the people I shall return." He made the common folk feel that he was one of them and they were part of him.

"Today," wrote Hitler in *Mein Kampf*, "I am acting according to the intention of the Almighty Creator. By resenting the Jew I am fighting for the work of the Lord." In 1929, when I was in Jerusalem during the bloody riots incited by the Mufti, the Mufti said the same thing, but instead of fighting against the Jews "for the work of the Lord," he claimed to be fighting them in the name of Allah.

Hitler's speeches all said, "Follow me, for there is no other way. I cannot go wrong. The forces of history and the Lord Almighty are on my side."

Kafka helps us understand the mind of a man who is obsessed with the belief that he alone is right. In his "Letter to My Father," Kafka writes: "Your opinion is right. Every other opinion is crazy, unbalanced, not normal. And with all this, your self-confidence is so immense that you have no need to be consistent at all—when you have no opinion whatsoever about anything, all possible opinions on the matter are wrong without exception. You run down the Czechs, the Germans, the Jews, not individually but wholesale, until nobody is left but you."

Unlike the underground outside of Germany, which ran printing machines and radio broadcasts during the war, the German underground produced only a few pamphlets appearing here and there, which revealed a small part of the actions of the leaders of the Nazi regime.

On September 12, 1936, I reported on the closing ceremony of the Olympics:

> The Nazis could not have wished for a better method of blinding the eyes of the throngs that have come to Berlin. The Olympiad is so masterfully organized, every detail is so skillfully prepared, that one need not be an athlete to be profoundly impressed and thrilled at the magnificent sights. The beautiful Berlin is more beautiful than ever. Never have I seen a city in a more beautiful, festive garb. Its people are the most painfully polite and 'gastfreundlich' people in the world. All tourists see a life that belies 'the false rumors' of oppression and want that are circulated in the U.S. and Western countries. Many tourists told me that on their return to their homes they will be able to tell the 'Truth' about the splendid, new, revitalized life that Hitler brought to Germany. Shameless in the impudent theatrical displays, so perfectly staged, one feared to question their reality.

I then proceeded to tell of the Berlin that the tourists didn't see. In the workers' quarters, fifteen minutes' ride from the stores laden with the richest foods, we saw half-empty stores where for weeks there were no eggs, no meat, no essential provisions. We heard quiet complaints of high prices, low standards of living, and low wages. All this was in the non-Jewish areas.

From a Jewish physician who once had a large practice, but was now forbidden to heal Aryans, I learned of the Friday night services conducted in the large synagogue. It was the only place where "I, a nonbeliever, find some comfort," said my acquaintance. I asked the doctor if he would care to have a Sabbath meal with me before I joined him on Friday night. "No thanks," he said. "I cannot risk being in the company of a foreigner. I may not even sit next to you in the synagogue. You must forget that we met or that I told you about the synagogue."

On Friday night the large, old synagogue was filled to capacity. After a beautiful, plaintive opening by the cantor, the young Reform rabbi, Dr. Max Nussbaum, asked the congregation, as he did every Friday night, to try to desist from crying on the Sabbath day. Our Sabbath, we were told by the rabbis, is a day of joy, a day of light and blessing. That was one of the last years that Rabbi Max Nussbaum officiated in the Berlin Synagogue. As a great Jewish orator, he, who was born in Poland, was asked not to risk his life in the service of a decreasing congregation. Dr. Stephen Wise arranged to bring him to America, and on the death of Rabbi Harrison, he assumed his place as the Rabbi of Temple Israel in Hollywood.

When the services were finished, I introduced myself to Rabbi Nussbaum, who asked me to meet him in his study on Saturday morning. He wanted me to tell him all about Palestine and said: "You can do it in Hebrew, instead of your tortured German." I gladly complied with his request. As much as I told him, he told me much more very cautiously. I had to infer a good deal from what he said. He was too close to the scene. What he saw was as blurred as what all other good, patriotic, German Jews perceived.

Through Rabbi Nussbaum and Dr. Eric of Berlin, and my cousin Boris in Zerbst-am-Inhalt, I met a few who displayed courageous resistance. Boris was drafted into the Russian army in 1910 when I was seven years old. In 1915 Abraham Boris was captured by the Germans and was sent to Zerbst-am-Inhalt, where he met and fell in love with a German girl named Martha. She converted to Judaism and they were married. Boris prospered in his small tire business with his brother-in-law as partner. It was Martha and Boris who adopted the two small boys from Shumsk, the children of Boris's widowed sister. As a result of the Nazi terror, Boris took the eldest of the two boys to the French border in the dead of night. They never saw each other again.

I had written to Boris from the United States. I wanted to visit him during the Olympic Games in Berlin. He answered me with a letter in Yiddish, Hebrew, German, and Russian, giving me specific and complicated instructions of how to contact him. I wrote back in the same confused language to indicate that I understood his instructions.

When the Olympic Games were over and many tourists began traveling through different parts of Germany, I, too, went to the ticket office of the railroad station. I bought a ticket for a town that was one station before the town where Boris lived. Near the ticket office I could discern two plainclothes men scrutinizing the foreigners who were buying railroad tickets.

When I arrived at my destination and left the train, I looked for a man with a leather jacket standing not far from his car. I walked over to him. He smiled. The man was my cousin's brother-in-law. In the half hour's ride to Boris's home, I learned more about the Nazi regime. The situation was deteriorating, and without the boys, Boris and Martha were lonely. Only two members of Martha's family continued to visit them: her brother, Max, and one of Martha's sisters-in-law. The others were all pro-Nazi.

After I was embraced warmly by my cousin and Martha, Max removed his jacket and his shirt. "Look," he said. "Look at the stripes on my back." I saw the dried skin around the red lashes that had been inflicted on Max by some of his townspeople for his outspoken opposition to the Führer.

Formerly Zerbst-am-Inhalt had about two hundred Jewish families. Now only six families remained. The attractive little synagogue, nearly eighty years old, had no quorum for its traditional public services. The rabbi and the cantor were among the last to leave. Martha had the keys to the synagogue and she acted as sexton. During the two days I stayed in the town, we only walked outside late at night when the streets were abandoned. Martha and I passed several hallways where we heard the voices that Martha waited to hear. They were the voices of her sisters-in-law, her only means of communication with her family outside of Max. Her other brothers were active members of the Nazi Party. When I asked Boris why he hadn't left, he shook his head and said: "I did not leave because I was sure that things would improve." Now his business was ruined, and with no available funds of any kind, he could not think of leaving. Here, he at least had a home. Late at night he was able to do a little work for Max and earn enough to buy food.

Martha did some sewing for her sister-in-law, but this too came to an end. Eventually Max found a way to get Boris and his wife out of the country at the eleventh hour. Several weeks before the outbreak of the war, they reached Palestine without money or possessions. This was in 1939, when Hitler said to the German people, "The annihilation of the Jew, our common enemy, is the reward and deliverance I offer you for following me into this war."

I had but a few isolated rays of light to bring back with me to a free America. One was Max, my cousin's brother-in-law, his courageous partner, who was later murdered by the Nazis, and a number of German soldiers and civilians whom I read about. Two sergeants wrote a pamphlet, calling the murder of Polish Jewry "the most terrible crime against human dignity, a crime not to be compared to any similar one in the history of mankind."

My difficult two weeks in Germany sapped my strength. I was not well on the last day and my first three days aboard ship were spent in the cabin, which I shared with a quiet Jewish refugee. He was an intelligent, understanding man and spared me the tales of horror that he had told to the other passengers.

When my brother Izzie met me at the dock, he gave me a lift when he said that I didn't look any the worse for all that I had undergone. "You must be thriving on trouble," he joked. In New York I had just enough time for a visit to the Metropolitan Museum and a good play in the evening. I was anxious to get home to my wife and my little daughter, Hedvah.

The Santa Fe train brought me to San Bernardino. Vera and my two-year-old daughter were on the platform. Hedvah did not rush to embrace me. She stood aside and looked at me wonderingly. My heart sank within me. I rushed to her, embraced her, and kissed her, but there was no response. I then lifted her high, very high, and suddenly I felt the light of God's merciful benevolence. Hedvah smiled, laughed, and put her little arms around my neck. I held my tiny daughter tight on my lap until we reached our home on Edgehill Road.

The following two weeks I was busy with preparations for the High Holiday services. No one, not even my wife, knew that those were the last High Holiday services that I was going to conduct, because I arrived at this decision during the last five quiet and isolated days on board the vessel which brought me back to America. In reviewing much of what I saw and felt on my travels, I realized that my direction pointed to other areas. The peaceful life in San Bernardino, the affection and respect that I enjoyed in the community, were not enough to engage my restless soul. When I was absorbed with my duties in the adminstration of charity during the height of the depression, I felt the satisfaction of fulfillment. Moreover, I was able to comply with Rabbi Harrison's request that I go to San Bernardino, where I could "lift the souls of the people." Now that brighter days had arrived, and the country, thanks to Roosevelt, was back on its feet, there were others who could take my place. The San Bernardino Jewish community was starting to grow again and it needed more than a makeshift, part-time rabbi. The college was a different matter. During the years of my teaching and lecturing, I had learned a great deal, but as Zarathustra said: "Behold, I am weary of my wisdom, like a bee that has gathered too much honey; I need hands outstretched to receive it."

No one in the Temple or in the community sensed that my work would come to an end before the advent of the coming Jewish year. I, myself, became more abosrbed than ever with my duties and with my two public interests: the struggle against Hitler and the fight against the British Government's restrictions on Jewish immigration to Palestine. For months I appeared on one platform or another, very seldom before the same kind of audience. I felt that both issues were closely related but, unfortunately, even the best of people live compartmentalized lives. The liberals and radicals who formed a "United Front" had their hearts and minds set on one thing, the struggle against Nazism. My most important address against Nazism was before an overflowing audience of over 2,500 people at the Philharmonic Auditorium in Los Angeles, and the main anti-British speech was given at a large auditorium that belonged to a church.

Bruce MacDaniel, a successful lawyer, heard me speak and wanted to meet me. We were introduced by a mutual friend and I gladly accepted his invitation to dinner, and thereby changed the course of my life. Bruce MacDaniel ran the affairs of the second largest orange growers' cooperative in

California, the Mutual Orange Growers' Association. He was a man about forty years of age, who looked more like a professor or a writer than a president of an association of orange growers. MacDaniel loved music. He played piano and delighted us with his fine renditions of Schumann and Mozart. He was a man of ideas and vision, which did not diminish his talents as an organizer and administrator.

MacDaniel told me that he had heard me speak about the art and culture of China. China, he said, fascinated him in another respect. He believed that China would ultimately determine the fate of humanity. With the hundreds of millions of her slumbering people, she would achieve wonders when fully awakened to her tremendous potential. As the conversation on China progressed, Bruce MacDaniel told me that he wished to extend the activities of his organization to the Far East, where there was a market for California oranges.

Before parting, MacDaniel invited me to have lunch with him at the end of the week, and it was at this fateful lunch that MacDaniel said that he gathered, in view of my interest in Chinese art, that I might be interested in living and working in China for a few years. He had an opening for someone to help develop a market in the Orient for the Mutual Orange Distributors. "The Sunkist Organization of Citrus Growers is quite well established in the Orient," he said, "but not the Mutual Orange Distributors." Would I accept the assignment? I would be provided with films, literature, a sample shipment of oranges, and all necessary contacts. I would work closely with the U.S. agricultural attachés in Japan, China, and Manila, and arrange dinners and talks for prospective dealers and distributors of citrus fruits. My period of service would be for two years or longer, depending on the progress I made. Since most of the work would be done by native employees, MacDaniel told me, there would be ample time to pursue my interest in studies, and travel. He also agreed that I could, if I wished, continue to be engaged in a part-time journalistic effort.

When MacDaniel asked me to think it over and discuss his proposition with my wife, I told him that as far as I was concerned, I accepted his offer without hesitation, and that since my wife was not used to living in a small city, she would also agree to what promised to be an interesting adventure. I called Joseph Cummings, the publisher of the *B'nai Brith Messenger*, and one of the principal figures in the American Jewish Publishers' Association. When I told him of my planned move to China, his instant reply was, "Great. We need someone for the J.T.A. and the World News Service in the Orient. I will call you tomorrow." The next day I had two jobs.

XVI
JAPAN

Bruce MacDaniel arranged for our passage to Japan on board a Japanese liner and said: "Your life in the Orient will begin on the boat." It proved to be more than a beginning. Most of the passengers were Japanese or nisei, the native Americans born of immigrant Japanese parents. Soon after our ship left the San Francisco skyline, I met a Japanese-American, who recognized me from the days when we both attended classes at the university. His name was Mara. It was through him that I was able to enter the closed world of Japan. Although that world was not hermetically shut, it took great effort, preparation, and patience to penetrate its barriers. Tourists had neither the time nor the patience to do it. They used to come and go to many fascinating places on the four main islands of Japan and comment, "It is impossible to understand the Japanese."

Mara traveled with his wife, a three-year-old boy and his parents. Of the fifteen children on board ship, Mara's little boy was Hedvah's closest playmate. The others were Japanese who came to America on business or holiday and spoke only Japanese. It was Mara's first visit to the homeland of his parents. He was born in America, where he and his wife led a Western life, and was only slightly affected by the Japanese ways of his parents, which had not changed ostensibly after thirty-five years in Los Angeles. Mara spoke with his wife and son in English, and with his parents in Japanese, which he knew better than many of the Japanese businessmen on board. This greatly enhanced the respect he received both in Little Tokyo and on the ship.

Mara told his parents about the news item in the *Los Angeles Times*, which mentioned my appearance before the visiting Japanese trade mission, when I argued on behalf of a reciprocal trade. Reciprocal trade between Japan and America was of uppermost interest to the wealthy businessmen on the ship. This facilitated my approach to the people who, in a leisurely, holiday mood, spoke with me much more freely than they would have done otherwise. I found the Japanese to be very reticent in their communication with non-Japanese, but thanks to the accidental meeting with Mara, my eighteen-day journey enabled me to approach people openly and naturally and to observe the workings of their minds. It was not always easy to understand and follow the logic of the most intelligent Japanese, let alone the uncompromising, fixed views of the rich businessmen.

Sensing that my background was different than that of the Americans they met in connection with their business, they endeavored to impress me with the righteousness of the glorious Japanese mission in the Far East. Why, they argued with me, was it all right for Britain, America, France, and Germany to seize all the advantages of trade in China? Now that Japan, who is closest to China, has come in for her rightful share, she is blocked and threatened on all sides. Japan, having assimilated so much that was good in China, was most suited to export her enlightenment to China. It did not matter to my Japanese friends what price the Chinese would have to pay for this "enlightenment."

I avoided any arguments or discussions. "I know and understand very little," I would say even to Mara. "I only want to learn." It was true. I had fallen suddenly into a new world with totally different problems from the ones which had engaged me up to then. What I sought most was to understand and to adapt myself to the congenial, delicate, ceremonial modes of life, which went beyond the flower arrangements and tea ritual. In the eighteen days I ate together with the Japanese and walked around the deck or sat close to them in the deck chairs, I began to discern the great drama unfolding in the Far East which was ultimately to affect America and the world.

On the way to Yokohama, our boat stopped for two days in the Hawaiian Islands. Many passengers had friends and relatives on the island. Mara and two other English-speaking Japanese passengers took us with them on the visits to the first Japanese houses we had ever seen. The houses were light, airy, charming in their simplicity, and neatly arranged. Though outwardly at one with all Japanese, inwardly the Hawaiian Japanese were different. They were no more than one or two generations removed from their country, but I could easily perceive the difference in their thinking and their reactions to the Japanese conquest of Manchuria and the five provinces in northern China in 1933. Happy with the economic and cultural progress of their motherland, the Hawaiian Japanese leaned more towards the American political line, and even regarded themselves as Americans. This was a shock to my fellow passengers, but it was no surprise to me. It typified the experiences in America among the Italians, Irish, and other immigrants. In spite of indoctrination and blood ties, it is the economic and social life that matters. The Japanese in Hawaii were no exception. A few years later, during the attack on Pearl Harbor, most of them proved their loyalty to America.

On our way back to the boat, Mara told me that, whereas he and other young Japanese retained many of the traditions of their people and the deepest reverence for the emperor, they were opposed to the arrogant, militaristic stance of the Japanese army and navy. They hoped that the emperor would bring the warring classes into line. How an intelligent, Westernized man could believe that a feeble little emperor could change the course of history was difficult for me to understand.

Hedvah was the star on board ship. The Japanese have a boundless love for beautiful children. All the ladies fussed with her, and looked after her and the relieved *amah* (nurse), when Vera, now in her sixth month of pregnancy, was unduly upset by the rocking of the boat.

There were not many pleasures that Japanese women were able to enjoy. The pleasures were mostly for the men. The women were relegated to a secondary position. Children and the home were their main compensations in a life that, for the majority, was one of denial.

The marriages of the women who were on board ship were nearly all arranged. It was a sort of partnership. I seldom saw the men talking to the women. Men talked to men, and women had only women and children to turn to. The Japanese women were trained for marriage from early childhood. They accepted it, as they accepted many things, out of an exaggerated sense of obedience and duty.

It was hard to get to know the true feelings of many Japanese, especially of the women. Their blank smiles were deceptive, and often made one wonder what they were hiding behind their smiles. Notwithstanding all of the smiling, I found very little good humor among the Japanese. We sat and talked for hours at meals, which were delicately and esthetically served in dishes that added to the pleasure of the food, but we seldom laughed. This, in spite of the warm saki which made me want to burst out into laughter on the smallest pretext. Seeing how seriously my companions accepted all the joys and pleasures, I restrained myself from behavior that would be shunned in good company.

Despite all the fine things that we saw in the Hawaiian Islands, the older Japanese talked about nothing but the lack of loyalty and patriotism which they encountered among their relatives. When Mara tried to divert their humorless conversation to some pleasant subject, a fat, influential Japanese government official rebuked him in English, not wanting to offend his parents by talking in Japanese. An offense in a foreign language, I learned, does not have the same sting that it has in the native language.

In Yokohama I was glad to end the abundance of my social life on board ship. From Yokohama, and its impressive gardens facing the port, we proceeded to the Imperial Hotel in Tokyo. The Imperial Hotel was built by Frank Lloyd Wright. It was the only large structure that had fully withstood the disastrous earthquake of 1923, which destroyed more than half of Tokyo's buildings and took a great toll in lives. In 1937 the Imperial Hotel, and its most elegant lobbies and restaurants, was the main meeting place for the people who had interests in the East and in the West. The ten days that I had to spend in

Tokyo to follow up on contacts I made in Los Angeles were an extension of the first real holiday I had in years. My business calls required a lot of waiting. For business people, this would have been torturous. For me it was a blessing. It enabled the three of us to wander about the city, to see sights we had never seen before, and to luxuriate in a hotel with the finest accommodations and varied cuisines.

It also gave me my first opportunity to see the great art of the Orient, the unfolding of the vast spiritual and cultural riches of the early centuries of China, Japan, and Korea. On the third day of our stay in Tokyo, Mara, who had a fair knowledge of Oriental art, joined me on a grand tour of the leading art galleries in the city. He enabled me to form a close acquaintance with some of the art dealers. We also went to the Imperial Museum, which houses the largest and richest collection of Oriental art in the world. After the first visit, I knew that in my new life in the Orient I would not be isolated from the world of art. Given the short distance between China and Japan, there would be a greater involvement with art than ever before.

My fortunate contacts with people who were associated with the art world revealed to me the best side of the Japanese character. Unlike most of the Japanese, they had no reverence for their warriors. Their reverence was for the great creative forces of all time and of all lands. In art, there is no nationalism in the accepted sense of the word; Chinese or Korean art were on the same plane with Japanese art. Each nation was accepted for what it could express in paintings, culpture, porcelain, architecture, and other creative forms.

At a dinner, to which Mara invited a Japanese teacher and his wife, we learned a good deal about the many universities in Japan and the regard in which Japanese teachers were held by the students, the parents, and society. I told my friends that, as an American who was formerly a teacher, I envied them for having placed education on such a high level. At that charming and delightful dinner, Mara and his wife and son agreed to join us on a two-and-a-half hour trip to Kyoto.

For over 1,000 years, Kyoto was the seat of the emperors who ruled the country from a palace called "Peace and Tranquility." There was still a feeling of peace and tranquility seldom found in other cities. It was not only the remarkable, wooden architecture, or narrow winding streets, or the shrines and temples that contributed to the peace and tranquility; it was the age of the city and the indescribably beautiful gardens.

When America made its fateful decision to force the Japanese military to surrender in the war and used the atom bomb, the U.S. Secretary of War, Henry Stimson, gave strict orders not to bomb Kyoto. It had to be spared from any damage, said the American Secretary of War, because it was a shrine of Japanese art and culture. In a world in which the Germans indiscriminately bombed centers of culture, and where the Jordanian Arabs deliberately destroyed all the ancient synagogues and schools of learning in Jerusalem, the action that Stimson took to preserve the treasures of Kyoto is worthy of being remembered till the end of days.

In Kyoto, Hedvah and Mara's little boy enjoyed the first puppet show they had ever seen. The puppet shows, like other forms of art and folk art, were originally brought to Japan from China, and they combine the manipulation and the chanting of dramatic ballads with music. They vary somewhat in the different countries. They are to this day the most popular form of entertainment in the villages. In China, puppetry has developed into a skillful form of art that moves to tears and laughter. It deals with the problems of the little people fighting the evils of their lives and championing the good. The dancing movement and the gestures of the performers rivet the attention of the little children. The puppets are superior in their artistic craftsmanship to those seen in the West. I never knew which puppets to admire more, the Japanese or the Chinese. The carving, painting, and varnishing is all done by master craftsmen. Every part of the puppet moves in the direction the manipulator envisages. They could dance, sing, talk, jump, smoke, or spit in a coordinated manner that raises puppetry to a fine form of art.

After the puppet show, I was eager to see the theatre. The Japanese national theatre is more intelligible to the Western viewer than its Chinese counterpart. It is called the Kabuki Theatre. Here, too, as in the puppet shows, the dialogue of the play is spoken to the accompaniment of music.

We parted from our cordial Japanese-American friends on our return to Tokyo. They were moved by my effusive expressions of gratitude for having helped us to see Japan a little more deeply.

It is difficult to sum up one's impressions of a complex country like Japan after thirty intensive days of study among the Japanese people. On the basis of all the reading I had done, and with all that I saw, I departed from the country an admirer of the unique qualities and traditions of the people, despite my dislike of their sense of duty, unity, and superpatriotism. The continuity of life for over 2,000 years, wtih Emperor Hirohito as the 124th ruler, and the ability to absorb all that was good in art, science, industry, and remold it into a distinctly Japanese pattern, is more than one can find in any European country. Above all, I loved its natural beauty. Nowhere are there such gardens as those I saw in Nikko, Kyoto, and in the surroundings of Tokyo.

D. Suzuki speaks of the Japanese poets who love nature so much that they feel at one with it and can sense every pulse beating through the veins of nature. One need not be a poet to feel at one with nature in Japan. Hokusai, Hiroshige and all the other great masters of the Japanese prints helped me to attain that oneness with Japanese nature before I had set eyes on it. For over forty years, four of Hiroshige's prints, hung on the walls of our bedroom, were like the light of morning, the first to greet my awakening eyes. His incomparable "Thirty-six views of Fuji" have added a new dimension in viewing the outstanding mountain of Japan. Alongside of Hiroshige is the other famous master of Japanese prints, Hokusai, whose "Wave" was among the first important Japanese prints I acquired. He, too, left thirty-six views of Fuji among some 30,000 other drawings. His prolific work is due to his long life and great mastery.

"Real work," he said, "began with me only in my seventieth year. At 75, the real appreciation of nature awakens in me. I hope that at 80 I may have arrived at a certain power of intuition which will develop further to my 90th year."

When he was near death at 89, he said: "If the gods had given me only ten years more, I could have become a really great painter."

All the more reason why I was saddened during the following years, when I felt a vehement aversion for the military "manly flower of Japan." With all of the brutality and inhumanity of that military that I witnessed in the years ahead, still, my love for the islands of Japan and for most of its innocent children, women, and old men has not diminished.

Jacob Alkow with his business associate Irving Marantz, China, 1938.

XVII
CHINA

May life never be empty and without meaning as a weary procession of worthless days. From the Reconstructionist Prayer Book.

It was in a land with a distinct pattern of life for 4,000 years, larger than all of Europe, and with three times as many people as America that I embarked on a new career. China has a heritage more ancient than that of my people, and as the two oldest peoples on earth, we share a long, patient, pragmatic outlook on life and on history coupled with respect for the rights of others to be different. In three years of close contact with the Chinese, I never found a trace of discrimination, and this was at a time when the Chinese were being woefully exploited by the Europeans and the Americans.

Their dealings with me, contrary to the malicious reports that the Chinese are "cheats," were always honorable. When I offered some uneducated, simple Chinese men a receipt for moneys they had given me in advance, they said, "No wanchee receipt. We writee for us."

China was the only country where the Jews were never persecuted and never suffered from discrimination or intolerance during all the 1,800 years they lived there. Once the Chinese had allowed the Jews to enter, they granted them the fullest freedom of religion. In 1250 A.D., when the world was drowning in utter darkness and all light was snuffed out in Europe, the Jews built a magnificent temple in Kai Feng Fu.

The Chinese Confucian philosophy, like that of the Jews, was based on humanism, and it penetrated into many lands without the use of armies or missionaries. When the Chinese were unable to subdue their uncivilized neighbors, they tamed them through their enlightened ideas, by their language, literature, and calligraphy. Vietnam and Korea adopted the Chinese language, and it was the Chinese writing and art that opened the eyes of the Japanese.

For a long span of time, the country was governed by men of learning, wisdom, and experience. Learning, for the Chinese, was like learning for the Jew; one of the supreme values of life. The learning of the traditions of old and the appreciation of art was not the sole privilege of the church and its functionaries. It was shared by the humblest of people. Their bowls and jars and vases were not made only for use, they were made for the delight of the soul.

Thousands of artisans decorated their pottery with exquisite colors, the like of which we are unable to reproduce today. A man in old China could be an important man of affairs or a leader in government, and in his spare time be a painter or one who formed beauty out of clay.

Printing was invented in China in 100 B.C. Thus, the books of Confucius were the first books in the world distributed in printed form. His philosophy spread throughout the length and breadth of the vast country and far beyond its borders. The Chinese were the first to invent paper, which they made out of rags. The Arabs learned the art of making paper 700 years later from the Chinese, and the Europeans learned it from the Arabs in the thirteenth century.

In the year 1100 B.C., the Chinese invented the compass and gunpowder, which they used for the making of firecrackers. Though gunpowder was used for hundreds of years in a pleasurable form in China, Arab tradesmen brought it to the Saracens, who used it to kill people.

The Chinese never accepted the dominating ways of the "barbarian Europeans." They despised them even when they silently and begrudgingly used their needed help. Nothing irked the Chinese more than the way the Europeans had made them lose face. The Europeans called the Chinese, educated and uneducated alike, "Chinks" and prohibited Chinese government ministers from entering the British Shanghai Club.

America is beautiful and great because of its willingness to allow anyone to enter within the precincts of its greatness. China is beautiful and morally great because, socially, none of its parts is estranged or opposed to another. There are no sharp divisions in China between blacks and whites. Confucianism, Buddhism, and Taoism abide by each other. One can be all three or none, and not be rejected or ousted from "decent society" for nonconformity.

It was in this eastern world that I found what had already existed in the world of my ancestors, a reverence for learning. In the *shtetl*s of Lithuania and Poland, the poorest of Jews managed to have one or two sets of books of holy writ. Most of them were unable to read any of the books which adorned their crude shelves, but they would not live without them. People have called it a worship of the Book.

In this respect the Chinese were very much like the Jews. The poorest farmer or worker dreamed throughout the ages that his son might be part of the government so that he could be with learned people. It was a tradition of the Chinese government not to accept anyone in its service who was uneducated.

Immured in their beautiful homes, the "foreign devils" seldom saw the integrity, the patience, the love of people, regardless of race or religion, and the perseverance and good humor of the Chinese. A sign was posted in the exclusive foreigners' park in Shanghai, with the words "No Chinese or dogs allowed."

I found a number of my fellow Jews, the old settlers in China, from Bombay and Baghdad, who took offense at the way the Chinese were treated. The spark of Judaism was faithfully retained on a foreign soil. The Talmud had taught them that to humiliate a man is a grievous sin. "One who humiliates a man is like one who sheds blood," says the Talmud. To save face, not to make your fellow human being feel inferior, is one of the spiritual laws of China.

I hired a clerk who was hopelessly incompetent. I knew that he was a good man and that he tried hard, but without any background or experience he was totally useless. I asked one of my friends, Ruby Abraham, what to do, and he told me how to dismiss my clerk without causing him to lose face. I greeted my clerk with a bright good morning in Chinese and then said to him, "Ho, it grieves me to see that your job is too taxing for you. It may run down your health. I suggest you leave it for someone else and that you take a vacation. I will give you an extra month's salary plus the customary bonus." He bowed and thanked me for my generosity.

After the darkness of Europe, China, in spite of having been ravaged by war, starvation, and floods, was like a sun desperately trying to break through the clouds. When we arrived in Shanghai, the future of the wealthiest city in the Far East was bright. The war-ridden countryside was united under the leadership of Chiang Kai-shek, who had subdued the warlords and ruled over the provinces for more than twelve years. He had realigned himself, at least ostensibly, with the Communists, whom he had been fighting for fourteen years.

When we settled in Shanghai, we heard a great deal of praise for Chiang, who was regarded by many as the Roosevelt of China. My Chinese Communist acquaintances took a different view of Chiang, who had "betrayed" the trust they had in his leadership.

Chiang's pragmatic approach was that "if we perspire more in time of peace, we will bleed less in time of war." The Kuomintang government carried on its activities separately from anything that was going on in the International Settlement and the French Concession.

The total population of Shanghai was four million; approximately 70,000 Europeans and Americans resided in the extraterritorial sections of the International Settlement and 40,000 Japanese in "Little Tokyo." This International Settlement was ruled by a committee representing thirteen foreign countries, including Japan. It was a miniature United Nations, each country trying to get the most out of the wealth of China.

In the 30s, a few years before we came to China, there were great floods and famine in the villages. Children were sold as household slaves and little girls as prostitutes. Through changes in welfare legislation and good organization, life was slowly returning to relative normalcy in 1937.

In Shanghai, at that time, there was actually a period of prosperity. The docks were filled with merchandise brought down the 1,600-mile Yangtze River to the wharfs of Shanghai by large junks, or wooden vessels. The junks were pulled along the narrow paths of the Yangtze by countless, poor coolies. Once every two years, the river boy reached Shanghai. It took him one year to navigate the river for 1,600 miles and another year to bring back the produce.

The clinking of bells mixed with the sounds of rickshaw boys, bales carried on bamboo poles, wheelbarrows pulled by rope, all formed a theatrical pageant unique to the port of Shanghai. I would walk around the streets enjoying the graceful movement of the slender bodies of the men and women who crowded the port, its entrance, and all the streets around the port.

The people, said Mao Tse Tung, are "a mine of raw materials for literature and art." The people were also a mine of raw materials for music. Nowhere have I heard such a multitude of sounds so unlike the customary sound of noise. It was a musical noise, the jovial noise of an energetic people.

The smell of the ducks and sausages, which wafted in the air, and the aroma of all the prepared foods from the open kitchens on the sidewalks near the port of Shanghai, were as delightful as the smells of the broiled lobsters on the Fisherman's Wharf in San Francisco. One of the inescapable sights near the different restaurants was the little tables with their letter writers. Each letter writer specialized in a particular field of letter writing. Those in love would go to the ablest writer of sentimental letters, while the small businessman sought the guiding hand of one versed in the clarification of business proposals.

Right in front of the sprawling port and its masses of people was the imposing, majestic Bund, a long row of stately buildings. It included the vast, massive Shanghai Bank Building and its large bronze lions, a symbol of British financial strength and power. Not far from it was the Shanghai Club, which had stairs, high windows, and the longest bar in the world, to which no Chinese could be invited.

The international quarter of Shanghai was a leisurely city, well protected by a special police force as well as the armies and navies of the thirteen foreign powers who controlled its destiny. Many wealthy Chinese citizens and intellectuals preferred to live there.

In the lovely Jessfield Park in the international zone, there were always concerts. The orchestra was composed of musicians of many lands, though the violinists and cellists were nearly all Russian refugees.

In Shanghai the wealthy paid no taxes whatsoever. The Chinese government of Chiang Kai-shek had no control over the affairs of the international zone and the French Concession. The government extracted all that it possibly could from the poorest farmers and workers. It received not one cent in the form of direct taxation from those who ran the most profitable shops, businesses, or industries. There was no income tax and no inheritance tax.

The British, Americans, and French dominated the foreign areas with their clubs, polo grounds, golf courses, and race tracks. The clerks and messengers of the foreigners made the arrangements, bought the tickets, and set the appointments for their "mastehs." All one needed to do was change one's suit twice a day during the summer or don one's tuxedo to see a five o'clock movie, go to a concert, or attend some social function.

We frequently patronized a Russian restaurant, which had a Hungarian quartet of international fame. Like many other artists, the musicians came to Shanghai because it was the only city in the world where they could live in freedom.

Yanosh was the violinist and his father, aged 65, was an excellent cellist. A widower, Yanosh had no one but his son in his life. I was told the son had murdered his wife in a jealous rage. He had loved her passionately and one day, on finding her in bed with an unscrupulous musician, he lost all reason. The murder was not premeditated and, according to the father's story, it was entirely accidental. The police took a different view of it, and the quartet had managed to escape Hungary to the only open city in the world which attracted rogues and scoundrels on the run for their lives.

The violinist did not enjoy the pastimes of his colleagues—playing cards, going to the dog races, or betting on the swift, dangerous ball game, jai alai. He developed a love for Chinese art and for a beautiful Russian woman, whose parents had belonged to the nobility. Unlike many of the other beautiful women who could only live through the sale of their bodies, Anastasia was watched and guarded by her strict Russian parents. Her father was an outstanding cook and able to support his family in style. Anastasia loved Yanosh deeply. Yet, though Yanosh loved Anastasia, he was unable to erase the memory of his wife.

Among other people I met during the first two months of quiet and peace in Shanghai were two well-known scoundrels from Los Angeles. One, who was more than a scoundrel, was a man named C.C.Julian. Everyone in the California financial world knew of Julian and his fraudulent oil operations. He bilked people out of millions of dollars. I, too, was a small victim of his stock manipulations before he escaped from the jaws of the police. I attended the horse races only once during my stay in Shanghai. There I saw him, busy studying his cards.

The other scoundrel I knew well. He, too, came to Shanghai seeking asylum. He was Louis B. Mayer's brother. Louis B. Mayer's brother, whose name I do not remember, had once asked me to help him cash a check for $200. The banks were closed and a merchant cashed the check for me. It took me several weeks to get the money back. The San Bernardino police knew how to contact Louis B. Mayer's business manager, who had made good many checks of his errant brother.

While the Anglo-Saxon, French, and other foreign nationals lived in the

134 / JACOB ALKOW

lap of luxury, there was a sizeable population of disenfranchised people. Nearly 20,000 of them were White Russians. Many were of the former nobility or were officers in the Czar's armies. They had escaped from the clutches of the Russian revolution and the Communist regime which followed. Among them were some former conservative professors, landowners, and a goodly number of well-educated people. They had left everything behind and brought only their memories and their sad songs. They were neither absorbed nor integrated into the rest of the foreign community. Their language, manners, and habits did not blend with those of the British, French, and Americans; the latter lived in a superior world, just as these Russians had once lived in a superior world devoid of real contact with the people. They had neither money, special skills, nor business sense, and were compelled to compete with the Chinese as workers, elevator boys, errand boys, and watchmen. The more fortunate found work as musicians, or in the gambling casinos, dress stores, race tracks, the local police, and as body guards for the rich Chinese.

The least fortunate of all were street peddlers and those who hung around the boats. A very large percentage of the Russian women were whores. There were many unmarried Europeans who were sent to Shanghai to serve as clerks in the large companies that established banks, insurance firms, and export and import offices. For the Russian women, this large reservoir of paying clients, plus the rich Chinese, was the best source of income they could find.

There was an unreality about Shanghai. Yet within this unreality one could find amazing pockets of sound, down-to-earth, self-respecting, good, honest, wise people. On the third day after our arrival, I went to visit one of the respected old-time citizens of Shanghai, who was advised in advance of our coming to live in his city. His name was Ruby Abraham. Abraham's chief clerk informed his "masteh" of my arrival and I was immediately ushered into a spacious, bright office with large old Chinese paintings on the wall and rare Chinese vases of the Tang Dynasty.

Ruby was about 40 years old. He headed one of the largest real estate and housing companies in Shanghai. This business had been developed by his father who, at the time of my visit, was semi-retired and devoted most of his time to the study of the Talmud and ancient Hebrew literature. Ruby's mother was a Sassoon, which was the wealthiest foreign family in India and China.

Ruby and his two teen-age sons were taught by his father every morning from 6:00 to 8:00 A.M. They were proficient in their knowledge of the Talmud and Bible and classical Hebrew, but knew nothing about the modern Hebrew cultural development, whose riches I was glad to share with them.

Ruby told me about the Sephardic community of 2,000 souls, an upper-class community which, for its size, played the most important role in the financial and economic life of the city. He described the other, larger community of Ashkenazic Jews numbering about 3,000 souls. The latter community consisted almost entirely of Jews who had left Russia after the First World War, arriving in Shanghai via Harbin. It was mainly a lower middle class community and there was virtually no contact between the two.

Then Ruby asked me if I knew his Chinese clerk. "No," I said. "I managed to meet very few people and I have not yet had the pleasure of meeting your clerk." He smiled and said, "I did not ask you if you met him. I asked if you knew who he was." This was quite a puzzle to me. Then he said, "Before you left America for China, did you, by chance, read anything in the Jewish Encyclopedia of Funk and Wagnalls about the Chinese Jews, and did you see any pictures in the article on China?"

"Yes," I said, "I did." I remembered a full-page illustration of a typical, traditional, Chinese family in Chinese garb with long queues: the picture of a Jewish family which had lived in the city called Kai Feng Fu.

"The little boy that you saw at the feet of his father in that picture is the gentleman who brought you into my office," said Ruby. To me the clerk was undistinguishable from other Chinese, but my brother Jew grinned and bowed to me, returning my Westernized handshake very warmly.

The Jewish-Chinese clerk was a descendant of a respected family which was said to trace its origins to 874 A.D., when Jews entered from Persia and Central Asia. Very little of their history is known previous to the twelfth century when Kai Feng Fu was a prosperous city in the Hunan Province. In the eleventh century they had built a large, beautiful synagogue patterned after the temple in Jerusalem, but in Chinese architectural style. They observed all the Jewish laws and rituals, even though they were already greatly assimilated with the Chinese. Their language and prayers were in Chinese except for some early Hebrew prayers. In 1950, the synagogue was discovered by Christian missionaries. By then, it was a ruined and abandoned edifice, but in the seventeenth century there had been at least 1,000 Jewish souls who had used the Kai Feng Fu synagogue as their place of worship. This population had been dispersed by the great floods.

After studying the history of the Han Dynasty (220 B.C.–220 A.D.), I arrived at a hypothesis that the Jews of China had first crossed into China from Rome, where many had engaged in the Roman-Greek world of art. The Jewish ships which brought the grain of Egypt to Rome had also carried other valuable cargo. With the cargo went the men who, though loyal to their Judaism, had enabled the Hellenist culture to penetrate into different parts of the civilized world. There are many signs that the Han Dynasty had welcomed the art of Greece and Rome, and with this art, I contended, came the first Jews, some 800 years earlier than the accepted date of their arrival.

My uncorroborated assumption that Jews had entered China around the first century seemed quite plausible to Ruby's father, who had heard that Jews lived in Kai Feng Fu since the destruction of the Temple in Jerusalem. Later I read Hans Wetzel's biography of Lin Shao-Chi, who was one of Mao Tse Tung's principal lieutenants. Lin Shao-Chi was a descendant of the Jews who lived in Kai Feng Fu. He heard from his grandfather that the Jews came to China from Ceylon during the Han Dynasty and lived there for many centuries before becoming Chinese like the others. His view differs totally with that held by nearly all historians, who assume that the Jews entered China at about 850 A.D. from Persia and India. The migration of Jews to China in 850 was, therefore, probably not the first.

China's long history of floods, fires, and military sieges caused the loss of many valuable buildings. It is quite possible that among the lost buildings there were other synagogues in Peking or in Kai Feng Fu that were utterly destroyed. It was fortunate that the great synagogue built in Kai Feng Fu in the twelfth century had left memories and a good deal of archeological evidence of its continued use for over 700 years.

Because of floods, the synagogue was reconstructed several times. It had a "Chair of Moses," on which the Torah was placed during the services. On a high tablet was the inscription in Hebrew, "Hear O Israel the Lord our God the Lord is one." Ruby's clerk told me that his grandfather worshipped in that synagogue in Chinese, reciting only a few passages in Hebrew, which was all the boys had to learn. He was dressed like all the Chinese, with a long queue common to every Chinese Jew, much like the earlocks of those who had come from Poland or Hungary. His grandfather, Li told me, ate only kosher food and every male in his family was circumcised. Neither his father nor any member of his family ate pork. On one of the monuments that was found in Kai Feng Fu, there is a lengthy inscription of the similarity between Judaism and Confucianism.

After leaving Ruby, Vera and I went to see the apartment that Ruby had rented for us. It was on the ninth floor of a building on Rue Winling in the French Concession. It faced a little park designed for small children and their *amah*s. It had an unobstructed view of a great part of the Chinese city that extended several kilometers beyond the French Concession. There were six spacious rooms and a private elevator opening in the foyers of each apartment of the twelve-story building. In addition to our living quarters, there were two rooms in the rear for the servants, who had a separate elevator. My wife and I looked at each other in surprise when we saw the large living room, exceptional layout, and wood paneling of the library and its built-in bookcases. What I had first thought was a somewhat excessive rental now appeared to be a bargain. When the months passed and the value of the Chinese dollar decreased, our rent was a relatively small part of our living expenses. The minimal number of servants that a man in my position had to have was also a small financial item.

On the following day, when I returned to the apartment with a number of suitcases, I found a little Chinese man with a hatchet and a rope at the entrance of the building. Without ceremony, he said he was "Sorry." Actually, he meant to say "Charlie," but to my ears it sounded like "Sorry," and "Sorry" he was called for the following years. He showed me several letters written in English attesting to his competence and ability as "Number One Boy." I promised him that if all went well with his references, he could begin work in two days when the shipment came from the docks. He grinned and informed me that he would also bring the new *amah* for Hedvah and his Number Two Boy to assist him in the kitchen and do the cleaning of the house. When I asked about their references, he grinned again, saying, "No neccesli. All me familee." The references I called all knew Sorry very well. When he worked for his former employers, he often had changed places with their Number One cooks.

If French people were invited to dinner and good French cooking was required, the Number One Boy, who knew how to cook good American dishes, would change for the night with his companion, who was an expert in French cooking. Such was the case with the Russian, Dutch, or any other cooking. The Number One Boys were organized and belonged to a special guild. The same was true of the *amah*s of the foreign children.

Early in the morning of the second day, my household employees arrived in time to receive the shipment and unpack the crates of furniture, dishes, books, and paintings. They handled it all masterfully. Whenever necessary, they had at their disposal Number One and Number Two boys from the building, who were only too happy to cooperate.

When I also wanted to get into the act and place my books on the shelves of the library, Sorry very politely told me, "No, Masteh, me clean book first. Putee on shelf. You fix lateh." How he was able to lighten my task in putting the Hebrew books on one shelf and the English on another, without knowing how to read either language, was one of my first mysteries in China. Once I had arranged the books the way I wanted them, I always found them in the place I had originally put them.

Sorry and his helpers were remarkably well organized. Any one of them appeared when he was needed. None of them was ever in anyone's way. Like shadows they would flit by silently during their call of duty. The apartment was looked after day and night. There was at least one servant on duty at any time during the twenty-four hours. When not in the house, they were in the servants' quarters, the streets, or the markets.

In addition to his cooking excellent meals to our American and Lithuanian tastes, Sorry did all the purchasing. This was a chore he loved most of all. All Chinese Number One Boys loved it. It was their second most important source of income. It was known by an unkind foreign appelation as the "squeeze." Whether it was food, flowers, or other essential items for the house, the buyer squeezed a copper or two for himself from every purchase. In a rationalized manner, they never really cheated on their mistresses. They would ask the price of an item and then go from vendor to vendor until they found a more reasonable price. The difference between what they paid and the going price remained in their pockets. We never begrudged or questioned Sorry about his "squeeze," and only regretted that we had to be part of an opulent, extravagant, unconscionable form of society which encouraged such petty dishonesty. What else could one expect when all the three servants, plus the chauffeur whom I had to engage later on, cost me less than the amount we had paid our one servant in San Bernardino?

With the furniture, books, and paintings in place, the family was settled. I went to see another Shanghai resident who had received word from Los Angeles about our move to Shanghai. His name was B. Hollzer and he was the brother of Judge Harry Hollzer of the Federal United States Court in Southern California.

Hollzer was a stockbroker. He was a bachelor, and when I met him, a very lonely man. He had no interest beside his work in a Shanghai branch of a New York Stock Exchange firm. Like most of the American and British representatives of foreign banks, insurance companies, and large businesses, he was not in the least interested in the art, culture, or history of China. For him and most of the other foreigners, all "Chinks" were alike. Where Hollzer lived and worked could have been anywhere—Malaysia, Africa, or South America. What mattered was how well he was able to live. When I took Hollzer for my first ride around Shanghai, I was not quite used to the way one had to skirt people. They would literally run in front of a vehicle. I nearly hit a young Chinese. "Hey, be careful," Hollzer said to me, "you could have killed that Chink and it would cost you $20." Twenty Chinese dollars for killing a human being!

It was this sort of insensitivity to the life of the Chinese people that made it difficult for me to become fully integrated in the easy-going, pleasure-loving life of the International Settlement and the French Concession. Hollzer was basically a good man. He was kind and very helpful. He added much to my understanding of the ways business was conducted in the Orient. He knew the life of the many ports of China from a business point of view, and he knew Shanghai and Hong Kong best of all. One of the first things he told me to do was to get a chauffeur. When I asked him why I needed a chauffeur when I enjoyed driving my own car, he put the answer briefly, "For business reasons. You cannot afford to 'lose face' with the people you will be dealing with by driving your own car." I accepted Hollzer's advice and engaged a chauffeur who, of course, was a relative of Sorry. All that the chauffeur did at first was to keep washing my car, morning, noon, and night, and sit by my side when I drove, so that everyone knew I had a chauffeur. Later on he became useful in bringing me to places where there was no parking. He would drop me off and pick me up.

Hollzer took me to the jai alai games and I joined him one day at the horse races. After that I told Hollzer that I had had enought sports to last me a while.

"Yes," he said to me, "you are like my brother, Harry, who finds all his pleasures in books. Incidentally, there is a job waiting for you. Our American Club is in need of a chairman of its library committee. I will propose you as a member this evening. I know all the people on the membership committee and two of them come every day to my firm. You will be accepted quicker than you know."

Several days later a messenger boy brought me the acceptance of my membership in the club, and a month later I became chairman of the library committee. The other two members of the committee knew more about sing-song girls than about books. The library was a large, beautifully panelled room with a high ceiling. It had a narrow balcony along one of the walls with many shelves, which were only half-filled. Most of the books had never been removed from their places. They were books which remained in Shanghai when their original purchasers returned to America. There were very few books on China or its rich heritage. With a fund of about $5,000, which a generous member had left for the acquisition of new books, the picture was changed. My first achievement in Shanghai was to purchase the American Club's books, of which I was the main beneficiary. The American Club was one of my islands of refuge. I enjoyed it infinitely more than the British Club, which boasted of having the longest bar in the world, or the frivolous, sporty French Club, with its beautifully dressed women in search of excitement.

Most of the foreigners, including the Americans, had little time for their clubs except when offered lavish parties, dances, or other attractions. The important people were all busy running from one cocktail party to another during the afternoons, and from dinner parties to cabarets in the evenings.

I limited my cocktail parties to one a week at the official receptions which the mayor of Greater Shanghai gave for the press. At these gatherings, I heard most of the information presented by the nationalist Chinese government of Chiang Kai-shek. On occasion I would also attend some of the diplomatic dinners and receptions to which I was invited as a correspondent and as a chairman of an important committee of the American Club.

As chairman of the library committee, I was also asked to greet and welcome distinguished American professors and writers visiting Shanghai. My popularity seemed to have spread beyond the small American colony. I was frequently invited to speak before the Rotary Club, the Chamber of Commerce, and various Chinese-American associations.

For ten days before each Christmas, the stately American Club was saturated with a spirit of joy and gladness that surpassed any Christmas spirit I had ever experienced elsewhere. This was due, in large measure, to the aroused longings and memories that the beautiful decorations and Christmas carols stirred in the hearts of those who were thousands of miles away from home. It was a time when all Americans wanted to be among their countrymen. The dining rooms were never more crowded, and even our library was no longer the forgotten room of the house.

Vera and I, too, were captivated by the Christmas spirit. For me it brought back memories of another distant land—Shumsk of my youth, when the Russian priest invited my family to his annual Christmas party, and his son and I received similar Christmas gifts.

On the Wednesday before we were fully settled in our new apartment, our Number One Boy, Sorry, advised us of our first social visitor. It was the mother of Ruby Abraham, who came to welcome us to the Jewish community. Knowing that we were not yet fully set up for the observance of the Sabbath, Mrs. Abraham asked us to come to their home on Friday evening at sunset and to bring Hedvah and her *amah*, who would be looked after by her own servants. Mrs. Abraham, as I later learned, was not only devout but learned as well. On Friday we all walked to the home of the Abrahams who, as observant Jews, never rode on Sabbath. The Abraham home was a three-story wooden house in a compound surrounded by a well-kept, trimmed, English garden and enclosed by a high stone wall. It was like an ancient, well-preserved monastery, an island isolated from the gross and corrupt world around.

We were warmly greeted by Ruby, his wife, his daughter, his sons, and his mother and father. Ruby's parents lived in this home from the time they were married. Ruby and his children lived in it all their lives. It was a house with many rooms and with sufficient privacy for every member of the family. Ruby asked me to join the men in the study, where we all individually received the Sabbath by saying the traditional prayers. Since their home was some distance away from the Sephardic synagogue, the members of the family went to synagogue only for the Sabbath morning services.

After the short service, Mr. Abraham placed his hands on Ruby's bowed head. He blessed him with the threefold priestly blessing, and he then blessed the eldest son, the youngest son, and Ruby's daughter. After the blessing, they invited us to the traditional Sabbath meal served by Chinese waiters. The sacramental wine, which would not be touched by a heathen, was served by Ruby's wife.

When Mrs. Abraham had spoken of the traditional Jewish Sabbath dinner, my wife Vera envisaged gefilte fish, mandel or chicken soup, some form of boiled or roasted chicken, and honey cake. At this typically Jewish meal there was a first dish of some very spicy curry with ingredients that I couldn't identify. Our mouths, which were burning from the first delicacy, were then treated to a dish that was even more spiced and God knows what was in it. It was a kosher Jewish version of a Indian food.

I gradually familiarized myself with the ways of the businessmen in Shanghai and then laid the ground for my main source of income, the distribution of "Pure Gold" oranges throughout the Far East. Before embarking on plans for the vast area which I was to cover, I established contacts with the Chinese dealers and distributors of citrus fruits in Shanghai. They had their fingers on the pulse of all the markets where the Chinese lived. That included one-third of the globe. The junks of many of these dealers carried imported fruits to various cities on the Yangtze River. It was vital for me to secure a strong foothold in the market of Shanghai. The large buying power of the foreign population, including some 40,000 Japanese and four million Chinese, was of paramount importance. After sifting through and interviewing many possible candidates for my chief assistant, I selected one of the youngest of the applicants, who was of a good family which had connections throughout China.

Yeng was only 23 years old. He had received a thorough schooling in one of the best Christian missionary schools, but he did not abandon the Buddhist faith of his family. Most of Yeng's family was in the wholesale produce business, and two brothers worked with his father. Yeng preferred to strike out on his own. He was a most likeable, intelligent, honest young man. He was loyal, and he told his father he was happy to work with me because we "both like to laugh." Yeng had more than the spontaneous laughter of youth. It was a reflection of accumulated experience and understanding of people in all their foibles, wisdom, and foolishness. Not to have laughed would have spelled defeat.

Yeng knew how to discount much of what traders and businessmen would tell him. One dealer told me that my man "sees mo den me see." I agreed with him. Yeng would sense the slightest lie or deviation from truth. He knew how to maneuver and jockey his positions. His analytical mind was what I needed in overcoming the obstacles of breaking into an established, conservative market that kept all outsiders at bay. With Yeng, my job was simple and full of fun from the very start. My main task was to say, "Yes, Yeng," or "No, Yeng," and no matter what I said he grinned, even if reluctant to accept it. When he disagreed he would say, "You much older."

One of Yeng's duties was to organize the dinners that we gave for the leading men in the trade. There was always a film, prepared in Redlands, California, on Pure Gold oranges, showing how they were raised and how well they were accepted in various parts of America. The dinners were elaborate affairs lasting many hours. With Yeng's translation I kept the guests alert with brief remarks. A year later I did not use Yeng as a translator. My Chinese was good enough to dispense with this part of his service. This made him feel very sad and he did not laugh. However, during that first year Yeng taught me many trade expressions that my learned Chinese teacher did not know. Having attended a dinner with Yeng's brothers, similar to those I would give in the future, I told Yeng that I would allow him to invite sing-song girls but that I didn't want them to sit on the laps of our guests who, as a part of their pastime, would play around with the girls' breasts. After he had failed to convince me that my prohibition would fault the success of the endeavor, he finally agreed with, "You older than me. You like Christian missionary priest. I know you too were Christian missionary priest in America."

"Yes, Yeng, I was," I answered, "but not a Christian missionary, a Jewish one." It took him a long time to figure out the possible difference between Jewish and Christian missionary priests, but he consented, "OK, I tell them sing-song girls OK. No sittee on laps and no touchee breasts." In spite of Yeng's fears, the first dinner was a success. We made a dent in the barrier that was set up by the established, entrenched, heavily advertised competitor of the Mutual Orange Distributors, the Sunkist oranges. "No one," they had said before I started, "will buy your oranges without a Sunkist label." Yeng and I were to prove them wrong and we succeeded beyond our wildest expectations.

We developed a strategy to follow in the wake of the favorable reaction of the main citrus dealers, who came largely at the advice of Yeng's father. While I had no confirmed orders for any quantities of fruit, I dispatched a cable for a large shipment of oranges and grapefruits. It was a calculated risk and a gamble. We had no assurance as to who would buy the fruit or as to what price the fruit would bring. Bruce MacDaniel, who was fully informed of what I did, backed me to the hilt.

During the weeks we waited for the shipment to arrive, Yeng was busily running to all dealers from Shanghai to Nanking, telling them of the large shipment of the finest and "joosiest" California oranges that were on the way. Many dealers were thrown off balance. They didn't dare order too much of their Sunkist oranges in advance. They limited their stocks and waited to see what our prices would be and how the quality of our fruit would compare with the only fruit from California that they had bought for years. A week before the fruit arrived, I placed ads in foreign and Chinese papers, advising people to buy our Pure Gold oranges from the fruit stalls in Wing On and Sincere, two large department stores. We had set up special, inviting booths in these stores in readiness for the arrival of our fruit. The dealers never anticipated such a novel approach, especially after Yeng had told them of the beautiful Chinese girls who would serve the delicioius samples of sliced oranges to the thousands of people visiting the department stores. When Yeng told me of some dealers who were now ready to place orders and pay in advance, I told him not to do anything until the shipment arrived. Within two days after our large shipment had arrived, it was sold out at the highest price that California oranges had fetched in those weeks. The dealers who bought our oranges, and paid for them in cash before delivery, charged higher prices for the better "quality of fruit." They were very happy. This was my first surprising experience in the illusion that can be created in the minds of consumers and merchants alike through good advertising and promotion.

To celebrate our victory and to carry our business to greater heights, I allowed Yeng to make a bigger party with more sing-song girls and "no sitting on laps." Yeng enlisted the help of his brothers to take offers and advance payments at the prices we established for the fruit.

I sent the confirmed orders via cable, and two days later Shanghai was bombed, first through stupidity and ineptitude of the inexperienced Chinese air force, which mistook the targets, and then a lot more seriously by the Japanese air force. We were instantly isolated and cut off from the world for long, long months to come.

All the British, American, and French women and children in the international district and the French Concession were ordered to evacuate to Hong Kong. I relayed the call of the American Embassy to Vera and told her to get ready for departure. She refused to leave. She remained in Shanghai during the worst bombings together with a very small group of American women, who had also refused to leave their homes. I canceled the shipment and told Yeng to return all the money to the fruit dealers who had given us orders.

With my business stopped dead, I turned to my work as a journalist. I sent the first cables after the bombing of Shanghai. Ironicaly, one of the victims of the bombings was the only Jewish matzo factory in the Far East. My cable became a journalistic scoop. Nearly all the papers in America and Europe carried it. After that, and with the help of a friendly Associated Press correspondent, I had no difficulty being invited to any press conference. Since Shanghai had only a small Jewish community and hordes of prominent world journalists flocked to the city, I had relatively little to report. Nevertheless, in 1937 I found myself at the center of the greatest excitement in the world.

The bombing of the Chinese sections of Shanghai reverberated throughout the International Settlement and French Concession. Their homes destroyed, countless Chinese sought refuge in the International Settlement and French Concession, which were already overcrowded with the joint population of nearly two million foreigners and Chinese. Among those looking for a place of lodging was Yeng's family. I appealed to Ruby Abraham. Fortunately, he had a small residence that he could offer Yeng's distraught parents. This was only one of the many kind deeds Ruby felt it was his religious and humanitarian duty to perform. I told Yeng to meet me at the grocery, where we arrived almost at the last hour to buy whatever was still available in food and canned goods. The shelves were nearly empty, but there were a few cases of food that we hurriedly threw into our baskets. They were a great help in varying our limited diet during the following three months of the siege of Shanghai. I was able to share some of what I bought at the last-minute shopping expedition with Yeng's family. It was more difficult for them to find provisions during the height of the war which, during the span of four months, claimed the lives of 500,000 Chinese men, women, and children.

Chiang Kai-shek had been thrown off guard. He had been sure the Japanese would not attack before the end of the year or even later. The first weeks of the war were harrowing. Through our living-room windows, we could see the Japanese planes emptying their arsenal of bombs on the homes of the Chinese section surrounding the French Concession.

When my little girl overcame her great fright and became used to the sound of the whizzing bullets, she would run to the window, shouting in her pidgin English, "Go vay Japnees!" Her language and emotions were strongly conditioned by her Chinese *amah*. When everyone became a little more placid and when the foreign capitals repeatedly assured us that the end of the agony was within sight, I was able to visit the news-gathering places and learn what was going on.

In the meantime, I was making all necessary preparations to take Vera to the county hospital, which was situated near a heavily bombed Chinese area. When Vera went into labor, it was relatively quiet. Sorry insisted that my chauffeur should drive the car.

An hour or two after we arrived at the hospital, the nurse told me to bring the doctor. The doctor was a Hungarian Jew who spent more time in Shanghai gambling joints than he did in his office, and it was not in his office but in a card-playing parlor that I found him. It was getting dark and the bombing resumed in earnest. The doctor was a brave man. In spite of his weakness, he had a fine sense of professional duty. When I kept apologizing for dragging him through the dangerous streets, he was very nonchalant about it. We had to leave the car at a little distance from the entrance to the hospital, which was reserved for ambulances. As we walked along the wall, there was a shattering explosion. Though it was probably a few blocks away, we could hear the shrieks of the Chinese wounded.

The hospital itself was one of the relatively few safe places in that area. The Japanese were very careful to avoid bombing the immediate sites of the foreigners. They wanted to finish off the Chinese before tackling the big powers.

My wife gave birth to a son on the last day of Succoth, the Festival of the

Booths. My visits to the hospital were accompanied by the sounds of gunfire and whizzing bullets overhead. We named him Michael, after the first important painting that I had bought, the Archangel Michael.

Returning home, I drove close to the bombed-out Chinese areas and saw the devastation, which was only a prelude to what happened the following months. I asked myself the same question that was asked among the old China hands, who had never experienced anything like it. Who started it? Why didn't the big powers stop it? What meaning do all the rights of thirteen foreign flags and individual armies have in Shanghai when such wanton slaughter is allowed to go on? What kind of joke were the 1,800 American Marines and 3,000 French soldiers, when all the American and British women and children had to be evacuated? Had this war been prevented from spreading wildly, a yet bigger war might also have been prevented, World War II, which came in its wake.

It is noted by historians that August 9, 1937, was the "Sarajevo of the Far East." On that day two young Japanese naval officers were on a presumed inspection tour. Their bodies were found riddled with bullets. The Japanese navy began to "teach the Chinese a lesson." Chiang Kai-shek, who always had been patient and cautious, lost his calm and agreed to a massive counter-attack by the Chinese Thirteenth Army, which was lying at the outskirts of Shanghai. The tragic result is part of history.

Because of the war, I had a great deal of free time on my hands and I looked for a good Chinese teacher who would devote two or three hours a day to concentrated and intensive lessons in the Chinese language and literature. One day, on my way from the county hospital, I stopped at the Y.M.C.A. I knew the secretary of the place and I told him my problem. After some thought he said, "I think I know just the man you want. A few weeks ago a distinguished Chinese scholar who had recently arrived from Hunan Province asked one of my associates if he knew of any work that would engage him for a few hours a day. I will try to get in touch with him and send him to you."

Two days later Sorry informed me that a Chinese gentleman wanted to see me. I was unable to communicate with my caller. He knew no English or any other language except Chinese. With the help of Sorry's peasant Chinese, I expressed my great satisfaction in accepting my guest as my teacher. Having taught Hebrew in the "natural method," where the target language is used exclusively, I was delighted to be able to learn Chinese in the same way.

My teacher, Ho Ming, was a man close to 70 years of age. He was well versed in the classics of China. In his gentle manner and soft, thoughtful speech, he began to reveal the ideas contained in the words he taught me. It was a fascinating way of learning the language, one that enabled me to understand the soul of China. In addition to his erudition, Ho Ming had an understanding of the art of ancient China. He knew the work of the Tang period better than some of the art dealers, and after a month of strenuous, daily lessons, my teacher accompanied me to those galleries which had somehow managed to keep their doors open, even though trade in art had come to a virtual standstill.

When I was able to converse wtih my teacher intelligently, I told him of the similarity of some of the Chinese expressions to the Bible. He smiled and told me he had heard the same thing from a Christian missionary in the city where he once lived. He then asked me how I knew the Bible, and I told him in Chinese that I was a Jew. He smiled again and said, "You do not look like a Jew. The Jews that I knew as a little boy looked the same as we did. They wore the same clothes and they had long queues, but they disappeared many years ago." He knew all about the synagogue of Kai Feng Fu. His father remembered it as a boy, but by the time Ho Ming was in Kai Feng Fu, the synagogue had already been destroyed. He had heard about Jews from India and the West, but he had never seen one until he saw me, and I was more like an American of the Y.M.C.A.

One Friday, Sorry was surprised to hear that he had to prepare an extra dish of gefilte fish for my teacher, whom I invited to our Sabbath meal. "No eatee gefilte fish. Me cookee rice." "No," I said to Sorry, "my teacher will eat what we eat." He did and he liked it very much. After years of eating Chinese food in America, I enjoyed having a truly distinguished Chinese philosopher eat Jewish gefilte fish and kreplach, which Sorry could cook better than my wife.

By the beginning of December, the Japanese Army destroyed and conquered all the Chinese parts of Shanghai. The only sections which remained undamaged were the International Settlement, the French Concession, and Little Tokyo. The two million inhabitants of this protected area began to adapt themselves to the new rulers of the surrounding country. There were some foreigners who were not at all displeased with the change. Sipping their iced scotch in the clubs, where life had returned to normal, they expressed satisfaction and hoped to continue "business as usual" under the new Japanese regime. The evacuated wives and children, who in some cases had a more difficult time than my wife and daughter, were returning to their homes when a new, serious incident occurred on the Yangtze River. Japanese warplanes attacked, bombed, and sank the U.S. gunboat, *Panay*. They also attacked the British ships and destroyed a British oil tanker. Many American and British officers were killed.

The *Panay* incident brought near panic in the American colony and in our home. Upon hearing the details of the incident, I said, "Now we must pack quickly and try to get out. There will be no time for an organized evacuation." Everyone in our household was in tears. But once I obtained a more complete picture of the situation after filing some cables, I returned home reassured and changed my mind about leaving.

I began to carry out the plans I had made before the armies withdrew. I called Yeng and told him to rush to the fruit dealers for a reconfirmation of their old orders. I also told him to accept orders for the nondeciduous fruits of the Di Giorgio Fruit Company of Central California, which firm also asked me to represent them. Starved for fruit, the well-to-do in Shanghai alone could consume vast amounts of the "health-giving fruits of California." While Yeng and the man I engaged to run my office were busy with their contacts, I laid plans to extend my operations to Hong Kong, Manilla, and the Dutch East Indies.

All about me there was a new vitality in Shanghai. Barely a week later, the *Panay* incident was forgotten and all the warring armies removed to the interior. The old life of Shanghai burst out in all directions; the horse races were on again and so was the jai alai; cabarets were filled to capacity. After three and a half months of restraint, there was a release of tension, a freedom and joy which were not in keeping with the actual situation.

Ruby Abraham, with whom I had been in close contact during the entire period of the siege, maintained a philosophic calm and a deep religious conviction, stemming from his studies of age-old Hebraic lore, which made him my most valued friend. After my Chinese studies, with which he helped me on occasion, we used to pore over the Bible and the Talmud together. Now I came to him for a prosaic purpose. I needed an office. Ruby asked no questions. He lifted the receiver of the phone and told his Chinese-Jewish clerk to reach Mrs. Hardoon.

Mrs. Hardoon knew all about me. Shanghai, in spite of its size, was in many respects a small town. Nearly everyone knew everyone else. Ruby filled me in about Mrs. Hardoon, a Chinese lady who had married one of the wealthiest Jews of Shanghai. When Hardoon died, she gave him two large official funerals, one Buddhist funeral with a long procession, and one Jewish funeral for the "brothers of Hardoon's faith."

When I called on Mrs. Hardoon, she was in the inner chamber of her large, traditionally arranged offices; many clerks attended to her real estate operation. I was led through two beautifully paneled rooms until I reached Mrs. Hardoon's spacious private office. As I entered the room, she bowed with her head down and folded her arms. She welcomed me as a *chacham*, a learned religious teacher, and a dear friend of one of her closest friends, the Abrahams. Tea was brought in. After enjoying the atmosphere and friendliness as well as the tea cakes, I came to the point. "Yes," said Mrs. Hardoon, "we have an office of the kind you need." When I asked her about the rent and the terms of the lease, she told me that these things were handled by her managers but that she would recommend that I pay no rent at all for the first three months, until I was established.

Besides the Abrahams, there were several other families who befriended us. They all belonged to the exclusive, closely knit Sephardic Jewish community. Paradoxically, their rabbi was an English Jew born into a Polish Jewish family.

Then there was Horace Kadoorie. He was a bachelor when I met him and only a few years older than I, a cultivated English gentleman. We shared a love of Chinese art. He was one of the two sons of Sir Eli Kadoorie, who was reputed to be the greatest Jewish philanthropist of those years.

Sir Eli owned Marble Hall, a palatial home in the Far East. It was supposed to have cost two million dollars to build and more than one hundred gardeners and servants were needed to look after the huge estate. We were often guests for dinner there, and once, while we were waiting for Sir Eli to come down from his study, we amused ourselves by counting the sofas and chairs in the mammoth living room. There wre fifty.

Sir Eli was a pleasant man—shrewd, but also wise, kind, and patient. I had many sessions with him six months later when he requested me to serve as honorary secretary of the European Refugee Committee. I agreed and worked with Sir Eli and Sir Victor Sassoon, who were vice-presidents of the committee, whose function it was to receive refugees from Nazi Germany.

When invited to dinner on Friday nights, we ate in the main dining room on a large, historic English dining table, which came from one of the castles of Great Britain. Sir Eli suffered from gout, a condition caused by his extravagant life in France during his youthful years.

Before I explained to Horace and Sir Eli that, religiously, I belonged to the Reconstructionist movement (of which they had never heard), there was always a special bottle of wine from the Holy Land placed along my wine glass. When Horace and Sir Eli saw that I preferred the old French bottles, the Holy Land wine ceased to appear.

Sir Eli and Horace were not only genuinely charitable people, they were also very democratic. They never refused to come to our home for a Sabbath meal and shower Sorry with gifts for his unusual cooking of Ashkenazic dishes. In spite of their grand scale of living, these wealthy people made me feel that their humanity was not affected by the burden of their wealth. In addition to their home in Shanghai, the Kadoories owned a great part of the utilities and transportation in both Shanghai and Hong Kong. Sir Eli also had a large house in London. When Haile Selassie, the emperor of Ethiopia, was forced out of his country by Mussolini, Sir Eli Kadoorie turned over his home in London to the Emperor for the duration of his stay in England. Sir Eli was also an officer of the French Legion of Honor.

Another colorful man, to whom I could not warm up very much, was Sir Victor Sassoon, the most important figure in the foreign community. Sir Victor lived in Bombay most of his life. With vast holdings in China as well as in India, Sir Victor, still unmarried, decided to move to Shanghai in 1931. All the financial newspapers ran headlines of his move. The shares of the principal British companies in China rose. It was a clear indication to the world of the faith that big business had in the future growth and development of China.

The older Mrs. Abraham did not approve of Victor's lifestyle. "He is not a pious Jew," she told me, "and I trust God will forgive him because of the charitable work he does." I admired Mrs. Abraham and I could talk to her frankly, in spite of our different approaches to the same religion which we both loved. I told Mrs. Abraham what one of our American philosophers, Santayana, said about piety. He called piety "reverence for the sources of one's being." Mrs. Abraham, who knew English very well, smiled and said, "But what are the sources of Victor's being? Are they not those that come from our holy Torah?"

At his social events, Sir Victor was always a most impressive figure. He wore a monocle that seemed to shine down from his great height. His slight limp was the result of his service as a captain in the British Air Force during the First World War, when his plane was shot down by a German fighter plane. It in no way detracted from his stately appearance.

The man who was best able to divert my attention from the gravity of the world was the spiritual leader of the Sephardic community, Rabbi Mendel Brown. He was a stocky, pudgy little man who was full of fun. Raised in a Yiddish-speaking home, he was delighted to find a companion with whom he could exchange a few Yiddish words. No one in his congregation knew a word of Yiddish and I was the first of his old-world tribe to join the synagogue. He was not a learned man, but he made up for it by his pastoral activities, which included a genuine interest in the trials and tribulations of the members of his congregation.

The elder Abraham could not understand how a man could be a rabbi without a deep knowledge of the Torah. I told Mr. Abraham that if he had met some of the prominent American rabbis, he would not have been so unkind to my jovial friend and *landsman*. "Yes," Mr. Abraham conceded, "I suppose you are right. He makes up for his lack of learning with the kindness of his heart." I couldn't expect greater tolerance than that. Rabbi Mendel and Yeng were two men with whom I could laugh without restraint. Once Mendel begged me not to get too close to him during the services. He was afraid I would make him laugh.

Mendel's wife was just the opposite. She was an unhappy, sullen woman and out of place in Shanghai. Everyone about her was foreign, including the English foreigners. She was born in the East End of London and lived her early life among Yiddish-speaking immigrants from Russia. She had never heard of Baghdad or Bombay Jews and was uncomfortable with their customs and food. Since her husband was busy, running around to homes and meetings, Mrs.

Brown was alone with her three daughters. The youngest, named Peter, was the only one who took after her father. She was a jolly, young lady of 15 when I met her. While she, too, helped me laugh, she was unable to make her miserable mother smile even once.

However, it was not the China of the foreigners which drew me. It was the ageless, cultural, creative, artistic world that I learned to know through my Chinese teacher and through my independent studies and observations. To obtain a basic understanding of Chinese philosophy, painting, and other art forms, a knowledge of the religions of China is essential.

The Chinese religions are really three and not one. The mixture of the three, as observed by the Chinese, is based on both mysticism and rationalism. Like Jewish rationalist believers who bear a deep reverence for tradition, the Chinese Confucians worshipped the memory of their ancestors. In both instances, that reverence and worship gave their people a spiritual continuity and unity essential for the good way of life. The rationalist believers ascribed no divine powers to Confucius. The only divine power they recognized was the Supreme Ruling Force of the World. This is not very different from what Dr. Kaplan called the "Power that worketh for righteousness and justice."

For the masses of people, religion was a preoccupation with "otherworldliness," a world of good and evil spirits, whose good will and help could be obtained through prayers, offerings, incense burning, and other varied forms of worship. For nearly a thousand years, the rationalist Confucians were in opposition to the followers of the Taoist faith, both organized long before Christianity.

A new, foreign, religion was imported from India and it offered the people a more promising and hopeful outlook. Like Hassidism, which burst on the scene of Jewish history after centuries of suffering and despair with a new doctrine of "serving the Lord with joy," Buddhism brought joy, brightness, and hope to the masses who needed something to believe in. Though all three religions, pulled in different directions, China knew no real conflicts among them.

At the age of 22, Confucius became a teacher, and according to tradition, he was free of four things: he had no foregone conclusions; he had no arbitrary predeterminations; he had no obstinacy; he had no egotism. The legacy of Confucius is found in five books, known as *Five Ching*. It is not very different from much that is found in the Pentateuch.

In his teachings Confucius stressed that the whole end of speech is to be understood. It is as unequivocal as the *I* and *thou* of Martin Buber. An *I* and *thou* relationship cannot be established without understanding. Confucius was opposed to metaphysics and all of the Taoist precepts which encouraged otherworldliness. He is, therefore, regarded by many scholars as an agnostic. When

Confucius was asked whether one should serve the spirits of the dead, he answered, "Since you are not able to serve men, how can you serve their spirits?" In another context, he said, "When you do not know life, how can you know about death?"

Confucius said the ancients first regulated their families, then each one had to regulate and rectify his heart and cleanse it so he could see clearly. A Hassidic rabbi of the eighteenth century said, "He who comes to improve others must first improve himself." When my Chinese teacher taught me that Confucius said "Not to do unto others as you would not wish to be done unto yourself," I smiled and told him that those were the exact words of Rabbi Hillel, who said it in the same negative form, because it is easier for man to desist from a wrong deed than to attempt a good deed.

When asked, "What constitutes the higher man?" Confucius answered, "The cultivation of himself with reverential care. What the higher man seeks is in himself. What the lower man seeks is in others."

The Chinese people have kept the teachings of Confucius and others close to their hearts, but it is basically Buddhism and its rites which are followed.

Since religion in China was not taken as seriously as in some of the Moslem and Christian countries, I was not disturbed by many of the practices and superstitions of the Chinese people. They kept them to themselves, never forcing them on others.

The Japanese War Department declared, "War is the father of all creation and the mother of civilization." The war started in China in 1931 with the conquest of Manchuria, and it then spread to Shanghai in 1937, after which hostilities continued until the end of the Second World War in 1945. The war was fought in the remote recesses of the vast land, between the Japanese armies and the two armies of the Chinese people, the army of Chiang Kai-shek and the army of the Communists led by Mao Tze Tung. When the Chinese tired of bleeding each other, they fought separately and at times united against the main enemy.

We watched the fighting going on in the interior as though we were thousands of miles away from it. In the International Settlement, most of the foreigners were not overly concerned with the outcome of the struggle going on at their doorstep, since the business and profits they were making in Shanghai had not diminished with the Japanese occupation.

There were, however, a few Europeans and especially the old Jewish settlers who took a different view of the war. They knew the Japanese and they knew the Chinese better than the most knowledgeable residents of Shanghai. They believed and prayed that China would sooner or later repel the evil forces. They believed it because they knew that China, with its vast agricultural base, would better resist aggression than the industrialized areas. The morale of these Europeans and Jews, like that of China, was high; as a result, so was mine.

In addition to my wise Sepahrdic brothers, who were a source of encouragement and faith, I made the acquaintance of a number of Chinese intellectuals. I met one of them, Liu, in our American library. Liu was a professor of literature and he was in close association with many intellectuals who were among Mao Tze Tung's followers. They had small, underground cells and surfaced only when sure that neither the Japanese nor the Kuomintang agents were near.

They were the most refreshing people in Shanghai, but I had to be very careful not to be ensnared by their well-intentioned designs. They belonged to the highest class of revolutionaries imaginable, not at all doctrinaire. They were free of intolerance for those in the opposite camp. They never spoke of "Chinese destiny." Theirs was an inner form of revolution that called for raising the Chinese masses to a higher level of life.

Behind the fighting lines, these principled revolutionaries helped the people build new factories, industries, and schools. Education began to spread widely and it was in this phase of work that they sought to involve me. Prudence and good judgment prevented my participation. No matter how careful one was in Shanghai, there were eyes that kept watch on all activities.

Furthermore, I had agreed to serve as the honorary secretary of the committee formed to cope with the problems of immigrants escaping from Hitler's jaws. Within one year, 19,000 German-Jewish refugees arrived. Our committee found living accommodations for them in the burned-out and bombed Chinese sections of Shanghai. The physicians and professional people found employment. The other refugees were a serious problem. After exhausting all the funds which Sir Victor, Sir Eli, and other wealthy Jews in China donated, we were greatly relieved by the rush of funds donated by the Jewish Joint Distribution Committee of New York. Within months after the boats had brought us the first batch of human cargo from Germany and Austria, professional social workers arrived from America, and I was again free to give attention to my business, which developed rapidly and successfully, despite the little time I devoted to it.

Shanghai summers were oppressively hot and humid. Many of the foreigners took their families to the lovely, mountainous areas of Japan. In the summer of 1938, I, too, took my wife and two children to Unzen in the Nagasaki mountains, which surrounded the port. It was the shortest distance from Shanghai, only a twenty-four-hour ride by boat, and it was like coming to another world.

In spite of reports to the contrary, I found a calm, contented, and no less prosperous nation than the one I had seen in Japan a year earlier. All around us were peaceful, orderly, courteous people. They seemed like another race of men, so different were they from their kinsmen who were waging a brutal war on the other side of the Nagasaki Sea.

It was hard for me to curtail my great enjoyment, leave my family in Unzen, and proceed to Tokyo by train. All along the trip to the opposite side of the Japanese islands, I encountered people of good cheer and the same traditional courtesy with which I became enamored during my previous stay in Japan. I found tremendous contrast between the humaneness of the people I met during my nine days in Japan and the inhumanity of their soldiers in China. When I later heard that there were good Germans who honestly did not know of the Nazi horrors during the war, I believed it. The Japanese military establishment, like the Nazi establishment, was, through its evil ways, able to transform boys and men with weak minds into brutal robots with very little likeness to the people from whom they were drawn.

Here, in Japan proper in the midst of war, I saw a people whose faces were turned to an enlightened future, undaunted by what was happening at a time when the actions of the military were allegedly answerable to a secluded man who was the figurehead emperor. In fact, the military was answerable only to its own high-ranking, disciplined officers.

The progress I observed in most walks of life did not extend itself to the art world. I found when I made the rounds of the art dealers that sales of good art had dropped. I was received very warmly, and two gentlemen invited me to their homes for tea. They knew I was preparing to add to my business enterprise the exportation of Chinese, Korean, and Japanese art.

In spite of the gloom that had set in as a result of the war, they encouraged me in my venture, promising to help me. Most of the very knowledgeable and experienced art dealers were optimistic about the future possibilities of exporting the art of the Orient to America and importing the art of America to the Orient. The idea of a new mission in a cultural exchange fired my imagination in Tokyo.

After leaving my family in Unzen for the duration of the summer, I returned to my work in Shanghai. My business grew from month to month. Pure Gold oranges replaced the Sunkist oranges in most of the markets of China. Through efficient organization, Yeng, Ho (my officer manager), and I prepared to extend our operations to other parts of the Far East. Hong Kong was, next to Shanghai, the most promising area for the opening of a branch office.

During the year I was in China, I communicated with my cousin Irving Marantz. Irving was an artist, but he appeared to me to have a good sense of business. When he importuned me to bring him to China to engage him in my "prosperous business," it suddenly occurred to me that I could make him manager of my Hong Kong office. I wrote Irving, telling him all the pros and cons of bringing him and his wife, Evelyn, to China. In Irving's effusive acceptance of my terms and the check for travel expenses, he added, "You scoundrel, how could you have dared to consider any cons in becoming one of your partners?" I had never mentioned anything about Irving's becoming a partner. I laughed and made the necessary preparations for my first visit to Hong Kong, Manila, and Singapore. In each of these cities, we already had some contacts and representatives for the distribution of our citrus fruits.

When the Committee for European Refugees was appraised of my visit to the various areas of the Far East, I was given the added task of receiving German-Jewish refugees on their arrival in the ports. I met with boatloads in Singapore, Manila, and Hong Kong.

On one of these boats, bearing 700 passengers, I traveled from Singapore to Manila, and on another from Hong Kong to Shanghai. This was after I had returned from a hurried business trip. When I left Germany in 1936, I thought I knew all about the agony of my fellow Jews under Hitler, but much of what I heard in hushed voices then, I heard now in an endless flow of pain and tears.

I would shut myself up in my cabin to calm down and to collect my thoughts; the refugee committee had assigned me to give talks to the passengers. "It does not matter," the passengers would say, "whether the German that you use is more Yiddish than German. What matters to all of us are the words that are spoken from your heart."

There was one thing I asked the committee not to do, and that was not to use the German word "Achtung," in calling to order. That horrible word, which I heard so often in Germany, made me shudder. In my talks to the large crowds, I drew a great deal of inspiration from the words of the prophets and from the long history of the Jewish people. I also drew much from the heroic resistance and unfaltering faith of the Chinese people. One quote from the Book of Judges, which I would use with great passion, had a salutary effect on my listeners. I quoted the Hebrew slowly and I then gave the correct German version with equal vigor, "Oh my soul, march on with strength."

The agony in trying to establish a foothold in the destroyed areas around the International Settlement was very great, but the European refugees were able to move about without nightmares and fears for their lives. For us, their unexpected arrival in large numbers added many problems to our effort to solve the humanitarian problem of the tens of thousands of Chinese refugees who crowded into the International Settlement and the French Concession.

We, who taught that in suffering and misery humanity is one, could not discriminate between those who were ours and those who were not. Our help was extended to all. Sir Eli, who gave me a check of fifty thousand dollars for the European refugees, showed me his little notebook in which there were even larger sums for the Chinese children. We received similar contributions from Sir Victor, the Abraham family, and others for the needs of the people. Unable to measure up to their big contributions, I gave, in addition to my contribution, whatever I could give in terms of service and time.

With the advent of the High Holidays, I was asked to "lift the spirits" of the downtrodden at improvised services arranged for the newcomers. "Lift the spirits" were the words used by Rabbi Harrison of the Hollywood Temple Israel when he asked me to go to San Bernardino at the depth of the Depression. During the High Holidays, in China, I addressed several gatherings. Most of those who attended had seldom been at any services before. They were Jewish because they were forced to be. They were assimilated Jews who had to realign themselves with the faith of their ancestors. I addressed them as human beings whose Jewish awareness did not have much in common with mine. I quoted from the prayers of the Days of Awe which spoke of "one humanity," and "I shall make of you one family." On Yom Kippur I added a new version to the "Ten Martyrs of the Hadrianic era." I began with the traditional words of "*Eile ezkera,*" "these things do I remember."

"Oh, I pour my soul out for them. In all ages long hatred pursueth us; through all the years ignorance like a monster hath devoured our martyrs as in one long day of blood.

"This hath befallen us. All this I tell as I beheld it passing through the years of bygone ages. And subdued and crushed, we pour our hearts out, supplicating Thee. Lord, Lord, give ear. Oh pitying, merciful, make an end of blood poured out and wasted. Wash the stain away, Oh God, King who sittest on a gracious throne."

The motley congregation became one in heart and one in spirit. Religious and irreligious alike were moved to tears. Not since my childhood days during the prayers of our indigent cantor did I see so many men and women engulfed in tears.

I spoke for the Jews of Europe under Hitler and I spoke for the Chinese under the heel of the Japanese, without mentioning the Japanese by name. Even at a Jewish service I had to be cautious. I called on the Europeans who had anything to contribute in medicine and other fields to fill the places of the Chinese who were killed. I reminded them of what the rabbis had said, "One who saves one life is like one who saves the whole world."

For the intellectual members of the congregation who knew Shakespeare better than the Bible, I quoted in English, "How far that little candle throws its beams. So shines a good deed in a naughty world." Then I translated this into German. I thought of what Rabbi Kaplan would have said if he had heard me speak not as a rabbi, but as a layman, "You gave the right message at the right time."

Irving Marantz and his wife arrived. The groundwork was laid for a flourishing, diversified business in the import and export fields, and I charted the direction we were to follow. Yeng was to be in charge of our extension to the imports. Irving and Yeng's experienced cousin, Lin, were to proceed to Hong Kong, where I opened an office, and were to look after our import and export business in Hong Kong.

Irving, with his knowledge of Oriental art acquired in New York, was to assist me with the sale of Chinese and Japanese art to potential buyers from America and Europe. I was not to be burdened with administrative problems. For this we had good and tried Chinese help, from whom I learned a great deal on how to run an efficient, smooth organization. It was not long before Irving surprised me with his dexterity in handling shrewd Chinese art dealers. When Irving came to the Shanghai office in connection with some old jade and bronze transaction in Shanghai, Yeng said to Irving, "You all right, you good Number Two Man." To which Irving, who was not versed in good Chinese manners, said, "No, I good Number One Man. You good Number Two Man."

Yeng was flustered. What he really meant was that Irving was the Number Two Man in the family. When Irving realized that he had made a *faux pas*, he embraced Yeng and kept repeating to him, "You Number One Man in all China." They became good friends. This gave me a chance to lay down a rule in our business. There was not to be any such thing as Number One or Number Two Man, and that I was only a mediator and nothing else. All, and especially Irving, accepted my rule without protest.

After a few months of smooth sailing, I began to notice that in addition to Irving's healthy involvement in business, he and Evelyn found ample time in a new involvement, an involvement with the radicals and Communists who kept coming and going in Hong Kong. Irving was a former Communist, and when he was a student in the Art Students League on New York's 57th Street, he used to engage me in heated debates on communism. There was one time when Irving broke violently with two of his Communist friends. Annoyed by what I said, they had blurted out that when the Revolution would come in America, I would be the first to be shot. At this, Irving's blood began to boil. The thought that his favorite cousin and friend would be placed before a firing squad by his own comrades made him forget all his Communist doctrine and discipline. I had been sure that he was going to strike his friend dead. That was ten years earlier, when Irving and his comrades were 22 years old. I had been amused by the incident but now, nearly ten years later, I was not amused by my cousin's emotional impulses. He knew of my own deep sympathies for what many of the Chinese revolutionaries were doing, therefore he graciously accepted my chastisement and advice not to meddle in the ideological and political conflicts in China for as long as he was associated with my firm. He knew that we were watched by the agents and double agents of the Kuomintang, the Japanese, the Russians, the Americans, and even the British.

Shanghai and Hong Kong were infested with spies from every major country. Everyone was under suspicion and one had to watch every step. Before they were employed, all the workers in my organization were carefully scrutinized. I was unable to trust Irving's judgment in the hiring of help for the office, so I sent either Yeng or Ho to select with care the people who would be employed in Hong Kong. The caution we took paid off. We dealt not only with the Chinese but with the Japanese as well. We obtained the agency for the distribution of Pittsburgh Paint for its products used on land and sea.

As for the Chinese, we had no problems. The Kuomintang agents of Chiang Kai-shek knew that some of our shipments were earmarked for the Communists of Chou En Lai. However, that did not stop any Kuomintang representative from doing business with our firm. People knew that we allocated some of our profits for the relief of Chinese children and no one questioned it or doubted our sincere motives. We were respected. Our business was on the up and up.

Absorbed in business, which by then included the Oriental art world, I had no time for journalism. The Jewish field was too limited and the compensation I received was not worth the effort. The Jewish community in America had no interest in the rich, cultural heritage of the Orient. It barely had any genuine interest in its own heritage. America was an easy, pleasant place to live in. *Life, Look*, the sports pages, and sometimes an occasional juicy novel was what most of the readers of the Los Angeles press needed in the way of culture.

I enjoyed a peaceful family life, until suddenly Hedvah became very ill. A disease she had suffered in her first year in San Bernardino struck again, more seriously, in Shanghai. One of the outstanding German-Jewish pediatricians, who knew the symptoms of this illness from research abroad, advised us to take Hedvah to another climate.

The top of the rock of Hong Kong appeared to him to be as good a place as any for the change he prescribed. We were to do this in about two weeks after medication and a close daily observation by the doctor. I dispatched letters to Hong Kong, Manila, and the Dutch East Indies, advising them of my arrival a month or two earlier than expected. I told Irving and Evelyn to have two rooms ready for Hedvah and her *amah* for four to six weeks. Vera stayed at home with Michael.

Hedvah's illness made me realize how deeply concerned my mother had been when I became seriously ill. Hedvah was my first child. I loved her for the priceless joy she brought into the home. She enlarged our life and filled it with a brightness which penetrated through all the rooms. Absorbed with the books in the library, I was always unconsciously aware of her playing with her *amah* in the bedroom. One of the pleasantest sights I remember was when I stood near the window and watched Hedvah walking along next to her brother's stroller in the little park across the street from our apartment.

When she was well, she was always jovial and playful, even rambunctious. And now, seeing her beautiful little eyes turned to the ceiling in incontrollable fits tore the heart out of us. Waiting and hoping for the miraculous end to Hedvah's illness, which the doctor said would come any time, I was unable to concentrate. I would have done whatever was asked of me for the restoration of my child's health. Vera, who was as a rule very unemotional, felt the same way I did. Neither of us said much about the way we were feeling. Not even the best poets have learned enough words to express a parent's agony when a beloved child is seriously ill.

When the two weeks were up, I took Hedvah and her *amah* to Hong Kong and, in three days, saw a remarkable improvement in Hedvah's condition. The doctor informed me I could leave my four-year-old daughter and safely proceed with my trip for about three to four weeks, depending on Hedvah's progress.

As I received daily reports from Hong Kong on how Hedvah ate and ran and played, my joy in seeing new, fascinating parts of the world became as lively as it was during the first months, when I faced my new adventures in Japan and Shanghai. How quickly man is able to change from utter despair to hope and joy! This change, which I experienced in a matter of two weeks, was also responsible, to a large extent, for another change I noticed in the lives of the German-Jewish refugee physicians. They, who were utterly despondent on their arrival, were now using their skills and were absorbed in the varied hospitals of China.

I was very glad the doctor had advised me to take Hedvah to Hong Kong. The top of the rock where Irving and Evelyn lived was 1,700 feet above the sea. On the last day of my visit, Hedvah was well enough to go with me to see the thousands of Chinese families who lived all their life on the fishing boats. The fish fascinated her. We walked over the planks to meet the many Chinese children who seldom touched land. They grinned when Hedvah gave them hard candies and she responded to their grins like any normal, happy child.

In my frequent visits to the ports of the Far East, I was one of the last beneficiaries of the glittering world on the high seas. Not one of those fine, mighty ships, including the *S.S. Victoria*, which I boarded in Hong Kong, remained to tell the tale of a remarkable, lost grandeur, which is now buried at the bottom of the sea. My voyage on the Italian *S.S. Victoria* came right after the most trying, painful days of Hedvah's illness. The Jewish Sages observed that a beautiful wife, beautiful objects, and a beautiful home broaden a man's horizon. Had they traveled with me on the *Victoria* over the calm, quiet sea, they would have added a beautiful ship to their list.

At that time, the boats were filled with businessmen traveling alone or with their mistresses, very few of whom had any love for the sea. They were bored and waited eagerly for the time when they could walk down the gangplank. Many years later I met one of those gentlemen, who flew in from Tokyo to Los Angeles and spoke glowingly of the new, marvelous form of travel by air. His story of the flight, which appeared to me to be long and tortuous, only awakened in me deep longings for those slow, easy, happy voyages on the limitless seas of the world.

On my return home some weeks later, Irving, Evelyn, and the *amah* brought Hedvah to meet me at the dock. With some coaxing from the *amah*, Hedvah ran up the plank and fell into my arms. We went up the hill, where Hedvah had a last meal before parting with the mountain that had restored her health. "No more fits. No more fits," were the first words of the *amah*'s greeting.

After I had spent a joyous hour in Hedvah's company, Irving opened some folders and brought me up to date on the progress that had been made in the Hong Kong and Shanghai offices. "From here on," he said, "we should sail full steam." While I liked Irving's optimism, I was sorry that I wasn't able to share it with him.

Toward evening we boarded the boat, where our happy trip to Shanghai erased the agony of our voyage to Hong Kong. Hedvah's return to good health was an occasion for festivity. The servants were all dressed in their holiday clothes, the house was decorated with banners and flowers, and Sorry prepared all of Hedvah's favorite dishes. Hedvah ran around embracing everyone, her mother, her two-year-old brother, and all the servants.

During the following months I was immersed in our far-flung, growing business. Our offices were expanded and we engaged additional help. Yeng and Ho were in the best of spirits. Suddenly, without any warning, we were struck by a thunderbolt. My office manager, Ho, was seized by the Japanese police for questioning about our business and our connections with Hong Kong, Manilla, and Singapore. They wanted to know all about our imports and exports and the nature of our competition with the Japanese and other firms. Each time his answers displeased the interrogators, they beat him. For several days he was unable to come to work.

I lodged a complaint with the American Consul. About a month later, my driver was taking me through an area in Shanghai that was evidently under the jurisdiction of the Japanese military. He passed a slow-moving vehicle with two Japanese officers. When our car pulled ahead of the officers' car, it was stopped. The driver was told to get out. I immediately asked the officer if we had done anything wrong. "Never mind," was the senior officer's gruff answer, "we will teach the swine a lesson not to pass a car with soldiers of the

Japanese Imperial Army." While the officer said this in perfect English, the second officer began striking my Chinese driver across the face. The driver turned to me pathetically and I saw blood running from the side of his mouth. I felt helpless, until I remembered what another American had done in a similar case. I lowered my head as low as I could in front of the officer. This satisfied him. He had achieved what he wanted—the humiliation of an American. My head was reeling and I could make no reply to my driver who continued to mumble, "Thank you, Master, thank you."

A few weeks later, the Japanese blocked the China coast and closed the Yangtze River to foreign shipping. The U.S. Ambassador to Japan, Joseph E. Grew, sent a report to the State Department in Washington, in which he stated, "Japan has become openly and unashamedly one of the predatory nations and part of a system which aims to wreck everything the U.S. stands for." This was still a year before Pearl Harbor, and there were not many who took the words of the ambassador to heart. Few among the foreigners in Shanghai could imagine that Japan would defy the might of America. I felt the ambassador was right.

I advised Irving and the Shanghai staff of my decision to transfer some of our operations to Los Angeles. I asked our offices to reduce our inventories and use all available funds for the purchase of Oriental art to be shipped to a new wholesale and retail distribution center which I planned to establish in Los Angeles.

Everyone understood that my motives for limiting our Chinese operations went beyond commercial considerations. It was not easy to terminate the growth of a business when it was reaching the zenith of its success. My stockbroker friend, Hollzer, thought I was being an alarmist. My other financial acquaintance, Chester Fritz, who represented one of the largest New York Stock Exchange firms, saw no justifiable reasons for the curtailment of my business and my return to the U.S. on account of the Japanese threats. Five years later, coming down the steps of my home in the Hollywood hills, I saw near my garage a man whom I did not recognize. It was Chester Fritz of Shanghai. He had just returned from China, where he had spent four years in a Japanese concentration camp.

We form strong friendships in times of stress. When parting from the Abraham family, Horace and Sir Eli Kadoorie, Rabbi Mendel, the Yeng family, and all my American and Chinese friends, I realized how much good friendship I stood to lose in leaving them behind. "True friendship," said a wise man, "is like sound health. The value of it is seldom known until it is lost."

Jacob Alkow with the noted philanthropist Sir Eli Kadoorie, Shanghai, 1939.

Jacob Alkow with his wife Vera and their children, Hedvah and Michael, 1942.

XVIII

THE WAR ERA

Unlike some of the foreigners whose departure from the comfortable life of China was traumatic, my feelings about departure were ambivalent. I was sorry to leave all the parties, the clubs, and the dutiful servants that Shanghai offered, but I was at last able to appease my conscience.

From the first day I set foot in China, I was deeply disturbed to see human beings instead of horses pulling rickshaws. The other human beings who sat in them were indifferent to the creatures who pulled them, but I could never reconcile myself to this institution, which had been first established in Japan by a missionary for the sake of his sick wife. The thought that the rickshaw boy's life span was only six years made it impossible for me to ride in one. No rationalization, such as helping poor Chinese gain employment or saving them from starvation, allowed me to condone a world in which my family enjoyed the best things, while thirty percent of the population hovered on the verge of starvation.

Regardless of the Japanese cruelty, and in spite of the financial success I achieved, I doubt that I would have been able to live permanently in a society so blatantly based on exploitation. It was fortunate that I did not need to exploit others, but it was impossible for me to be oblivious of a system in which I occupied a prominent place. It was in this ambivalent mood that my family and I parted from the rich life of China.

On our arrival in Los Angeles, we were warmly welcomed by our family and old friends. The scars of the bitter Depression were gone and they were all in a healthy, buoyant mood. I had sufficient means to buy a beautiful home on top of a hill north of Sunset Boulevard. To reach the house, there were seventy steps along a terraced hillside covered with almond, orange, and avocado trees as well as flowering bushes. The many steps that led to the entrance of the house had greatly reduced its commercial value. For us, each step enhanced the charm and the beauty of the home and its spacious grounds. From the top, there was a panoramic view of the western part of the city and the Pacific Ocean.

Since real estate rentals were at low ebb, I had no difficulty in finding a spacious store with a mezzanine floor. It was located in a block of fine shops on Wilshire Boulevard. The store had built-in showcases on its two long walls. With suitable lighting installed, they would be ideal for the display of the art objects that were a part of the first shipment. The finely carpeted store, attractive neon sign, and large window displays drew attention, though very few of those who marveled from the outside had courage to open the door and step inside. This was an unfamiliar world, even to the more cultured people.

For some days I wondered whether I had allowed my enthusiasm for the sale of Oriental art in California to lead me into a path of no return. Within a few weeks, the picture changed. Some people from Beverly Hills and Bel Air found the objects in our store to be suitable "adjuncts"' for their Western art collections. Barbara Hutton, the multimillionairess, decided to redo her home in Chinese style. She was among the first who made considerable purchases of our rare Chinese and Japanese art. I helped her select many fine Hiroshige prints from our large collection of Japanese prints. Then there was a wealthy oil magnate from Dallas, and a retired attorney of one of the leading railroad companies. These were people of means who knew how to evaluate our art.

Others began to come from La Jolla, Pasadena, Huntington, and the surrounding wealthy areas in California. This enabled me to order two more shipments, which arrived before Christmas. The third shipment consisted mostly of colorful ware, which was within the reach of many who could not afford to buy the more expensive art. I engaged two attractive, knowledgeable young women, and one gentleman to look after the sales on the ground floor. On the mezzanine we exhibited works of modern American painters.

Saturday, when I did not come to the store, we did the best business of the week. In dedicating the Sabbath to my God, my children, and my books, my greatest reward was a special kind of peace of mind worth more to me than the business itself.

Our upper gallery was not a profitable operation. It was, however, able to maintain itself.

After Irving and Yeng made the first shipment of art, Yeng found a fine craftsman of the old school who had a large supply of mahjong sets painted with 14-karat gold lettering. They were ordered by an exporter whose business was ruined by the Japanese. After a great deal of bickering, Yeng and Irving advised me to act quickly in acquiring the supply on hand. I sent them enough funds for a third of the shipment, which they dispatched at once. I told them to tie up the balance and hoped that the quality and sale of the first third would enable me to raise enough capital to pay for the rest. When the mahjong sets arrived, they created a sensation among the mahjong players at the height of the short-lived fad. They were really exquisite works of art. Our prices were three to four times the price of the ordinary machine-made mahjong tiles, and never before was our large store jammed with so many ladies waiting to be served. When our first shipment was sold out within two weeks and department stores clamored for some of our sets at any reasonable price, I had no difficulty raising the money to pay for the balance of the available supply. It was sold out throughout the country in less than a month. Once the mahjong fad declined, all shipments from the Orient stopped.

Calm returned to our normal operations and all loans and debts were fully repaid. I was concerned, nevertheless, with the second large shipment of Chinese and Japanese art for which there was no large demand. Statues, sculpture, large paintings, and exquisite Japanese ceremonial robes very rarely interested those who ventured to come into our Wilshire store. With the advent of the Christmas season, I decided to bring part of my large stock into another area. I rented a store in Westwood next to one of its principal theaters, where there was a great deal of foot traffic. To my pleasant surprise, some of the stock that remained unsold in the Wilshire store sold very well in Westwood. Business increased daily, and I negotiated with the landlord for a three-year lease. When the lease was ready to be signed, America received a shock. The Japanese Air Force had attacked Pearl Harbor. It killed thousands of our best fighting forces and sank the finest and proudest ships of our Navy. The nation was dismayed. Close as I was to the possibilities of war between Japan and America, I had never really visualized such a tragedy. For the next day or two, I did not much care what would happen to my business and to the large shipment of Japanese prints, cloisonne, porcelains, ivories, and brocades that were to reach Los Angeles harbor in three days.

A few days after the initial shock and President Roosevelt's words to the nation, Americans gradually resumed their normal life. Though no one touched our Japanese art, most of which we removed from the shelves, the sales of Chinese and Korean objects continued better than we expected. With the lull that followed the Christmas business, I closed the Westwood store and reconciled myself to a quiet life in the midst of our national turmoil.

One day our sales lady came to my office to advise me that Mrs. Anna Prinzmetal wanted to see me. I knew Mrs. Prinzmetal very well. She was a tall, cultured lady, who devoted her time to educational institutions and to Hadassah, of which she was one of the leaders. She was the only one who could pull me away from my business to deliver lectures before Hadassah and other organizations. I was sure she was coming to see me for a lecture, and I was ready at this time to say yes immediately. When I received Mrs. Prinzmetal more warmly and joyously than I ever did before, she couldn't figure out what had happened to me.

"Are you so overjoyed that you closed your store in Westwood and that your business is not so good?" she asked. "That is right," I said to her, laughing. "Now I have much more time to talk to you." Mrs. Prinzmetal was slow in disclosing what she came to see me about. Previously she had always called me on the phone for whatever lectures she wanted me to deliver.

"I am here on behalf of the Committee of the Modern Center in Boyle Heights, of which you were the first director," she said. "The present director had to resign because of some complications, and the board wondered whether you would be interested in filling the place of the director. The Center's board has been discussing plans for an expansion of its activities throughout the city. Now with additional U.S.O. work and programs related to the war, the board felt that you can render the Center's movement a great service." The thought of returning to social activities in the crucial days of the war appealed to me. Nevertheless I told Mrs. Prinzmetal that I would have to think about it. I had never considered going back to this work again.

On the third day after Mrs. Prinzmetal called on me, I met with the committee at my house to discuss the offer that they made me. The head of the committee was Julius Fligelman, with whom I shared a mutual interest in the Reconstruction movement of Professor Mordecai Kaplan. Seeing my large home filled with Western and Oriental art, the committee was a little hesitant to discuss the terms of its proposal. When some members began to explain to me the limited budget that the committee had at its disposal, I quickly assured them that remuneration was not my primary concern. What I wanted was a free hand to carry on my activities till the end of the war, or at most for a period of no more than three years.

I found a good man who was able to run the Wilshire store without me. We had sufficient merchandise to sell for several years to come. I spent several weeks in quickly disposing of the more valuable objects to art dealers.

For the next seven months I plunged into my new work with zeal. I seldom found greater joy in any work. Five years after I left public service in San Bernardino, my long-dormant need to work for people (and not necessarily with people) filled me with happiness. I was free of material concerns, free to engage in larger tasks than those of making money. I became more occupied than I was during my large business operation in China or America. Unlike those who are busy for the sake of being busy, or because others expect it of them, I was busy because of what I expected of myself. Thoreau said, "It is not enough to be busy.... The question is what are we busy about."

I became busy because of the children who were in need of a better environment than what they found on the streets or in their spiritually impoverished homes. I became busy giving adults an opportunity to play, socialize, find friendships, and to lift themselves culturally. The new Singer Building, the large gymnasium, and the auditorium that were built during the years I was in China answered the needs of a mixed population of Jews and Mexicans in Boyle Heights.

For those who had migrated to the Beverly Fairfax area, I found by chance a group of buildings that was eminently able to answer the social and cultural needs of the growing community. I went to the real estate brokers who were handling the sale of the complex buildings formerly used by the Curtis school. They had slashed their original price by half because the buildings had been vacant for a long time and no one wanted them. I heard that Judge Isaac Pacht, who was a leading figure in the Jewish community, had a sum of $45,000 that one of his clients willed for an educational and social institution. I told Judge Pacht of the low price that the real estate brokers were asking for the school building. He was skeptical. He said that if I could really get those buildings at the price I had quoted, he would give the money for the center. Judge Pacht and the Committee of the centers were surprised when I presented the written sales offer, which was even less than the amount first mentioned. My friend, Max Zimmer, a leading contractor, whose sister-in-law was employed as one of my first Hebrew teachers in Boyle Heights, got on the job of renovating the building for use as major community center in Los Angeles. In addition to the fine gymnasium, swimming pool, lecture halls, club rooms, and concert hall, which doubled as a theatre, the committee agreed to dedicate one of the small separate buildings as an art gallery and library. Edward G. Robinson, the motion picture star lent us some of his priceless Impressionist paintings. His latest acquisition, a Diego Rivera "Revolutionary," attracted many people to the center, for whom both our concerts and our gallery became a focal point of interest.

A month after I was well settled in my new office at the Beverly Fairfax center, I was faced with a deteriorating situation in the operation of my Wilshire Boulevard store and I was forced to liquidate my business in a public auction. Thomas William Kilshaw of "Kendall England established in 1790" was the auctioneer. For nearly a week I attended the three sales a day that disposed of all that we acquired in two years. The auctioneer, who was an intelligent gentleman with a genuine appreciation of art, sighed more than I did when many of the valuable items were given away. On my last visit to Tokyo, I had acquired a rare collection of twenty court kimonos that were woven with pure gold thread. Each one was like a rare painting. We had previously sold only two of them, to a collector from London. Eighteen of these irreplaceable kimonos were auctioned off at a time when I was not present at the store. They were sold for a price less than the value of the gold thread. The auctioneer, who was an honest man, was powerless to stop the sale. I was sick at heart.

We didn't do so badly on the sale of the Chinese art. Many collectors from all over the state competed for the select items and raised the total sum to a satisfactory figure. The auctioneer encouraged me to remove a number of important Japanese bronzes, porcelains, and prints from the sale and keep them in storage until after the war.

All traces of my business were now gone, and I turned all my energies to work in the community. Some of it related to the war effort. There was a remote possibility of having to evacuate the population of Los Angeles. I was appointed as the evacuation officer of part of the western section of the city.

At the beginning of February 1945, I unexpectedly received a long distance call from New York from my old friend Meyer Weisgal. More than three years had passed since I had heard from him, but neither his voice nor his spicy salutations had changed. "I am calling you on behalf of Dr. Stephen Wise," he said. "Dr. Wise asked me to tell you that we need you in New York right away. We are faced with an emergency. The American Zionist Emergency Council is without an Executive Director and you were selected to fill the place immediately." I told Weisgal that I knew from the press what happened, but I had no wish to get involved in any political quarrel between two of America's outstanding Jews, Dr. Abba Hillel Silver and Dr. Stephen Wise. Aside from that, I had already made plans to return to private business. Weisgal, who was a very shrewd man, though usually impatient, knew now how to wait for his turn to talk. Relying on his powers of persuasion, he talked with me for a half hour. Everything he said made sense.

The American Zionist Emergency Council was the overall umbrella of all the major Zionist bodies in America, who were then engaged in a political struggle to establish a Jewish Commonwealth in Palestine and open the gates of Palestine to Jewish immigration. Dr. Wise and Dr. Silver differed in their respective approaches to the means of attaining those ends. the former relying on the Executive branch in the government, the latter relying on the people and legislature. When Dr. Wise's position was accepted by a majority of the Zionist organizations, Dr. Silver, and the three main executives of the Zionist Emergency Council, stepped out and formed a small opposition party. The office of the Zionist Emergency Council had a large staff of political analysts, journalists, organizers, and a vital program that had to be implemented. It now was without guidance or leadership. Meyer Weisgal stepped into the breach until a new director could be found, but Weisgal could not do it for very long. He was committed and dedicated to Professor Chaim Weizmann, the president of the World Zionist Organization. Weisgal was Professor Weizmann's right hand for the building of a scientific institute in Palestine, which, thanks to Weisgal, has now become one of the greatest educational centers in the world.

Like the wedding guest in the *Ancient Mariner*, I could not help but listen to what Weisgal was saying. When Weisgal ended by telling me that this was the most crucial period in Zionist history, and that in spite of my personal hardships, it would be the greatest challenge of my life, I believed him. I told Weisgal that I would be in his office the day after tomorrow. Soon after my arrival in New York, I spent several days in committee meetings and in familiarizing myself with the operation of the organization which Dr. Stephen

Wise had formally asked me to direct. I knew Dr. Wise previously as America's greatest orator, but not as the indefatigable worker that he continued to be in his advanced years.

As the most beloved and renowned figure in Jewish life in America, he possessed a nobility and a lofty approach to human problems that inspired every one who worked with him. Until I met Dr. Wise in our daily conferences, I was only familiar with his deep, resonant voice, which was heard from one end of the land to the other. Not only Tammany Hall but many others in high places quivered when he spoke out against the corruptions of our society. I heard of his close friendship with President Woodrow Wilson, Justice Brandeis, and President Franklin Delano Roosevelt, who respected him greatly. In my new contacts with this remarkable man, I realized that the fulfillment of the Zionist aspiration was the most absorbing interest of his life. The spell that Dr. Theodor Herzl, the founder of Zionism, had cast on him remained until his dying day.

Our new apartment on the West Side of New York was not far from where Dr. and Mrs. Wise lived. On Saturday afternoons, during the warmer days, Dr. Wise and his very kind and scholarly wife would sit on a bench in Central Park. Several times during our walk with the children in the park, Dr. and Mrs. Wise asked us to sit with them. They loved our children. On these Sabbath afternoons, he never discussed anything pertaining to my work in the office.

The first week of my work in New York was probably the hardest week I ever had in my life. After meeting with the heads of the different departments, I sensed some resentment, lack of cooperation, and unwillingness to help me with the information I needed for my work. There was a lack of loyalty to the elected leaders of the Council. Arthur Lurie, who was the political secretary of the Council, and later the Ambassador to Great Britain, and Professor Benjamin Aktzin were the only ones on whose support I could count. It was from them that I learned that some of the members of the staff remained loyal to the executives who had left their positions to join Dr. Silver. Some, they said, were also resentful that the committee of the Council did not bother to consult them or to include them in their deliberations.

The next morning I dictated a memorandum requesting all the members of the staff to meet with me at 4:00 P.M. After dictating the memorandum, Dr. Haim Greenberg and Herman Shulman, who were Dr. Wise's cochairmen, came to see me. They were upset about some leakage to the press of confidential information. They also said that the decisions of the Board weren't implemented. I told them that I was fully aware of the problem and asked them to give me two or three days to go into the matter more fully.

At 4:00 P.M. the entire staff was present at the meeting. I began by telling them about their important work and how much I admired what they had done until my arrival. I told them quite truthfully that I did not come to replace anyone or take sides in any political squabbles. "I am here," I said, "to work with you, to help you, and to listen to your legitimate grievances. Please do not punish me. Give me a chance to do the job for which I was called by a duly elected body and let me go home as quickly as possible." After a friendly discussion that followed my remarks, I excused myself and allowed the staff to go on with its deliberations concerning the program of activities that I outlined for the coming months. An hour later, a committee of three came to my office to advise me that the staff was unanimously behind me and that it approved the program and was ready to meet with me the following day to discuss the details for its implementation. That night was the first night in three days that I slept well.

My duties as an administrator and organizer required my coming to the office an hour ahead of any other member of the staff. It was part of my job to open the confidential letters or cablegrams, to discuss some of them with Arthur Lurie, and to relate them to Dr. Wise and Dr. Greenberg. Some of the cables that arrived from Moshe (Shertok) Sharett, who was later the Premier of Israel, were of the most disturbing nature in Jewish history. It was not until these early months of 1945 that we learned of the magnitude of the great calamity that had befallen European Jewry. Each report brought us closer and closer to a realization of what had transpired in the darkest years of the life of European Jewry.

But it was the last confirmed report of the vast number of our people who were exterminated that made me shudder. For days I lived under the spell of horror that was cast on me by Shertok's long cable. I knew and loved many of the people that the telegraphic letters referred to. They were my flesh and blood. They brought joy to my heart when I saw them in 1937 on the railroad station in Kenna, when they waited for the arrival of their close relative from America.

Thoughts of their inexplicable fate suddenly changed some of my daily habits. For weeks I searched the newspapers for any item that described the last days of European Jewry under Hitler. I went to meetings where people came to unite with others in common grief. I was attracted to books, music, theater, and art that aroused deep sorrow, a sorrow that I could relate to those dear, dear people who were suddenly wiped off the face of the earth.

I renewed my familiarity with YIVO, which is now located on Fifth Avenue and 86th Street in New York. It was this institute with its rich archives of Jewish history that was moved before the war from its home in Vilna. I first came to the YIVO institute on my visit in 1937 to Lithuania. It was there that I met many illustrious Jewish writers who were known to me through their creative work.

Now they, too, I lamented, and my uncles, aunts, cousins, and all other innocent fellow Jews had disappeared. For days I listened to the sad whispers of my colleagues. And the grief and pain was endless. My Zionism had taken on a new dimension.

Roosevelt, who was genuinely sympathetic to the plight of European Jewry, was either too ill or too tired and despondent to carry out some of his initial good intentions. This had also become obvious in his attitude toward Palestine. He opposed Great Britain's policy of 1939, when the gates of Palestine were closed to Jewish immigration, but he never stood up to the Conservative Party or the Labor Party of the anti-Jewish Ernest Bevin for the abrogation of that policy. Every day the immensity of the job that was lying ahead of us became more and more clear to me.

I soon began to question the wisdom of Dr. Wise's approach, which relied so heavily on the help of President Roosevelt. Dr. Silver's approach of turning directly to the people of America and to its legislative bodies, the Senate and the House, was, I felt, the only logical one. We were still at war with two bitter enemies, Japan and Germany, and all our plans had to be thought out very carefully. There was no clear unified policy that we could follow.

Eliezar Kaplan, the very able treasurer of the Jewish Agency in Palestine, arrived in New York soon after I assumed my position. He followed the line of Dr. Weizmann, and at our meetings he stressed the need of emphasizing our activities for opening the gates of Palestine to the Jewish refugees from Europe.

Several weeks later, David Ben Gurion arrived from Jerusalem. His strong voice commanded the utmost attention and regard. "A Jewish State in Palestine must be our primary consideration," he clamored as he raised himself up and down from his seat. His appearance before our Council was an unforgettable experience. It was the first time that I saw the likeness of a living prophet in Israel. While I personally accepted every word of David Ben Gurion, the staff agreed that we should devote our time to the implementation of both parts of the program, that of Dr. Weizmann and Dr. Wise, and that of Ben Gurion and Dr. Silver, at one and the same time. One called for the opening of the gates of Palestine for the refugees of Hitler's extermination camps, and the other for the establishment of a Jewish State in Palestine. This work had to be started in a hurry before President Roosevelt left for the historic Potsdam Conference with Stalin and Churchill.

One of my pleasant tasks after Ben Gurion's arrival in New York was to call Ben Gurion and relay to him the information that I passed on to Dr. Wise. It was not always easy for me to get Ben Gurion on the phone in a hurry. He had a powerful intermediary who screened every one of his calls. Her name was Paula, the indomitable wife of the man who became the actual founder of the State of Israel and its first premier. "Why do you need Mr. Ben Gurion so early?" she would ask, "can't you wait a half hour?" "I can wait, Mrs. Ben Gurion, but your husband won't let me wait," was one of the many answers that I had to give to Paula before getting her husband on the line.

No man I ever heard of had a more protective wife than Ben Gurion. Many years later, I stayed at the President Hotel in Jerusalem. In the next room were David Ben Gurion and his wife. Once, when I walked into the corridor, I saw Paula on a chair outside the door of their room. When she saw me, the first thing she said was "Shalom, and so you are here. I remember how you woke Ben Gurion every morning when we were in New York." "But not today," I said, "not today." It was nice to see Paula smile at me for a change.

Spurred on by the tragic news of the fate of the Jewish people in Europe, we determined to use every means at our disposal to arouse the conscience of all Jews and all Americans. We formulated a plan for the largest demonstration possible to launch our twofold program: the opening of the gates of Palestine and the creation of a Jewish State. We sent a call to the representative leaders of all the leading Zionist bodies in New York to consider the plan which we prepared for large mass demonstrations throughout the country. The first and most important was to be at the Lewisohn Stadium and its adjacent sports field. Some of the leaders of our Council and of the Zionist Organization of America failed to attend the conference. They dreaded the vociferous opposition of Dr. Silver's group, which could turn the conference into a political confrontation. When a people is aroused, frightened leaders are not needed. Courageous ones are hard to find. More than 300 representatives of all organizations filled our conference room to capacity.

The meeting took place one day after the death of President Franklin Roosevelt. While some of the things that President Roosevelt did or did not do were disappointing to many Jews, all Jews deeply mourned the loss of a great American leader. The death of the President on April 12 added to the solemnity of the meeting.

Rabbi Wolf Gold, one of the leaders in the Religious Zionist Movement, who knew me from the days when my parents worshipped in his synagogue, introduced me to the audience. I began with a quote from Jeremiah, "Weep not for him who is dead. Weep for those who are living." I then told the representatives of our objectives and I informed them that before coming to the meeting I called Dr. Silver in Cleveland, at the suggestion of Dr. Wise, and that I invited Dr. Silver to join Dr. Wise as one of the two principal speakers at the large demonstration. Dr. Silver had graciously accepted the invitation, and in this solemn moment in our history, I told the conference that we were all united now. My last words were drowned out in an outburst of applause. The meeting, which had opened in an atmosphere of doubt, now ended on a high note with the loud singing of the Jewish national anthem, *Hatikvah*.

The results of the mass demonstration in the Lewisohn Stadium and in its large sports grounds hit the front pages of all the New York papers. Meyer Weisgal, who was one of those who embraced me warmly after the demonstration, said, "You see, we showed them what we can do." It was he who had the faith in my ability to take the first step. The following steps were no easier. None of us had time to relax for a single day. With the relatively unknown Harry Truman as President of the United States, we had to accelerate our efforts in gaining the support of the House, the Senate, and all major public bodies to affirm the purpose for which the demonstrations were instituted throughout the land.

A letter to the President of the United States was sent to every congressman and every senator for his approval and signature. The letter petitioned the President to use his influence with Great Britain to open "the doors of Palestine to unrestricted Jewish immigration" and to urge the other governments to join the United States "in establishing Palestine as a free and democratic Jewish Commonwealth in the earliest possible time."

This action had to be carried out with maximum speed before President Truman went to meet Churchill and Stalin in Potsdam. We worked day and night contacting all influential friends we had in the country to call on their congressmen personally to expedite the signing of the petition. After a week's work, we were sorely grieved when all we had to show was a hundred signatures. This called for a redoubling of our efforts. We used all our powers of persuasion to overcome the objections to the letter by members of our State Department. After five weeks of hard work, we finally received signed petitions from two-thirds of the members of the U.S. Senate and 300 petitions from our congressmen.

Heaving a sigh of relief, some of our staff who worked the hardest were able to take a day off. I went to my hotel and stayed in bed all day. A week later my family arrived from Los Angeles. During the last year of the war, there was not a single apartment in New York. For over two months, I had to live in a small hotel room. Luckily I found a sublet of a furnished apartment for them.

On our return to our jobs, we continued with the organization of 136 meetings in nearly all of the sizeable cities of the country. The National Broadcasting System offered us one hour's time gratis to present "The Letter to the President" from coast to coast. It was dramatized by leading motion picture actors. We were told later that President Truman, who listened to the broadcast, "enjoyed it."

While we were at work with the Senate and the House, we did not overlook the governors of our forty-eight states, who wield considerable influence on the political affairs of the land. The annual governors' conference was scheduled to take place at the inaccessible Mackinac Island in the State of Michigan. The president of the conference was Governor Maw of Salt Lake City, who was a good friend of the Zionist movement. I sent Gerald Frank and Hyman Getzoff, who were on our staff, to Salt Lake and they later found their way to Mackinac Island. The results were announced in headlines in the papers, "38 Governors Petitioned the President for the Establishment of a Jewish State in Palestine."

Six days before President Truman's trip to Potsdam, I went to Washington. I wanted to discuss the details of the official presentation of the petitions to the President with Senator Wagner. We made all arrangements for a large press conference. Senator Wagner was to make the presentation jointly with two other senators of the Republican and Democratic parties. After agreeing on all the details, Senator Wagner telephoned the President. President Truman told him that he preferred to see Wagner and discuss the matter with him at lunch the following day. My associate, Mr. Stein, a veteran Jewish lobbyist in Washington, turned to me shaking his head. I do not think either of us slept very much that night.

On the next day at 2:00 P.M., we arrived at Senator Wagner's office. Soon thereafter Wagner appeared, "Boys," he said, "Harry asked me not to publish the results of our petitions from the Senate and the House because he does not want to upset the State Department, the British, and the Arabs. However," the Senator continued, "the President was glad there were so many signatures." He promised to present our request in Potsdam as firmly as he could, providing that we would not issue any statements to the press about the President's conversation with the Senator.

We were dumbfounded. All our hopes were shattered and anything we could say was of no avail. The Senator looked at me with pity and added, "Go back to New York and tell our friends that our efforts were worthwhile. I know Harry for many years and I know that he will keep his word."

I then asked the Senator to call Dr. Wise and tell him in his own words what had happened. I did not know how I would be able to face my people in New York.

Several months later we learned that President Truman had kept his faith. He demanded of the British that they allow the entrance of 200,000 Jewish immigrants to Palestine at once, and only after pressures from the other participants, Churchill and Stalin, did he agree to reduce his demand to 100,000, a number that many had accepted as a realistic figure for that year.

In Dean Acheson's book *President at the Creation*, which was hailed as a "great political document," Acheson wrote that President Truman was one of the few thirty-five presidents who managed their offices with eminent benefit to public interests. Acheson then admitted that, as the chief architect of America's foreign policy, he did not agree with the President. "I did not share the President's views on the Palestine solution to the pressing and desperate plight of great numbers of displaced Jews in Eastern Europe.... A million homeless Jews saved from the crematoria and the persecutions in Arab lands would exacerbate the political problem and imperil American interests in the Near East. The problem before me was clear, but not simple, to bring Truman closer to Attlee's position." (Atlee, the head of the British Government, was opposed to a Jewish immigration.) Our own State Department followed his line, but a little man from Kansas City with a conscience, great vision, and a warm heart was able to stand up to all of the polished professionals of his own State Department. When Ben Gurion told President Truman that the Jewish people will never forget what he did for them, "there were tears in Truman's eyes."

At the end of July, Dr. Abba Hillel Silver returned to the leadership of the American Zionist Emergency Council. With Dr. Silver's return, Harry Shapiro took over my activities. What my immediate associates and I had been doing in the previous ten months was continued under his direction. At the time of the changeover, Dr. Silver was vacationing in his summer home in Maine. Mr. Shapiro asked me to go up to Maine for a few days as Dr. Silver's guest. Dr. Silver wanted to hear all the details of our operation from the time I came to New York.

During the two full days I spent in the exhilarating country, which refreshed my soul, I learned to admire the qualities of a fine intellect and a brilliant mind. As an orator, Dr. Silver appeared like a volcano, but in private life he was a warm human being.

When I told Dr. Silver that I was preparing to return to Los Angeles, he asked me to stay on for at least another six or seven months. He felt that I would be useful to him and the movement in the critical months ahead. I agreed to change my mind about leaving New York.

Following the six hard months, I was rather glad to undertake the relatively easy assignment of editing a new edition of Dr. Theodor Herzl's *The Jewish State*, which included articles by Alex Bein and Louis Lipsky. Bein and Lipsky were the most eminent and competent men to write the articles. The book was published in paperback under the auspices of the American Zionist Emergency Council. About a hundred thousand copies were sold in six months' time at a nominal price. Before I began my second assignment, I spent seven days of mourning for my beloved father. This brought me back into the arms of my brother Izzie and his family and all my relatives in New York.

I then embarked on my last assignment of directing the activities of the American Palestine Christian Committee in a few cities in the south and in the west. This entailed my appearance as a speaker before various church groups, a reminder of my old days in San Bernardino.

I returned to New York with a clear mind. My work at an end, I spent two weeks at the Metropolitan Museum, the Broadway theater, and at some of Dr. Mordecai Kaplan's lectures.

XIX
TELEVISION
1946–1953

Fully involved in intense work in New York, I paid scant attention to the great developments in the new housing programs in Los Angeles. Wars always brought on shifts in population. Soldiers who had passed through southern California, traveling to and from the war theaters of the Pacific, discovered that the California sun was warmer and brighter than in the midwest or the east or even in their own hometowns. When dischaged from the service, they flocked with their wives and families to Los Angeles and its surrounding areas.

Industries followed. Jobs were created and the demand for housing escalated. This brought a revival in the real estate industry, which had never recovered from its Depression slump. The new demand for housing benefited everyone, including myself. My properties, which had suffered during the war, were now in line for rehabilitation. I found it to be in my best interest to devote a year to this end.

I never regarded property as anything more than a desirable means of support in time of need. I was never proud of what I possessed and only a very few people knew what material goods I had. The visible things I derived pleasure in were few. In addition to my family they were my garden, my art, and my dog. Other things I kept out of view, much as Japanese keep their paintings rolled up and hidden.

My feelings about material acquisitions engulfed me at a fund-raising affair organized by Dr. Shlomo Bardin, a very able man. He had previously raised funds for the construction of the Brandeis Institute of Jewish Learning in Simi Valley, California, near Los Angeles. For three years after my return to Los Angeles, he invited me on weekends to lecture before young men and women of this institute. This stimulating activity balanced my absorption in business. Many years later, when my name appeared as a successful head of a financial institution, Bardin invited me to a fund-raising gathering for the enlargement of the Brandeis Institute. It was a gathering of wealthy, well-known heads of industry and finance. Everyone was called on to introduce himself and each one stated with pride the name of the industrial plant or business he headed.

When my turn arrived to introduce myself, I blanked out. At an affair which involved the Braindeis Institute, I couldn't think of business. My only thought at that moment was of the activity with which I had subconsciously associated myself throughout the years. So in all candor and in a forceful voice, I announced, "I am a Hebrew teacher."

I have never seen so many eyebrows raised. Dr. Bardin and those who knew me for a long time and had watched me rise on the ladder of financial success could not understand what possessed me.

At that meeting I realized more than ever where I really belonged. None of the financial or social rewards that would come my way could obliterate my deep attachment to the Hebrew schools in Boyle Heights and Williamsburgh at the time when Hebrew teaching was for me the noblest profession on earth.

To avoid preoccupation with the many properties I had acquired over the years, I turned them over to a management agency established for the purpose of freeing people of unnecessary burdens. I was then able to turn my mind in other directions. I abandoned the thought of returning to the Orient. China was now a Communist country and Japan was impoverished. The new type of business in the Far East required a new breed of man. It lost its former charm, elegance, and grandeur.

A world that preceded some of my previous worlds began to beckon to me again. It appeared in a new guise and in a new cloak. It was the world of television films, combining entertainment and education. A few of my old acquaintances shared my views on the use of film and two of them joined me in the production of a half-hour film and one fifty-five minute program.

There were no reliable precedents for our work. We were shooting in the dark. When we finished our historical and art films, nearly everyone who saw them approved of their high quality and predicted their success. This, regrettably, did not come to pass. Neither of them was commercially viable. My partners abandoned me and I was left alone amid a lot of useless reels. I didn't blame them. I was ready to follow suit.

A producer of religious subjects for use in churches was in search of a producer of Biblical films for television. He had all the necessary contacts and the capital. He approached me and gave me a few of his ready scripts to read. They were horrible. My first impulse was to withdraw from the project.

The gentleman was kind to me when I explained my dilemma to him. He very nicely allowed me to make some "reasoable changes." This made the project more palatable. The first five half-hour Old Testament films surprised me with their immediate acceptance, even though in my opinion all the films were qualitatively poor. Aside from being well compensated, I was rewarded by the project in another way. It put me on the right track. It enabled me to obtain some experience and make contacts for work that was to follow.

As I was evolving plans for a continued engagement in the field, I suddenly had to leave for a short visit to Palestine. It was in connection with the program of the Palestine Economic Corporation, of which I was a director.

It was thrilling to be in Palestine again and to see the progress made in a single decade. I was moved by a few of the notices in the papers concerning my arrival. They mentioned the work I did for the creation of a state in Palestine. This was eight days before the great Sabbath of November 29, 1947, when the United Nations, meeting in Lake Success, New York, had by a majority vote recognized the right of the Jewish people to establish a state in the greater part of Palestine.

On the day the notices appeared in the papers concerning my arrival, I was asked by the president of the General Zionist party in Palestine to address a meeting planned in connection with the contemplated decision at the United Nations. It was a time when excitement in Palestine was at its highest pitch in history. At the meeting, which was attended by an overflow audience, Mr. Joseph Serlin, who was later a minister in the Israeli Government, introduced me as the principal guest speaker.

My address was in Hebrew. I worked a whole day on its preparation. It was not so much what I said that moved the audience. It was the emotional way in which I used every carefully chosen word that electrified my listeners. That night I was so excited that I couldn't sleep. At seven o'clock the following morning, a taxi was waiting to take me to Haifa to meet with two of the heads of the Palestine Economic Corporation. We were going to inspect the buildings erected for industry with the money I helped raise on the West Coast through the sale of securities of the American-based Corporation for Economic Development in Palestine.

I looked at the fine, modern, expansive buildings but nothing registered. My mind was still on the exceptional meeting I had addressed at the most unusual time in the history of the Jewish people. I returned to Tel Aviv and finally got a good night's rest. I stayed there long enough for some warm visits with old acquaintances and two good plays. Then I went to Jerusalem.

I could think of no more fitting place to be on the historic Sabbath of the United Nations decision. I never thought that my visit to the Western Wall, the holiest shrine in Judaism, would be the last visit any Jew could make to the Wall for the next twenty years. Immediately following the festivities of the U.N. decision, the Arabs sealed off the eastern part of Jerusalem from the rest of the city. The most sacred, historic places were liberated by the Israeli armed forces in the Six-Day War in 1967.

There was still another night when neither I nor many people in Palestine closed their eyes. It was the night after the announcement of the U.N. decision allowing the Jews to establish their own independent state on the soil of their historic homeland. At long last, we lived to see the culmination of the dreams of the Jewish people, the fulfillment of the words of their prophets. People danced in the streets of the country which, in less than a year, was changed from Palestine to Israel. When I finished hugging and embracing people, I prepared for my scheduled trip back to my family and my work.

At home I evolved a plan for the production of films which would compete with the large studios. I observed that the old, existing studios like those of Hal Roach, where television films were made, were very wasteful. The large stages with their tremendously high ceilings were built for big productions. They wasted space, consumed too much electricity, and were too expensive for the production of television films during the early stages of development.

I came across a vacant building that, if converted to a television studio building, would allow a more economical form of film production. I told this to my friend, Isidor Lindenbaum, who was one of my first supporters in the campaign for the Board of Education.

Lindenbaum was an attorney. He had inherited a good deal of money and he was prepared to make a sizeable investment in my project if I would agree to take in another partner and join him in a project of his own. One of his clients was an inventor, who had patents for a new sound machine for films. Lindenbaum believed it would replace all existing sound machines. I saw the machine and I met the inventor, Ferenz Fodor. I knew nothing about machines so I consulted people who were more knowledgeable. They did not think very much of the invention. All they could tell us was that we might not lose too much money on the development of the first model. Lindenbaum disagreed with them. He had a mind of his own. I had no alternative. I accepted his package deal.

Having been assured that I would have no interference from any source, I became general manager of the newly formed Filmcraft Productions of Hollywood. It was not long before we discovered that Fodor's machine was a failure and our total investment in it went down the drain. However, we retained Ferenz Fodor, the inventor of the machine, as our sound engineer. He made up for some of our loss by his economical installation of the best sound equipment available.

After purchasing the vacant building on Melrose Avenue, which occupied the entire lot, we very quicky converted it to the use for which it was bought. Its large open space in two-thirds of the building became the first studio in the world for the exclusive production of films for television. On the mezzanine were our sound machines and equipment; below were our bright, modernized offices.

In spite of the rosy outlook, our beginning was slow, costly, and painful. We gradually became busier as time went on, but the net results of our pioneering effort during the first year were very poor. It was a far cry from the terrifically successful first year I had had in China. The television film industry was young and the demand for its products at the outset was not very rewarding. The people who were attracted to the medium had neither the knowledge, the means, nor the foresight that a vital, promising industry needs. Many of the pilot films which we made for independent producers never got off the ground. Like some pioneers in other areas, I felt that we had entered the field too soon to reap any of its benefits.

While I was pondering over my future personal developments, the most significant development of all finally took place. On May 14, 1948, the Jewish State of Israel was established. Much that I have done in my life has been for the realization of this great hope. Since my earliest childhood, I have never wavered in my faith that Herzl's vision would become a reality.

My first two years in films gave me insights into the lives, aspirations, successes, and defeats of the people I had worked with twenty years earlier. On the surface, nothing had changed in Hollywood. The buildings were by and large the same and so were all its streets. The new faces and the youthful, bright eyes still to be seen in the crowds were like those of their predecessors, attracted to the glamor of Hollywood from all parts of the country. For them, like for those before them, it held out the promise of fame, wealth, and limitless sex.

For me this Hollywood had no appeal whatever, either in the past or in the present. I was in it by chance, without having made any real effort to be a part of it. Because it surrounded the pleasant home which I loved, and it had touched on the lives of the people whom I liked, I found myself in its midst. It was the only place where I could use my energies.

Twenty years after DeMille, I found some changes in Hollywood. It was still as glamorous as it was outwardly, with unlimited opportunities for people with and without talent. It continued to be a pleasant place for work, play, and a free association with people of varied backgrounds, but it also had become a sad place, one of the saddest in the world. Those who did not shut their eyes could see the sorrow in the faces of the old actors and actresses, directors, and cameramen. It was evident in the Clifton Cafeteria on Vine Street or in the small, one-room, furnished apartments and their cramped, grimy kitchens. In their bizarre dress, sauntering listlessly and aimlessly along Hollywood Boulevard, these people carried little more than the ashes of their younger, brighter days. They clung to the sidewalks of Hollywood Boulevard, which for them had once been one of the most cheerful places in the world. They looked at the windows of the shoddy stores, without having the means of patronizing them, and they glanced at the names and footsteps of the heroes of their past. These names and footsteps, which bring fond memories to the forgotten and abandoned old men and women, were ceremoniously imprinted in the wet cement of the sidewalks by the famous stars themselves. Today, like the old people who gaze at their names, they are no more than a memory. Only the tourists and the old thespians look at the names with any attention. The others step on them.

I didn't have to walk along what was once called "The Boulevard of America" or eat in cafeterias to see the faces of those whom I still remembered from earlier times. Some of them appeared outside my office. As I walked out one day through our small waiting room, I saw an old actor whom I knew very well. He was a talented man who achieved some fame. He came to find work, a small part in a short subject filmed during the week. When I looked at his eyes I knew pretty much all that he told me later. He was surprised and taken aback when, in the presence of other waiting actors, I rushed over to him and embraced him warmly. He was a good man and he needed and deserved more than my embrace.

I turned back to the office and asked my secretary to arrange a postponement of an actor's interview until after lunch. I then told one of my co-workers that I could not eat with him that day. I had, I said, "a very important visit by a great artist." While my chance meeting with a fine talent was a sad one, I told my family how good I felt in having lunch with a poor man, who said it was one of the most enjoyable lunches he had in a long time.

In one of the last days of a year's trying and unrewarding results, there unexpectedly appeared a ray of light. It was the opportunity we were waiting for. The Pabst Blue Ribbon Beer of Milwaukee, Wisconsin, had a popular radio show which had been running for a long time. It was called "The Life of Riley" and the star was William Bendix. The aggressive beer manufacturers wanted to bring Bendix on the T.V. screen for the prospective drinkers of their beer. After meeting with several heads of the Hollywood Studios, the vice-president of Pabst Blue Ribbon Beer came to see me. I talked with him for over an hour and he asked if I could meet with him that evening for dinner. "Why, of course," was my emphatic answer. "I have not had a good dinner out in a long time." He smiled. I still remember the place we went for dinner. We had the toughest, most inedible steak I ever ordered.

Aside from the steak, I heard everything I was eager to hear. The studio with which William Bendix had a contract for a major film production was unable to release him for at least a year. The Pabst Blue Ribbon Beer Company therefore had no alternative. They had to find a good substitute for the television program which they wanted to sponsor without delay. The vice-president felt that our studio, with its fine equipment and good acoustics, was ideally suited to start their first series of thirteen half-hour films. He told me of some of the actors who were suggested to him for the part of Riley. I told him of a few that I heard of, including a fat fellow who was an entertainer in the Bandbox on Fairfax Avenue, a few blocks from our studio. His name was Jackie Gleason.

In a few days the vice-president had made a contract with Jackie Gleason. It was Gleason's first significant break. The contract with our studio was also the first chance for Filmcraft to have its name appear on film from coast to coast.

Gleason was a natural for the part he played. He was a born comedian who, with the gestures of an artist, wormed himself into the hearts of the plain people of America. His role as a bus driver, a misunderstood husband, and a good-natured father was what they understood and could feel. The supporting actor, Art Carney, was an unusually talented actor in his own right.

The show ran for years and it brought Gleason to the rank of the leading entertainers of the world. Not many years later, his earnings were more than a million dollars a year. Each week during the filming of "The Life of Riley," our studio supplied the National Broadcasting Company with copies of a completed 30-minute episode which was broadcast over its national network.

I admired the warm relationship Gleason had with his wife. She adored him and came frequently to the studio to wait until he finished rehearsals. When I was ready to go home, I asked her to wait in my large, comfortable office. Gleason's wife was a kind woman, a devoted mother, and a very pleasant person. I also thought her very attractive and when I told Gleason, he agreed with me wholeheartedly. Some years later when Gleason reached the zenith of his profession, I heard that he had divorced his lovely wife. For most people in Hollywood, this was not anything unusual. For me it meant a great deal. I saw in this particular divorce a break in the values and morality in life.

"The Life of Riley" attracted other worthwhile productions, which were well-cared for by Ferenz Fodor. I was once more able to enjoy the free time at my disposal with my family.

I never belonged to a country club because I had no need for it, but I did enjoy being invited for lunch at the Hillcrest Country Club by some of its active members. The Jewish cooking in this exclusively Jewish club in Los Angeles was the main source of Jewish identity for the members. It was an awareness that I, too, enjoyed very much. The chopped liver, matzoh balls, and other Jewish dishes reminded me of my mother's cooking.

There I met Gummo Marx. He was one of the Marx brothers and the only one of the brothers, beside Groucho, whom I got to know. Gummo was Groucho's business manager. He asked me what I thought of putting Groucho Marx on film in a quiz game to be called "You Bet Your Life." Some people thought that Groucho Marx, sitting on a high stool spinning his wise, cryptic, sharp remarks, could not be as funny as he was in the films for which he had achieved world acclaim.

I told him I wasn't competent to express any opinion, but I would be very happy to have the series filmed in our studio. Not long after my conversation with Gummo, Filmcraft Studios became the center for filming another great and successful weekly show in Hollywood.

The first months of working on "You Bet Your Life" posed some serious problems. Groucho Marx, who was a great artist, was not an easy man to get along with. He was intelligent and thoughtful, but his natural sense of humor didn't extend itself to those who disturbed his peace. Groucho had trouble with his eyes. His glasses didn't protect them. He was unable to stand in front of the strong lights needed for close-ups. We did everything we could to diminish the painful effects of the bright lights. Leading cameramen and electrical engineers were consulted, but nothing was able to bring Groucho the relief he needed.

Groucho was not a vain man, but he did want a good picture. I loved to watch Groucho calmly puffing his cigar, and raising and lowering his eyebrows as he regaled his audiences with incessant laughter. Countless people wanted to be the contestants on his weekly quiz show. They were never offended by his gibes and off-the-cuff remarks about their appearance, their names, clothes, or whatever else he thought of.

Aside from some of my difficulties with Groucho, I had no serious problems until I was operated on for gall stones. My recovery was slower than expected, and I decided to allow Isidore Lindenbaum to take over the operation of the studio.

After my full recovery and a long vacation in Yosemite National Park, I had a year in which I was free to "loaf with my soul." It was a free, unburdened year, a year in which I girded my loins for future undertakings. It brought me back to the early-morning, pacifying, invigorating hours of work in the garden. I read more than I had in a long time and I fulfilled my duties to society. During the second half of my free year, I met Pierre La Muir, who was basking in the glory and vast income which accrued after the sale of his successful novel, *Moulin Rouge*.

Moulin Rouge was the story of Toulouse-Lautrec, one of the greatest Impressionist painters of the nineteenth century. I knew the work of Toulouse-Lautrec and I was familiar with his sad life. La Muir adapted the book for a play, which he sold to a leading Broadway producer. He was very proud of his work and being wealthy, independent, and stubborn, La Muir did not allow the producer the right to tamper with his creation. He and the New York producer quarreled and the playwright's lawyers withdrew the play.

During my pleasant talks with La Muir, he indicated his willingness to allow me to produce the play in Los Angeles on a modest scale. The idea intrigued me and he offered favorable terms. I agreed not to change a single word in the play without his permission. La Muir also insisted on the right of approving the actors, although I would select them. He agreed with me on the choice of the Circle Theatre, which prevented my getting involved in a great called Pardes Hannah, where I saw a private school for boys that combined general studies with agricultural subjects. Michael, who loved my stories of Palestine, surprised me with his enthusiastic reply when I asked him if he would like to go to that school for a year and learn Hebrew.

Neither Vera nor Hedvah liked the idea. Though Michael pestered Hedvah on many occasions when she preferred to be shut up in her room, she was very attached to him. I told my two ladies that it was up to Michael to decide and that I would not change his mind.

At about that time I had to go to Oregon in connection with some land that originally belonged to my sister Lizzie. The place where I had to consummate the sale of hundreds of acres of forest was in Roseburg, Oregon, in the heart of the largest timberland in America and a thousand miles from where we lived.

Vera was not well. It was the beginning of one of her recurring nervous breakdowns. Hedvah was busy with her schoolwork. To Michael, his last few weeks of schooling did not matter. Both of us were glad to have each other's company during the long trek by car. It was as though I had a premonition that this might be Michael's last chance in twenty years, and mine in more than fifteen, to see the great western part of America.

We turned our trip into an exploration of fascinating areas that were at times reached through dirt roads or by foot. We waded, bathed, and fished in rivers all along the route. By picking up young hitchhikers, we shared their experiences and they shared our food.

When Michael and I arrived in the office in Roseburg, Oregon, Michael suffered a great disappointment. The man with whom I negotiated the sale told us that it would not be safe for anyone to go into the timberland. The land I owned was inhabited by unfriendly "wolves and lions." The more he mentioned wild animals, the greater was Michael's excitement and desire to get into the forest. Most of the night Michael couldn't sleep. He was waiting for me to wake up and go out in search of a group with guns to accompany us into the forest.

It happened to be a quiet time in Roseburg, when there were no people with any business or interest in exploring the remote areas of the difficult terrain among the mighty trees. Michael was finally placated when two forest rangers allowed us to accompany them to some of the forest areas not far from our camping ground. There were no paths or fire breaks. Our walk through the brush was difficult and we saw no wild animals. We did hear from a distance something which sounded like the calls of wild life. It was enough to fire Michael's imagination for the tales that he would spin for Hedvah and his classmates. This trip, which lasted only two weeks, impressed itself on Michael's memory more than any other event in his young life.

On our return home, we found a letter from Israel advising us that Michael was accepted in the agricultural school in Pardes Hannah. It left us very little time for long farewells. Michael's excitement about our trip to Oregon was quickly replaced by his excitement in the other adventure of going to a new school in Israel.

With all of his belongings packed, we sent him off to a new life. His departure from his mother and sister was not as traumatic as I had feared, because I promised them that if he was not happy in his new surroundings, I would bring him back within six months.

We all missed Michael. He added a great deal to our family life. When the six months were up and we received only scanty reports of how busy he was with his studies and his work in the fields, I was urged to keep my promise and bring him back. I did not want to do it without seeing for myself what progress Michael had made in his studies. I took a direct flight to Israel. When I arrived at the airport in Lod, I went straight to Pardes Hannah.

I never saw Michael happier and healthier than he was at that time. I spoke to the private tutor who taught Michael Hebrew and my heart rejoiced when he told me that Michael was the best pupil he had in twenty years. There was not a chance of my being able to bring Michael back.

Michael, who had upset me by his poor performance as a student up to the age of 14, became one of the best students in a school that had a rigid, intensive program of study in a language he never learned until he came to Israel. Many years later, the same poor student won the international award for scholarship at the oldest architectural university in the world, the University of Florence in Italy, where he received his doctorate in architecture.

This confirmed my early views as a teacher that a parent should be as lenient as possible. He should not be bent on conditioning his child to follow in the parent's particular interest in art, science, or religion. Surrounded by paintings, books of art, and regular excursions to museums and art galleries, my daughter now inclines toward music. The books and periodicals on Reconstructionism strewn about my house and my constant talk of Dr. Kaplan led my son to choose the path of the emotional Chassidic rabbis, with whom neither my father nor I had anything in common. Moreover, my son's converted, formerly gentile wife and my wonderful grandchildren are now more pious than I am.

My father never compelled me to go to his synagogue and I never compelled my son to go to mine. Though neither of us joined our respective parents' synagogue, both my son and I found our separate ways. We each joined synagogues that were diametrically opposed from a religious and philosophic point of view. The synagogue that is most conducive to my religious outlook is the Reconstructionist Synagogue, while that of my son is a small, Orthodox, old-world synagogue.

Having met a newly found, culturally revitalized son, I was also excited by other significant events that occurred in Israel since my previous visit. First there was the mass migration of Jews from all the lands of oppression, which included hundreds of thousands of men, women, and children who had escaped the Holocaust. And the number of immigrants swelled with those who escaped persecution in the Arab lands.

I recalled the days when I taught the words of Isaiah to my Hebrew class in Boyle Heights during the twilight hours. "From the east I shall bring thy seed and from the west I shall gather thee. I shall say to the north, 'Give,' and to the south, 'Hold not back. Bring my sons from afar and my daughters from the end of the earth.' They shall build the old wastes, they shall raise up the former desolations, and they shall renew the waste cities, the desolations of many generations."

In parting with Michael at his school, I noticed a sadness which I never saw before. A modern poet said that out of our sadness "we have made our world so beautiful." Michael's sadness, which came with our parting, enhanced for me the beautiful world in which he remained.

During my last two days in Tel Aviv, I met with one of the contractors, H. Einziger, whose partner drew the plans for the Z.O.A. House, which was being erected by the Zionist Organization of America. The contractor explained to me all of the novel features of the impressive building and its marble-covered walls, well-designed halls, and outer spaces, which gave it the appearance of a stately, ambassadorial mansion. When I asked him about the ultimate use of the house, he was unable to give me any clear idea. The people who had commissioned the architect to draw the plans were not sure how they were going to use this very costly edifice. Never before had I met with a contractor or architect who was not sure of how every part of his building would be used. Little did I think at the time that one of the burdens I would take upon myself a few months later would be to change the character of some of the lovely rooms and innumerable urinals for purposes other than those for which they were designed.

My return without Michael was a disappointment to both Vera and Hedvah, but they were glad to hear of the remarkable progress Michael was making in his new school. I brought them two long letters which Michael had written to his mother and sister.

During the following half year, I enjoyed the leisurely, contemplative life which I have always yearned for. Hedvah was preparing to enter college. Since Vera was in poor health, I was the only one who could help make arrangements for Hedvah's new life in a sorority on the campus. My prospects for a quiet, studious life devoted to teaching at the University of Judaism were short-lived.

I received a call from Dr. Emanuel Neuman, who was the guiding spirit of the Zionist Organization of America. He knew me well and I had known him since my boyhood days. He was Dr. Abba Hillel Silver's closest friend and ally. Dr. Neuman told me that he heard from our mutual friend, Abraham Goodman, who was a cultured, wealthy, and charitable man, that I had visited the Z.O.A. House in Tel Aviv and that I was very much interested in the project. Abraham Goodman was also interested in it. Would I care to visit New York in order to discuss with both of them plans for putting this building into operation? I accepted Dr. Neuman's invitation and came two days later.

I arrived in New York on January 14, 1953. All of the newspapers carried banner headlines about the nine Jewish doctors who "confessed" to killing two Russian political leaders. The nine doctors, who were accused of working with the American Jewish Joint Distribution Committee, had "also confessed to their plan for killing five of the leading Soviet generals." *Pravda* and *Izvestia*, the leading papers in Russia, revealed for the first time that three other Jewish doctors, who were not apprehended in time, "killed Maxim Gorki and two of the chief collaborators of Joseph Stalin."

For two days all of America and the free world was startled by the unbelievable turn of events in the Soviet Union. Everyone was accustomed to the Russian vilification of Zionism, but its unabashed, murderous assault on Jewry was incomprehensible. Not since medieval days, when Jews were accused of poisoning wells, said the papers, has a great power resorted to accusations like those made by the Soviet Union. Russia picked on the doctors because of the large number of Jews in that profession. Scandinavian papers spoke of the accusation as a dark, new chapter in human history, claiming that "Stalin has assumed the role of Adolph Hitler." Nothing could have prepared me better for the work I was asked to do in Israel to help the Jewish people become more firmly entrenched in their new homeland.

From my conversation with Dr. Neuman and Abraham Goodman, I gathered that the impressive Z.O.A. House in Tel Aviv was nearing completion without any clearer plans than those I had heard in Israel. Dr Neuman told me that it was first envisaged as sort of an embassy of American Jewry in the newly restored Israel. As such, it was intended to outshine all other embassies in the country.

I also learned that, of the two apartments which I saw, a luxurious one with built-in furniture was designated for the resident head of the institution. Neither Dr. Neuman nor Abraham Goodman were responsible for the initial planning and construction of the building. Now that the white elephant came within their jurisdiction, they asked me what I would do with the building, given a chance to use it to maximal advantage.

I studied the plans, the dimensions of the building, and the photographs of the different halls, lobbies, and rooms much more carefully than I had in Tel Aviv. I then arrived at a preliminary plan of how to use the building. It was not to serve as an "embassy" or a rest place for tourists. It could only be used as a cultural center for the inhabitants of Tel Aviv. I realized that for this purpose the building was too ornate. It had a great deal of wasted space and not enough space for the operation of a center commensurate with the size of the building and its location.

On the other hand, I visualized the use of the building for the reception of dignitaries and important personages who visited the new state. This was during the period when the government did not have a single attractive building for important receptions and gatherings. In all of Tel Aviv, there was neither a nice-looking hall, a suitable auditorium for musical events, nor room for good, noncommercial theatrical presentations. With some modifications in the last stages of construction, I told Dr. Neuman I could visualize a reasonably good chance of turning the Z.O.A. House, as it was to be called, into an asset.

After several meetings with Dr. Neuman, Abraham Goodman, and others concerned, I agreed to go to Israel and devote one to two years to the development of the Z.O.A. House and its program. I made one condition, however, and that was that I must be given a free hand. I did not think at the time that the project would last through three rich years of my life.

Jacob Alkow, 1950.

XX
Z. O. A. HOUSE
1953–1955

When I returned home, Vera, who was in poor health, was pleased that I accepted the assignment that would reunite her with Michael. Hedvah was settled in her new life at U.C.L.A. and Vera was lonely. The great privacy that surrounded our hilltop house was a refuge for me. For Vera it was too isolated. In spite of her frail, nervous condition, which began to reassert itself, she craved to be close to people and activity. She imagined that Israel would bring her back to a more normal society and greater physical strength.

In spite of her preoccupation with her studies and her new social life, Hedvah was depressed over the prospect of being left alone. My assurances that we would return in two years didn't lessen her sadness. This distressed me considerably.

After two months of preparations to leave for Israel, Vera suffered one of her worst nervous breakdowns. The doctor, who originally believed that the anticipated change would be good for Vera's health, advised me that she was in no condition to travel. The people in New York and in Israel were waiting and clamoring for my arrival in Tel Aviv to discuss last-minute changes with the architect in the final construction of the building and the preparation for my program of activities. I had to leave Vera in the care of Hedvah for what we hoped would be no more than a month or six weeks.

The metropolis of Tel Aviv and its suburbs had a population of 600,000 people of diverse habits of life, characterized by a conglomeration of languages, a loss of old values, and a search for new ones. In our prayers, we are wont to say, "The needs of thy people, Israel, are many." Not until I began this backbreaking job did I realize how numerous the needs were in those days, not only in housing, jobs, and clinics but also in the fields in which I was to be engaged.

Tel Aviv had no library, no university, no experimental theater, no home for the Israel Philharmonic Orchestra, and no modern school for the study of Hebrew by new arrivals. Many nights I lay awake thinking of what priorities to choose for my initial program.

The great centers of Jewish learning were destroyed. Even those I knew intimately, like the East Side of New York and Boyle Heights, were gone, but I was faced now with an opportunity and a challenge that filled me with excitement. Heretofore my contribution to the creation of the State of Israel was in the political and economic fields. In the political area, for twenty-five years I served as the president of one or another Zionist group and as director of the American Zionist Emergency Council. In the economic field, I addressed countless meetings to raise funds. I was also a director of the Palestine Economic Corporation, which invested millions of dollars in new industrial enterprises. Now was my chance to round out my varied activities by doing what was closest to my heart.

I moved into the elaborately furnished apartment on the second floor of the Z.O.A. House. It adjoined a spacious office with large windows and a specially built circular desk. I was not happy with my living quarters. They were superior to and out of line with other quarters, even those of the Premier, Ben Gurion. I was also uncomfortable because of the noise that reached me day and night from the activities I initiated. I was ashamed to invite Israeli guests, lest they think that only an American would use up precious space for his own personal indulgence. After two months of living uneasily in this well-designed, luxurious, modern accommodation, I told my house committee and the architects that the apartment should be converted into two badly needed classrooms. One was for a new Bible class, and the other to house the first Ulpan, which I organized for teaching Hebrew to new immigrants.

My next requet was that the architects tear out eighteen urinals and all the mirrors from an elaborate toilet and six showers that were originally designed for tourists. That space also was converted into classrooms and club rooms. There were very few tourists who stopped long enough to use eighteen urinals in addition to the toilets already there. These structural changes were approved by my friends in New York. There was still nothing I could do about the large, beautiful foyers and the costly, palatial circular stairs. In the end, even these began to serve a purpose when the Z.O.A. House assumed the role of a major attraction for important international personalities. In addition to my being the initiator and director of cultural programs, I was to function as host to distinguished Zionists and foreign visitors.

Ben Gurion said, "Only by being a model nation shall we preserve the love of the Jewish people and its loyalty to israel." The leaders of the Zionist Organization of America encouraged me in my effort to turn the Z.O.A. House into a model institution. They felt it would enhance the love of American Jews for the new, creative life that was being hammered out in Israel.

The response of the community to our effort was greater than I expected. Every available room was filled with activities that appealed to young and old, immigrant and native-born. One of our backers in America told me that we utilized our available space three times as much as the average center in America, which uses its facilities only during the prescribed hours of the day. Our activities started at 8:00 A.M. with classes for new immigrants and workshops in crafts, art, and music. They continued till 11:00 P.M., just allowing time for the rooms to be cleaned. The building was operating nearly every evening with some major recital, theatrical performance, or outstanding lecture. We had a first-rate restaurant and bar, with music for dancing. During the summer we had short musical programs at teatime on the patio. Tourists mingled with Israelis to fill all available space.

On Friday evenings several hundred tourists joined Israeli residents in special programs which included leading personalities in the theater.

On Saturday mornings, we instituted lighter programs when old residents and newcomers were able to join together in Sabbath songs, recitations, and inspirational talks. We timed these activities so that they did not conflict with religious services. It was good to see people remote from tradition, drinking the sacramental wine with those who came in their prayer shawls.

In the evenings the concerts gave many rising, young talents an opportunity to appear before music-hungry audiences. I recall a family of three who came to visit me in my office. They were new arrivals from Argentina. The father was a musician and the eleven-year-old boy played the piano. The father told me the boy was a prodigy and asked me to arrange a debut. I called my music adviser, Roman Messing, and we listened to the child's rendition of a Beethoven Concerto. Within a few days we announced in the press a special appearance we were arranging for the young, talented pianist. Some questioned the wisdom of exposing our discriminating audience to child prodigies. I was glad to hear the unbounded applause when Daniel Barenboim completed his debut performance. Mainly I remember the radiant face of his mother and her thanks when I met her casually many years later in Carnegie Hall. "I will never forget," she told me, "the time when Daniel Barenboim lived in Israel and the Z.O.A. House was always open and ready to receive him."

Among my most enjoyable activities were the drama classes led by one of Israel's leading directors, Moshe Halevy. Dr. Emanuel Neuman had asked me if I wasn't devoting too much attention to this particular activity, which was more expensive than the others. I said, "No other activity unites people so completely. Please show me an institution in Israel where young people of Yemenite, Iraqi, Polish, German, and Rumanian origin mix, study, and work as freely as those who come to us." Dr. Neuman, whose cultural appreciation surpasses anything that has to do with finance, smiled and answered, "I will tell our friends in New York exactly what you said." Out of these classes we established the first independent theater for the performance of Biblical plays.

I had to restrain myself from allowing this activity to absorb more time than I was able to spare. Israel was not America, and I could not allow myself to do only those things I loved most. I had an excellent staff whom I trained quickly in a country where there were no facilities for training professional group workers. I was thus able to devote time to expanding our work in novel directions.

In back of our beautiful building, we had over an acre of valuable land. This, as well as the land on which the Z.O.A. House stood, had been donated by the Jewish National Fund. The original planner who built the Z.O.A. House pictured this space as a garden with benches and a fountain for tourists, for whom there were originally very few facilities in Israel. He failed to foresee the rise of hotels with fine accommodations and swimming pools. He also failed to foresee the lack of free time, when tourists left their air-conditioned buses after traveling all over Israel. I looked at the few, paltry trees that already had sent their roots into a ground which I visualised for a quite different objective.

The Israel Philharmonic Orchestra was already one of the greatest musical institutions in the world, but it had no home. In winter it performed in a small, badly equipped, rented auditorium. It was not conducive to concerts in the summer. After a careful survey of the area I had at our disposal, I decided to build a Hollywood Bowl in the back of the Z.O.A. House with about 1,800 seats. The management of the Philharmonic Orchestra was elated with the idea and urged me to do all I could to get it ready in time for the summer concerts. I cabled a long, detailed description of the plan to New York and asked them to allocate $20,000 for the project. I received a return cable advising me that the idea was interesting and plans were fine, but that the organization was without any available funds. If I could raise the money in Israel, the Z.O.A. would pledge to return it as expeditiously as possible. I knew that times were hard and that the 1953 depression had cut many voluntary contributions. But hard as it was to raise money in the U.S., it was infinitely harder to raise it in Israel, where eggs and meat were rationed.

Having raised the hopes of so many people, I was crushed. In Israel it was hard to keep any secrets from the ever-watchful press. I faced my first crisis. Time was of the essence. I could not waste a day. The Israel Philharmonic Orchestra pressed for a commitment. I went to see my banker, Dr. Mirelman, who was also treasurer of the General Zionist Party. Mirelman was highly respected in the community for his philanthropic work. Both he and his wife, who was a physician, were people of culture. When I showed Mirelman the plans and the cable I received from New York, his first reaction was that I was pleading with him for a lost cause.

"The Zionist Organization of America already owes me a lot of money for advances I made on their behalf," he said. "$20,000 is out of the question."

"I will tell you," I said to him, "what I would like to propose to you. Take

$7,000 out of my personal account and add $7,000 of your own money. With this sum I will ask the contractor, who is a leader in your party, to build the concert stage without delay. I promise to allow him to take his share of the cost out of the first proceeds of the income we derive, providing that you convince him to forego his profit."

Mirelman looked at me and said only one word, "*Beseder!*" (okay). It was the best *beseder* I heard in Israel.

Everything that followed went on schedule, including the repayment of the loans and advances. For the first time in the history of the Holy Land, the Israel Philharmonic played the season's concerts under open skies to overflow audiences. Hundreds of people stood in the adjoining streets. Every available evening, the Tel Aviv version of the Hollywood Bowl was used for concerts, operatic performances, theatrical performances, and special events. After the first summer, we had sufficient funds from revenue for further improvements in the appearance of our open-air auditorium. The mayor of Tel Aviv was very appreciative and named the Z.O.A. House with its "Hollywood Bowl" among the principal assets of the city.

At the height of our summer season, I received a call from Hedvah. Most of her vacation had been spent looking after Vera. The nurse alone was not able to cope with her. Hedvah was totally exhausted. The doctor told her that I could now come to Los Angeles and take Vera back with me to Israel. He thought she would be able to make the trip without strain. I told Hedvah that I had planned to come earlier to relieve her of her responsibilities, but the home, which I bought in a suburb of Tel Aviv, would not be ready for a few months. I then spoke to Vera and told her I would come to take her and that we would live for the time being in a hotel. She said she would welcome living in a hotel near the sea.

I received a letter from Dr. Sidney Marks, the executive director of the Zionist Organization of America, asking me to attend the annual convention of the Zionist Organization in New York, because "your activities have already given us a shot in the arm." After five months of ceaseless labor I, too, needed a change of pace.

On my way to Los Angeles, I stopped in New York for five days, during which time I attended the Z.O.A. convention. The recognition I received from the delegates helped me continue and accelerate my work in Israel. I had a chance to make necessary contacts with people who planned to visit Israel. One of them was my teacher, Dr. Mordecai Kaplan. Others were writers, artists, and noted public figures. I extended to all of them opportunities to appear at the Z.O.A. House.

Vera's anticipated move to Israel had a good effect on her health. People who are ill are always in need of a stimulus, a change, a hope that does more than any medication. I found her calm and ready to leave for what would, hopefully, be a healthier place to live. When one believes strongly in a place for the cure of an emotional or nervous ailment, such a cure is within the realm of possibility. Israel enabled Vera to regain her strength and return to normal health very soon. Hedvah was much more resigned to being alone, and happy with her freedom from the care of a sick mother.

In spite of all the assurances by the contractor, when we arrived in Israel we found our new home far from livable. Two months passed before we were able to leave the hotel which was situated on the edge of the sea. Two months in the late fall in Israel can be a cure for many ailments, including those which affected Vera. She was content to watch the pounding of the waves and to listen to their roar. She preferred that to conversations with the resident tenants of the hotel.

In addition to the continuous changes and improvements in programming, my work at the Z.O.A. House called for an extension of my activities to other parts of Israel. A good deal of the talent for our special events and the Friday evening gatherings was recruited from the kibbutzim. One kibbutz, close to the Jordanian border, specialized in training its members in music, song, and dance. It was a youthful kibbutz and full of life. After spending a day at the rehearsals of one of their groups, I didn't want to stay overnight because of the unrest that existed in the border areas. The newspapers carried stories about nightly attacks by Arabs who crossed from Jordon, Gaza, and Syria. This was not the case in the vicinity of the kibbutz I was visiting, where it was relatively quiet. Though one of the older members pressed me not to drive at night, I ate dinner and started out for home.

I had been on the road about fifteen minutes when I heard the sound of bullets. There were no cars coming in either direction. I put on my bright lights and accelerated. A bullet hit the car above the rear window. In less than a minute, I heard the sound of more bullets and the crash of my rear window. The right side was in splinters. The shooting came from the invisible right side of the incline. It flashed through my mind how fortunate it was that my English-made Humber Hawk was built for foreign consumption with the driving wheel on the left. My greatest relief came from the fact that the poor Arab marksmen did not hit my tires.

That night I took two of Vera's tranquilizers. I never told her what happened. She didn't read Hebrew and didn't see the newspaper headlines, "Z.O.A. Head Miraculously Escapes Death." It was a time when not a day passed without a Jewish casualty. It was a time of undeclared war by the Egyptians and Jordanians on Jewish civilian outposts. It was only when we left the safety of the cities that we became aware of the sinister effects of that war and the hard life in the remote countryside.

The dozen fresh eggs I had brought with me from the kibbutz were still intact. At a time when we were rationed only three eggs a week, the fresh eggs I brought made up for some of our trouble. Michael, who was now living with us, asked me to take him with me when I would go to the kibbutz for more eggs. He, too, never knew what had happened because I immediately turned the car over for repair of the two bullet holes and the shattered rear window.

Michael had at first been reluctant to leave the agricultural school, but now he was happy with the new high school established on the edge of Tel Aviv. Our home was in Herzlia-on-Sea, about twenty kilometers from the school. On my return with Vera, I brought him a Vespa miniature motorcycle. He used it to get to school and to his special studies in Talmud.

It was not long before the Vespa began to serve other uses. Girls, who are awakened much earlier in Israel than in the West, quickly noted the handsome American boy on a machine, which at that period was a novelty. I was soon aware of it, and for the first time I was compelled to curb my son's aroused inclinations toward the daughters of Zion. Fortunately, he was an obedient son. Michael's stay at home with us was a help to his mother. It also enabled me to devote myself more freely to my work.

I have met great people in my time, among them Vladimir Jabotinsky. Twenty-five years later I was destined to meet a great woman, Eleanor Roosevelt. I was notified two weeks before her arrival in Israel to get the red carpet cleaned for the distinguished wife of the deceased President, Franklin D. Roosevelt. I wasted little time in arranging one of our finest welcomes, for which the Z.O.A. House was known. I did it with the cooperation of the Israel Government.

When Eleanor Roosevelt arrived at the rotunda of our building in an inconspicuous hired car, I had been standing at the door for ten minutes, waiting for the moment I would shake her hand. My first two words of greeting were in Hebrew, and I saw that her face was beautiful. When I asked her if she understood my greeting, she said, "One always understands a warm greeting."

I seldom have felt as small as I did when I walked alongside of Eleanor Roosevelt. She was about six feet tall, and I am four inches shorter. Later on, when I traveled with her through the south of Israel, I forgot how tall she was or how short I was. When I took her to our home, I was delighted to watch the expression on her face when she saw my paintings. She was very familiar with the art of contemporary America. Vera loved her and identified her life with Eleanor Roosevelt's life.

Eleanor Roosevelt had an unhappy childhood. Her beautiful mother died when she was eight. Her father, who was an alcoholic, died a year later. She was adopted by her grandmother, but she never had the blessings of love, which were denied to the unattractive, gawky orphan with the protruding teeth. She took no pride and found no consolation in the knowledge that she belonged to one of the most illustrious families in America. Her uncle, one of the dramatic figures in American history, was President Teddy Roosevelt. She married another of the great presidents of America, Franklin Roosevelt, who respected and honored her.

Eleanor, like some of the unloved saints, found her consolation and fulfillment in the service of the poor and the downtrodden. She found her warmest nest in the ranks of the dispossessed of all lands. When the wretched victims flocked to the Bonus Marches in Washington soon after President Roosevelt was inaugurated, Eleanor went to their encampment on the outskirts of the capital. She brought the disenfranchised victims of our society more comfort than any of the promises of a president. They would chant loudly, "President Hoover sent the army, but Roosevelt sent his wife." Eleanor never wavered in her devotion to the "Great Franklin." Eleanor found her fulfillment in her mission and dedication. There were some among the reactionary women's clubs who did not like her any more than they liked her husband. They called her a bleeding heart. During the memorable hours I spent in Eleanor's presence in Israel, I understood what some of her biographers meant when they said that Eleanor repeated an oft-quoted saying, "Back of tranquility there always lies conquered unhappiness."

I presented Mrs. Roosevelt to a worshipful audience, which filled the halls of the Z.O.A. building. At the close of her warm, sincere address about her great faith in Israel and its accomplishments, I gave her a gift, a beautifully molded silver *matzoh* plate used on Passover. The photograph of that plate and Eleanor Roosevelt hangs alongside my paintings. After Eleanor Roosevelt left Israel, I told our committee that when the prophecy of Isaiah would be fulfilled and all nations ascended to worship one God, Eleanor Roosevelt will be one of His saints. It was the first time an Israel audience wholeheartedly accepted a saint.

In 1954 David Ben Gurion and his wife lived in the heart of the Negev. Tired and depleted, Ben Gurion resigned as the premier of Israel and turned to the desert of his ancient prophetic guides in search of spiritual sustenance. When I was told that Ben Gurion wanted to see me in his new, humble dwelling in the undeveloped, southern area of the Negev, I wasted no time in making the four-hour drive to Sde Boker. For more than an hour before reaching my destination, I saw nothing but dried-up brush. There were no trees, no grass, and no place where one could quench one's thirst during a hot, summer day.

Paula remembered me from the days I worked for the American Zionist Emergency Council. She asked me to wait in the little dining room, and before I had time to make myself comfortable, I was given a large glass of hot tea with jam and cookies. "By the time you finish the tea," she said, "Ben Gurion will be ready to see you." Without losing time, refreshed after Paula's home-baked cookies, tea, and hospitality, I entered Ben Gurion's library. Though he recognized me, he said nothing about when and where we had met previously. For me it was an indication that I was wanted for a purpose. What it was I could not imagine.

While Ben Gurion was still arranging his papers and books in their orderly places, he saw my deep interest in the volumes that filled the shelves on all sides of the room from floor to ceiling. "You have not seen my library before?" he asked, and immediately explained to me the importance of keeping each book in its right place. I had never seen a private collection of Greek philosophy in the original, classical Greek. During his life in Sde Boker, Ben Gurion devoted as much time to these books as he did to the Hebrew volumes with which I was familiar. There were not many Israeli scholars who were able to read Isaiah and Plato in the fluent way that Ben Gurior read them. We talked for over half an hour about books. He was curious to know the reason for my attraction to the books that I studied so intently. Listening to every word, I watched Ben Gurion's changing facial expressions. They added a great deal to what he said. It was his face that reminded me of Walt Whitman's description of Abraham Lincoln, a "deep, subtle, indirect expression" that "there was something else there." I have read many descriptions but none ever told me fully what that "something else" is which Ben Gurion possessed.

It was about the future that he wanted to talk to me; the future of our youth; and the future of the Negev to which he dedicated the last years of his life. Ben Gurion, who knew of my former activities, wanted to know if I could help attract some of the youth in Israel and America to a pioneering life in the undeveloped area surrounding his home. Ben Gurion had established himself in the Negev because of what he first learned about it in the Bible. For him the Negev was the cradle of the Jewish people, the place where Abraham, Isaac, and Jacob envisaged the land of Israel as the eternal heritage of the Jewish people.

Ben Gurion's vision transcended the national boundaries of his people. His was a universal vision for those who could be inspired with humanity's loftiest aspirations and values. Not too many young people were responding to his call for the redemption of the Negev; those who did came from the cities of Israel, from New York, and Buenos Aires to join the "Old Man" with his eternally young vision.

At the end of my visit with Ben Gurion, I mentioned that now I was going to Beer Sheva to meet another man for whom the Negev was very dear. "Who is it?" he asked me. "Nelson Glueck," I replied, "Ah, your fellow American, Glueck, a good man. He has done wonders in bringing us a great understanding of the Negev. Give him my best regards."

It was one of the hottest days of the year. When I reached the hotel in Beer Sheva, Professor Nelson Glueck was already washed and changed after a hard day in the life of an archaeologist. I told Nelson Glueck of my special credentials from Ben Gurion, and that seemed to make it easier for me to talk to him. I wanted him to deliver a series of lectures at the Z.O.A. House on his explorations in the Negev. Glueck at first was not sure whether he could take time off from his archaeological digs and come to Tel Aviv. At that time, it took three hours to travel each way. However, when I combined the importance of his lectures with what Ben Gurion had asked me to do, he agreed. I assured him that his audiences would outshine any archaeological audiences in America. While he was somewhat skeptical of what I said, he liked my enthusiasm.

Nelson Glueck was one of the two Americans who made the greatest contribution to Biblical scholarship and archaeology. The other was F. W. Albright. Glueck was called "a trailblazer in Biblical archaeology" by the dean of Israeli archaeologists, Benjamin Mazer. Nelson Glueck was president of the Hebrew Union College in Cincinnati, and for over thirty years he spent his summers surveying Biblical lands in Jordan and in the Negev. Studying the potsherds strewn over many sites, he created a new picture of the early Israeli settlements about which we had known very little. He was the first to reveal to the world the fascinating Nabatean culture and civilization.

More than most archaeologists who worked in the Holy Land, he was in love with every inch of its ground. The knowledge that he was treading the earth where the patriarchs and the prophets had lived seized him with a sense of excitement. It was through Glueck's discoveries that Ben Gurion was able to hear the voices of those who inhabited the Negev in ancient days. Glueck made the Biblical figures come alive. He did not seek antiquities or discoveries for their own sake. "He sought solutions to problems," says Yigal Yadin, "he went to their sources, and there he struggled till he mastered them."

There were many affinities shared by the two men I met within those six hours. How often I had traveled through the world without finding one man comparable to the two men who were revealed to me in that day!

On my return to the Z.O.A. House, I called in my staff to consider the best ways of imparting the messages of Professor Nelson Glueck and the former premier of Israel, David Ben Gurion. Nelson Glueck's message was delivered directly by him to large, overflowing audiences. Ben Gurion's reached as many young people as it was possible for us to contact. It wasn't issued directly by him, but through various media that we employed. We made the Negev alive. There is no ideal universally accepted by all people. Each one views it from his own perspective, his own circle, his own situation. The emphasis that one group gives it elicits an altogether different response from another.

The Rotary Club, of which I was a member, asked me to fill the place of a speaker who was unduly detained in his governmental post. I told the chairman that I would speak on my last visit in the Negev. I had a prepared address which I had given to a large group of young people on the previous night. It had been enthusiastically received with loud applause and even cheers. When I finished the same address at the meeting of the Rotary, it was received politely. The well-settled businessmen, who constituted a large part of the membership, were not very enthusiastic. While some of them had been pioneers at one time, they were now too comfortably entrenched in their salons in Tel Aviv. They were far removed from the hard life in the undeveloped areas. A new generation and a new breed of men was needed for the new situation in the southern part of the country. It was this human material that absorbed most of my time.

When Hedvah arrived, we were once more reunited as a family for four weeks. This was her first visit to Israel and her first sight of our home near the sea. The trips we took with Hedvah, pointing to this and that place, were like seeing them again for the first time. Hedvah loved Jerusalem, and of all the times that I had watched Jerusalem's shades and moods, I never saw it quite like I did with her. She loved Caesaria and its Roman anphitheater, where we attended an operatic performance. In the background, we could see the waves of the Mediterranean. Like her, I was carried back 2,000 years.

After the beautiful garden in Hollywood where Hedvah grew up, I did not think our much smaller one would impress her. I was delighted in her reaction to the bushes, roses and flowers planted less than a year before. She did not imagine, she said, that I would bring to our new home the same beauty we had left behind. She also found pleasure in the clear skies and immense assortment of colorful birds. Added to this, she was struck by a gaiety in life that she never expected to see. She had been hearing and reading only of our daily hardships and austerity. Our strict rationing brought great enjoyment to what she ate at a time when she was watching the intake of her calories. She only wished that she could eat as much of the delicious Israeli bread that we offered her.

It was more than the material things that made her happy. It was the people who wanted to please her that made her stay one of rapture and delight. At twenty, and without the sight of the man she was to meet later on, reunion with her parents and her brother was the most important event in her life. It was also the best break that I could have had in my ever-increasing endeavors.

Toward the end of the summer, Al Epstein from Beverly Hills, California, came to see me. I had known Al for many years. He was a land developer and real estate manipulator, as well as a good Zionist with strong leanings to the right. He contributed much of his time and substance to the extreme right wing of the Zionist Organization and was bitterly prejudiced against the labor government of Ben Gurion and Sharett, Ben Gurion's successor. He knew that I didn't share any of his political views. In spite of Al's political idiosyncracy, I liked him. He was a good, generous man with a love for the land.

Al had a serious problem and he needed my help. He had organized a company in Los Angeles for the manufacture of a new type of building material, which he believed would cut the construction time in Israel. In 1953 and 1954, Israel was in a desperate need of the quickest way to build homes for the several hundred thousand people who were living in *maabarot*, shanties which were thrown together from tin, wood, and canvas. These *maabarot*, or transient dwellings, haphazardly assembled, were a blight on both sides of the main thoroughfares and were a cause of acute distress. Epstein enlisted the cooperation of prominent American Jews and non-Jews, who invested an appreciable sum of money in the building of a factory to produce the material. After preliminary studies by experts in the field, Al's finished product was approved as a feasible means to alleviate the housing shortage in the country.

There were other building-material factories with which Al's factory had to compete. These belonged to businesses and industries which worked in close cooperation with the government. The Minister of Housing and Labor was, for some unknown reason, reticent in placing orders with Al's firm. Al, quick of temper, and with no love for the Labor government, accused the ministries of "prejudice against anything that emanates from private initiative." This occurred at a time when political and economic conflict divided the socialist-oriented government and private enterprise in all fields.

Al invited me to go with him to his factory. He felt that with an unbiased judgment, I could be convinced of the wrong that the government's Labor Department was doing to his effort. At Al's factory, I met with the foreman, an architect, and a building engineer, who all agreed with Al's claims. I, too, without knowing all the facts, felt that Al was being discriminated against or pushed out of the market on account of his violent anti-government statements. Al was never known to be tactful or diplomatic. He ran to the American ambassador. The ambassador was apprised of the important Americans who backed the project, and he called Golda Meir, the Minister of Labor. Golda very tactfully asked that Al Epstein come to see her and her department heads, and place his grievances before them.

Al knew no Hebrew and did not want to take an attorney with him, so he asked me to come and plead his case. My first reaction was no. I was not going to get involved in Israeli politics. It was not within the realm of my activities. Al impressed on me the duty I had to important donors to Israel. He said I knew how to represent their interests without prejudice to myself or my political views.

When Golda Meir saw me with Al Epstein, the first thing she said in Hebrew was, "So you have nothing better to do than to come here and plead for Epstein?" No, I said, I did not come for Epstein. I only came to translate what Epstein and his supporters had to say. "So you think I have already forgotten my English?" she shrugged. When Al asked me what Golda said, I told him that she could understand him without a translator. Golda Meir was raised in Milwaukee, Wisconsin. She had been a teacher of English in grammar school and spoke English better than she spoke Hebrew.

Golda Meir called in a young lady to take down the proceedings stenographically. After twenty minutes of writing the presentations from both sides, Golda asked the secretary to read back a part of her notes. The stenographer started to mumble and fumble, and couldn't read a word of what was said. I started to laugh and it took me a long time to control it. Al Epstein also started laughing, but Golda was in a rage. I had never seen her more upset and angry. She rose, grabbed the pencil from the girl, and chased her out of the room. Then she returned to her seat and began recording all that was said by me, Al, and the heads of her department. When the proceedings were over and I was ready to return to Tel Aviv, Golda was calm and composed, as if nothing had happened. When I approached her to say good-bye, she told me that if I was not too busy, she would like me to come to her house for tea. She wanted to discuss a few things with me.

When I reached Golda Meir's neat little apartment, I saw Golda for the first time as a warm, kind, humble person. After we had consumed the fine cookies that she herself had baked, Golda asked me if I thought it would be proper to arrange a concert for her son, who was a cellist. "Strange," I said to Golda, "a few days ago Levi Eshkol asked me if I could arrange a recital for his talented daughter, who is a dancer." Golda asked me what I told Levi Eshkol, who was at that time Minister of Finance and, like Golda, was to become Premier of Israel. I answered, "I told him the same as I tell you—that it will be my pleasure to do it."

One morning I found a letter from my teacher, Professor Mordecai Kaplan. He was due to arrive from New York the following week. When I asked the director of public relations what he could do in a hurry to arrange a suitable reception for Dr. Kaplan, he shrugged his shoulders. What possible interest, he asked, could be aroused for an American religious leader of Reconstructionism, whose views run counter to the prevailing religious establishment in the country? The intellectuals, he pointed out to me, have very little interest in religion. No matter how progressive Dr. Kaplan may be, they would not come to hear him speak, and as for the general nonreligious public, there would be no way of arousing its interest in a philosophic discussion of Judaism at a time when the country was beset with more realistic problems. I told him that I knew all that and then I proceeded to tell him what to do. I asked him and the staff to contact the important Hebrew writers and scholars who appeared in our forums and have them sign a welcoming letter to Dr. Kaplan who, in addition to his great love of Zion, included modern Zionism as an integral part of the Jewish faith. After receiving more signatures than we expected, the letter was widely circulated and publicized.

The intellectuals, who were invited to hear a new interpretation of Judaism, were eager to find out what Dr. Kaplan had to say. Absorbed in their special interests, they gave little thought to the place of religion in an emancipated society. In their concept of a new civilization, Judaism had no major role to play; they did not know how to fit it into their lives and into the life of their society.

In a perfect, literary Hebrew, Dr. Kaplan captivated his audience at once. One idea led to another with startling brilliance. This presentation more than satisfied the cultural and religious curiosity of the three hundred listeners.

After a ninety-minute address, there followed more than an hour of what Dr. Kaplan termed "the most learned, profound questions" he had ever been asked. For me this event was a feat, the highlight of my last major activities in the Z.O.A. House.

Much of the work that followed in the subsequent months was routine. It lacked the challenge and creativity of my first two years of complete absorption. The beautiful Z.O.A. House was too small and limited for further expansion. I had done all I could. The job could now be taken up by anyone willing to replace me.

I sent a formal letter of resignation to Dr. Emanuel Neuman, who was rounding out his three years as American Chairman of the Z.O.A. House. Some political and administrative differences had developed between me and the head office in New York toward the end of my term. Dr. Neuman was magnanimously able to overlook these differences in writing to me as follows:

> July 8, 1955
>
> Dear Mr. Alkow:
>
> You have advised us that for personal and business reasons you will be unable to continue your activities on behalf of the Z.O.A. House in your present capacity. I cannot conclude this letter without an expression of deep appreciation on my own behalf and on behalf of the organization for the valuable services you have rendered during this period. You took in hand what was little more than a shell of a building and built up an important institution teeming with activity, which has won the most widespread commendation both in Israel and in the United States. You have done this under conditions which were difficult and at times most trying. You have, in fact, made a great contribution to the Z.O.A. and to the Jewish community in Israel. We are not only grateful for all you have done, but in time will give appropriate expression to our appreciation of your arduous labor and achievements.
>
> Cordially yours,
> Emanuel Neuman

Jacob Alkow presenting a silver Pesach plate to Eleanor Roosevelt, 1935.

Jacob Alkow presenting a gift of white jade to Governor Adlai E. Stevenson for his humanitarian work.

XXI
WALL STREET
1955-1965

Like a rubber ball tossed from wave to wave, submerged, raised, cast to the beach and drawn back to the billowing sea, time and again I found myself drawn into one world after another by chance or accident.

One day Irving Norry, an American business leader and philanthropist, came to see me in Tel Aviv with a "a proposition which might be of interest." He and a Washington banker, a railroad company president, a financier, and ten others were in the process of forming a Wall Street investment firm associated with the New York Stock Exchange. The firm was to be headed by Henry Montor, formerly the executive head of the United Jewish Appeal. Montor had launched the successful operations of Israel bonds throughout the world, and the UJA, in its present multi-billion dollar dimensions, was his creation. "Every Jew in America knows Montor and respects him" Norry said. In the estimation of many people, he was an organizational genius. Those who were prepared to invest in the new enterprise were largely American leaders of the Israel Bond Organization and the United Jewish Appeal. They all had implicit faith in the talents Montor possessed as an organizer and operator of large undertakings. He was so well regarded in America and Israel that Golda Meir would come to the airport to meet him.

Because of the ruling of the New York Stock Exchange, the corporation, which was to be organized as the Henry Montor Associates, had to have three active, full-time partners in addition to the investors. Would I consider accepting an active partnership? I would be offered a position as vice-president of the firm in charge of West Coast operations. It was understood that if I accepted the offer, I would have to spend several months of training in the Finance Institute of New York University and in the New York brokerage office before being qualified to serve as a broker and an active partner.

The thought of participating in a large economic venture with people of vast experiece appealed to me. It was a new field of endeavor, which I had never before contemplated. I arrived in New York to meet with Henry Montor, who filled me in on the background of the corporation and its plans for operating a Wall Street brokerage firm. Montor was an intelligent man, honest financial risk. The Circle Theatre was a small hall, similar to the off-Broadway theaters, and was located in Hollywood and run by George Boroff. It had always attracted good productions.

Because of La Muir's interference, the work was more difficult than I expected, but I took my time and La Muir finally approved of the cast. Some of those who were chosen were motion picture actors of note. The union wages which I offered were of the least interest to them. For the time they devoted to rehearsals and the weeks that followed after the rehearsals, they could have earned ten times as much in the studios. What they wanted most of all was exposure before a live audience. Since we had no matinees, their participating in the evening play did not interfere with their regular work in cinema.

A crisis occurred when an actress of great talent answered the call from her lover in New York. She met him on occasions when he left his wife and children and his work for a "business trip." She dropped out of the rehearsals without giving any notice, and flew to Las Vegas to indulge in love and gambling. Basically she was a good woman with a sense of honor. We followed her to Las Vegas and asked her to return to the final rehearsals. She complied. Because of her conscience she wanted the play to open on schedule.

One other lady with talent who made her debut on the stage was the beautiful daughter of the world-famous pianist, Artur Rubenstein. It was a delight to watch Rubenstein's face during rehearsal, when he looked at his gifted daughter on the stage of the Circle Theatre.

The play was a smash hit. The critics gave it unqualified, good revues. It ran for twenty-seven weeks. In the films, I had very few opportunities for the creative work which I enjoyed most. The theater was the fresh, living water for a parched soul. I was on the verge of being induced into accepting another offer to produce a play, but after some hesitation, I turned it down. I knew too well the pitfalls to which one is exposed in a theatrical production that can raise one to the heights or cast one down to the depths, whether one is a producer, director, actor, or investor. I was reminded by my family and friends that I had enough excitement and nerve-racking months in my life to last me a long while. My children were growing up and they needed more of my attention.

Hedvah was now 17 and happily absorbed with her studies and friends. Michael was past his bar mitzvah and it grieved me that I had neglected to give him a proper Hebrew education. He could not read my Hebrew books. Even the titles were a mystery to him. What he learned in Temple Israel was of no value. He was a wonderful, obedient child, but he showed no prospect of becoming a scholar. For a while I was unaware of where he acquired a smattering knowledge of literature. Later he told me that the druggist used to throw him out of the store after he had lingered too long over the comic book stories of the classics he was supposed to read.

In my last trip to Palestine, I remembered passing an agricultural village and convincing. He was not obsessed with money or wealth, but was more of an adventurer, who retained cool judgement. He impressed me as a very busy man, one who preferred to work alone. I did not mind, in fact, I welcomed his wanting to be alone. It would allow me the freedom of finding my way without undue interference.

During the first months in New York I familiarized myself with Wall Street, where I was to spend the next ten years of my life. It is a landmark in American history. On the corner of Wall and Nassau Streets, George Washington took his oath of office. At the head of Wall Street stands one of the oldest and richest churches in America, the Trinity Episcopalian Church and graveyard. Bishop Manning said about the church that one has the feeling that "the forms of Mammon surrounding it are like a circle of ravenous wolves waiting to pounce upon the only open space left in this section, the sole witness to the things of spirit in the midst of the great temples of materialism." Here the church stood since long before the United States was born, since the time when Wall Street was really a wall built to protect the city from the attacks of Indians and wild beasts.

It was in this small area of New York that I learned a geat deal more than I knew during the twenty-five years I was buying and selling stocks. What I learned were the nice things about investing, the things which are good, profitable, and essential for the country. Much of it was new and very positive. I was impressed by the statistics on modern materials, methods, drugs, babies, Medicare, and Medicaid, which all cause business to expand and raise living standards.

I learned that all this was made possible by those who bought stocks and bonds with funds which the companies funneled into the building of new industries and the acquisition of new machinery. "A share of stock is a share in America," was one of the constantly repeated slogans. From my experience, since the time of the Depression until I came onto the "Street," I knew that securities, on the whole, were the best investment over a long period of time. Later on I saw another picture, but basically, the philosophy, the reasoning of investing in the building of American industry, had been sound.

There were too many people who did not enter the market as investors. They were interested in it primarily as speculators and gamblers. They never studied the securities they bought. It was the fluctuation of the market which excited and attracted them. It was not the safety or gradual growth of their investments which interested them. They never bothered to know why stocks rose and fell. People like this, in their instability, have made stocks increase and decrease contrary to any logic or reason. I was destined to learn a great deal about the human factor in the complex machinery on which America depended for its life and well being.

After my preliminary months of apprenticeship, I left for Los Angeles to survey the field for the establishment of a branch office of Henry Montor Associates, Inc. This was to be done as soon as we received the green light from the New York Stock Exchange, which is the umbrella organization of its member firms throughout America. Every firm has to abide by its rules. More than half the business in America is listed with this mighty exchange. It includes nearly all the oils, railroads, steel, and airlines. In 1960, it embraced 1,100 large corporations. There are 1,366 permanent members in the New York Stock Exchange. All members have what are called seats on the exchange. Actually there are no real seats. The members on the exchange stand or shuttle from post to post where the trading goes on. Our firm of Henry Montor Associates bought one of those seats, which in 1955, cost upwards of $150,000.

The brokerage office I was about to set up on the West Coast was to serve as a clearing house for individuals who owned shares in leading corporations registered with either the New York Stock Exchange or any of the other exchanges, or over the counter. A customer who wanted to buy or sell his share of stocks or bonds would contact our office and place his order for "buy or sell." Our firm received a commission for the transaction.

After two months of searching for suitable personnel and arduously laying the groundwork for our branch office, I received a call from New York advising me to abandon all my work on the coast and to return to New York with my family. The New York Stock Exchange had refused to allow the establishment of a branch office at this early stage of our operation. I accepted the reason as a logical one. But I could not understand why Henry Montor and our knowledgeable associates did not foresee this. It was the first break in the confidence I had in the meticulous planning at our head office. In a sense, I was glad to have had the opportunity to spend two months with my daughter and to change the management of my property in Los Angeles.

We found a cheerful sublet on Central Park South facing the park. Little did I know at the time that I rented the apartment that, together with its location, it would be the only bright spot in the dismal, demeaning months which were to follow. My adjustment to my work and surroundings in the central office on Exchange Place near Wall Street was painful. Without defining my functions in the corporation, I was given a desk in the back office, which saw very little of the light of day. My work was such that any competent clerk could have done it better. Some of it involved research. My concentration on research helped take my mind off the seemingly unbusinesslike way in which Montor was running the firm, without consulting any of his active partners. Though he was both an idealist and pragmatist, Montor was a tough administrator with underlings. Unable to arrive at any evaluation of Montor's activities, I plunged into a study of how the listed corporations operated. Some of my discoveries were depressing.

One of the things that struck me was what Berle and Means had written in *Modern Corporation*. They claimed that the individual interest of the shareholder is definitely made subservient to the will of a controlling group of managers, even though the capital of the enterprise is composed of the aggregate contributions of perhaps many thousands of individuals. Through a proxy system, the board of directors could perpetuate themselves.

Then there was the work of Bernard G. Reiss, published in 1937, which contained startling facts of how the directors of most of the large corporations robbed the investors by taking exorbitant salaries for themselves. For example, the Consolidated Oil Corporation had an income of over $20 million in 1929 and the total compensation to the directors was $526,357. In 1932 the income dropped from $20 million to only $1,313,466, and the compensation to the officers and directors rose to $655,334.

Charles M. Schwab, chairman of the Board of Directors of Bethlehem Steel Corporation, received $150,000 in 1929. When in 1930 the corporation did half the business that it did in 1929, Mr. Schwab's salary rose to $250,000. In the darkest days of the Depression, in 1932, Bethlehem Steel lost $19 million and Schwab's salary was still $250,000. All of this data was obtained from the Federal Trade Commissioner. In checking the corporations, I found a number of exceptions to the general practice. Those were Union Carbide, Westinghouse Electric, American Car and Foundry, and two others.

Here then, was a fact to bear in mind. The stockholders who voted and elected the board of directors of the big corporations had very little control over the large sums that the officers and directors took out of the corporation for their own salaries.

There was only one consolation which enabled me to accept the way the officers and directors removed the cream from the top. When business was good, there was usually a good deal of milk left for the investor. That was not the case during the Depression, and that was partially the reason why I and millions like me lost all our money. By the time I was fully involved, I realized that with all its faults, Wall Street was still the best institution to serve the major economic needs of our society.

In learning something about the corporations, I was beginning to know how to advise people. I began to gather clients who recommended me to other clients, and I moved out of the back room to the main board room where I could watch the board and receive orders over the phone. While my work for the company progressed satisfactorily, my distress was increasing daily. Henry Montor's aloofness was probably the main cause of it. His extravagance and bad judgement led our firm more and more into the red. His attitude toward the staff and the sales force was cool, indifferent, and impolite. I was at a loss to understand him and explain his behavior.

Montor was basically an honest man where money was concerned, by far more honest than most heads of Wall Street firms, but he was ashamed to face those people who now saw he was not as able, sure, and confident as they were led to believe. He knew that for me and our other active partner, H. Fishman, he was a dismal disappointment, and he could not look us in the face.

One day, without informing me or any other partner, Montor disappeared from the office for several weeks. He had a faithful secretary, who shielded him and would not divulge his whereabouts. It was only through Montor's wife that I learned he was in Nevada for a divorce. On Montor's return to the office, he allowed me a freer hand in my work.

At long last, I found that some of Montor's supporters began to take note of my existence. For over a year, I had patiently waited for the opportunity to be able to talk to any of them. At the meetings with Montor, I would sit in the back of the room without saying a word. Confident that the firm would turn the corner and begin to operate profitably, they never questioned Montor's genius to change the bleak financial situation of the firm into one of great prosperity. I have never encountered such blind faith in all my life. Having studied the life of many of the so-called prophets of capitalism I knew that the disillusionment of the naive Jewish business leaders was not too far away.

One day I was asked to have lunch with one of them. He wanted to know if I had any ideas how to put the firm on a sounder basis. This was the opportunity I was waiting for. After explaining to our investor what had gone awry in our operation, I suggested to him that we talk to Montor and convince him to allow me to open a branch office in the diamond district on 47th Street near Fifth Avenue. I told him that I had surveyed the area and I felt I could give our firm a shot in the arm. I seized upon this opportunity to relieve me of the unhappiness of working in the same office with Montor.

Two days later, Montor agreed to let me go ahead with my plans to open the 47th Street office. This was a turning point in my life. For many nights prior to that time, I had tossed from side to side planning and praying for a way to escape from the unbearable situation in which I had found myself. To see all that was wrong and not to be able to talk to anyone about it was the most difficult. I knew that according to the rules of the New York Stock Exchange, I was regarded as second in command of our operation and answerable for anything which would displease the thirty-three members on the Board of Governors. I was aware of the way the main employees of the Stock Exchange watched every one of our moves. They disliked Montor. He ignored their petty rules of the game. At the start of our business, Montor was angry with their "unreasonable restraints." He referred to the management of the New York

Stock Exchange as "pious hypocrites," since they overlooked many serious infractions of the Securities Exchange Laws by some large member firms, and made a tremendous issue of nonconformance to some petty regulations by the little firms. Chairman of the Federal Securities Exchange Commission, William I. Cary, said, "The New York Stock Exchange seems to have certain characteristics of a private club." Montor may have been right in regarding the Exchange as a private club, but having joined the club, he should have known better than to antagonize its august members. From the beginning, I had a feeling that Montor and I would pay very dearly for some of the "little things" that no one had ever noticed.

I was given independence and freedom in the running of my new, modern office. The business I developed on 47th Street was the first indication of the ability of our firm to operate profitably. From week to week our clientele increased, and I was able to attract good men to fill all of our available desks. The investors in our corporation now sought my advice to prevail upon Montor to change his direction and bring about a rapprochement with the New York Stock Exchange.

In the summer, I rented a home which faced the Long Island Sound in Old Larchmont. Once again we could hear the waves and the splashing of the water, just as it was at the Israeli seashore in Herzliah. Hedvah came to stay with us during her summer vacation. We spent our evenings at concerts and plays, which were offered in and around New York in the summer festivals. During free days I used to fish through the bedroom window. Sometimes I brought in

Jacob Alkow (center) standing in front of the Beverly Hills, CA, office of Alkow & Co., 1960.

fish, more often I snagged an eel, which would wriggle along the floor and draw shrieks from Hedvah, "Daddy, take it away."

With the end of the summer we moved to West 81st St. near Central Park. This had been a large apartment, formerly occupied by the great opera singer, Enrico Caruso. It then had been remodeled into two apartments. We lived in the large one. In the other apartment lived the Israeli Consul, Esther Herlitz, whose father was a distinguished librarian in Jerusalem and a good friend of mine. During the Sinai War she used our phone for confidential calls.

Michael completed his high school studies and a year at the Hebrew University and joined us in America. While Michael liked his new environment, he found great difficulty in forgetting his old environment and especially Ada, a girl he left behind in Israel. He was consoled by my promise to let him go to Israel the following summer, and if his love for Ada endured until then, I promised also to buy her a ticket to come to America.

On November 29, 1956, I read about the alliance Israel made with Great Britain and France in the Sinai war with Egypt. The war between Israel and Egypt was understandable. The endless harassment of Israeli settlements by the Egyptian Army and the continuous sniping and killing of Israelis called for an Israeli retaliation. What I did not like about this was Israel's alliance with the two colonial powers, which shared no mutual interests with Israel. In their case, the war was for the preservation of their colonial rights and their freedom of navigation through the Suez Canal.

On the second day of the war, as we were all sitting in front of the television watching the first reports which came in on the battle around the Suez Canal, we saw some trucks with Israeli soldiers. In one of the trucks there were two boys whom Michael recognized. He jumped up excitedly and asked me how soon he could fly back to Israel.

We did all we could to calm him down. I talked with him and pleaded with him not to rush back. The war, I told him, would be ended quickly, and besides, it was unlike any other war when Israel fought for its life and its self-preservation. But logic was of no use.

There were no direct flights from the United States to Israel because of the war, but Michael called the airlines and found a plane which would take him to Italy. From there he could catch a plane to Israel. Two hours after the telecast, Michael kissed his sobbing mother good-bye. In driving Michael toward Idlewild to catch his plane, I lost the way and took the bridge which leads toward the Bronx on the opposite side of our destination. I looked at Michael and I was sure that he would be furious. I was surprised to see his dejected, resigned face. I quickly made a U-turn and reversed my direction. We reached the airport twenty minutes before the departure of the only plane he could have taken within the next twenty-four hours. I arrived in time, but lost my son for more than five years.

With the passing of the summer and the healthy operation of the 47th Street office, I opened a new branch office in the heart of the cloak-and-suit district on Seventh Avenue near the Pennsylvania Station. The start was a little slower than it had been at the 47th Street office, but with a steady growth it was another proof of our ability to operate successfully. One day, I was asked by a functionary in the New York Stock Exchange to discuss our branch activities. He referred to the way Montor had started running our business "noisily," and also used the expression "a cloak and suit operation." I was upset by the anti-Semitic overtones.

Nonetheless, I was happy with the progress of my work. When my office day ended at four, there were galleries, libraries, lectures, and concerts to absorb my time. In order not to lose the spark, which according to Bishop Manning, Wall Street seeks to extinguish, I joined the Reconstructionist Synagogue where Dr. Mordecai Kaplan and Dr. Jack Cohen delivered some erudite lectures. I was elected a member of the editorial staff of the *Reconstructionist Magazine* and served in this capacity for eight years. I was also selected to be chairman of some of the large dinners in support of the Hebrew movement and various educational institutions.

No one, however, can expect to have cloudless days indefinitely. Vera's rheumatism and arthritis began to assert itself and it was not easy for her to suppress the pains. This was at a time when the main investors in Henry Montor Associates, Inc., were suddenly aroused to the sad financial condition of the firm. Though the branches I had opened were doing well, the firm in general was ailing. One by one the investors came to see me and suggested that Montor leave the firm so as to preserve whatever assets remained. $600,000 were "wasted and squandered in three years," they said to me. As the largest active partner with an investment of $100,000, I, too, was worried. We were getting close to the red line, below which we would not be able to operate. To free the firm of Montor, Montor's closest friends needed my help. One of them was Sam Rothberg, the head of the Israel Bond Organization in America. No one was closer to Montor than Rothberg, and when he threatened to withdraw his deposits from the firm if Montor remained, I saw a cause for alarm. Montor thought that Fishman, the other active partner, and I were conniving with the investors to remove him. He sent Fishman and me telegrams advising us that we were discharged from the firm. The lawyer representing eighty percent of the investors told me to send Montor a telegram advising him he had no right to discharge us and to summon him to a meeting with the officers of the New York Stock Exchange. The Stock Exchange took immediate action by inviting both

Montor and myself, Fishman, and eight major stockholders to a meeting at its headquarters. Within an hour, Montor's seat in the New York Stock Exchange was turned over to me. Several of the stockholders raised the necessary money so I could pay Montor for his shares of stock, which were not worth one-third of the original value. Montor was out of the firm and the name of Henry Montor Associates was changed to Alkow and Co., Inc.

As soon as Montor left, I arranged to release any of the investors who wanted to leave the firm. They were paid the full value of the stock at that time. Their fears of serious repercussions were unfounded. Not a single registered representative left our new organization. I turned the operations of the 47th Street office over to a competent manager, and I moved into Montor's office in the downtown area of Wall Street. Surrounded by large bouquets of flowers, I sat at my desk for half an hour impassively, absorbed in the magnificent view of the East River and the bridges which span it.

The office was a far cry from the dismal, dark corner where I started my financial odyssey three years earlier. Throughout the morning of the first day, I received visitors and well wishers. How quickly we are hailed and accepted when we prove successful in the land where success is valued above all else.

I visited the offices of the New York Stock Exchange, where I was highly commended for the peaceful way in which I effected the transfer of the membership from Montor to myself. I then met with the president of the exchange, G. Keith Funston. He rose head and shoulders above anyone else who was involved with big business in Wall Street. After meeting him, I never again felt out of place in the cavernous world of the "great temples of materialism." Mr. Funston, prior to his election as president of the New York Stock Exchange, had served as president of Temple University. One of his great loves and hobbies was archaeology, and if it could really be said that anyone was out of place in the large, impressive building of the Exchange, it was this tall, dignified, solitary president. I learned that he was retained in his position as an ornament to the institution and only peripherally as a leader or business guide for its multiple manipulations. The thirty-two hard-boiled businessmen who, with Funston, comprised the Board of Directors, regarded him with the honor that was due him, but without much concern over what he thought, and felt, or knew about the operations of the 1,100 members of the staff he headed. Martin Mayers, in his book *Wall Street Men and Money*, said that everybody liked Funston but nobody helped him much. Even his own staff has, on occasion, taken the pleasure of "bamboozling him." On one occasion, Funston checked back to find that the staff had taken advantage of his ignorance. He was seldom informed by his staff of the habitual inattention of the Board to ram through one of his pet projects. Another eyewitness observes that nobody had told Funston about "the snakepit in which he would have to stand twelve months a year to earn $100,000." My grasp of what Martin Mayers described so poignantly was important to understanding what happened to me and to Montor two years later. For two years, I lived in a world of relative innocence and bliss, unaware of the problems that were to arise later on.

With good winds blowing in my direction, I laid plans for the strengthening of our business. I went over the lists of our brokers to make sure that they were all of a high calibre and able to render good service to our faithful clientele. Instead of a drop in the number of our clients, as the previous investors had feared, our customers increased in nearly all of the branches. On several occasions, I encountered the salesmen in our 47th Street office and asked them to curtail their business with people for whom the stock market was a roulette wheel.

My organization did not need to be reminded of what the Bible said: "He that loveth silver shall not be satisfied with silver nor he that loveth abundance with increase." Our objective was to impress prospective investors with the fact that no big profits could be earned overnight and that they should not be led into unwarranted speculation. In trying to follow a reasonable line, we avoided some of the clichés and slogans of the New York Stock Exchange, such as "People's Capitalism." I knew that capitalism didn't benefit all the people and that the vast majority could never have any meaningful part of it. It was fortunate that when making money, about which John D. Rockefeller said, "God gave it to me," the capitalists were compelled to return a great part directly or indirectly to the people to whom the money belonged. If it was not taken from the large capitalists through taxation for building roads or schools, large portions of their wealth were left to society. Our great national treasures, our immense libraries, museums, universities, and hospitals were built with the money willed by the Fricks, Carnegies, and Mellons.

I did not agree with what the President of the New York Stock Exchange said, "By merely trying to broaden the base of stock ownership, we strengthen the basis of democracy." I did believe that by owning good, sound stocks, one secures the economic basis of one's family, but I did not see how it strengthened the basis of democracy. Democracy, unlike stocks, can only be strengthened when it is shared by all the people of the land; it is not limited to those who own stocks, a mere twenty percent of the population in the last years of the 1950s.

I chose to tell our stockholders the truth. The truth was that people have very few places to turn for the preservation of their money. With inflation gradually eating away the value of their savings, and with the small interest they received from the savings and loan institutions, stock in good companies with ample assets and possibilities for growth was one of the very few means of protecting their wealth. Ideas about their share in the benefits of capitalism, or strengthening democracy had as much validity as dancing for the rain at a time of drought.

Momentum is an important factor in the building of a business that caters to the public. With it, the confidence it creates reaps the largest benefits. In my New York offices I welcomed my old friend, Meyer Weisgal and Dr. Samuel Blumenfeld, who sought my advice and help. Dr. Nahum Goldman and other Jewish leaders were worth more to me than others whose portfolios were ten times their size. They bolstered my morale and helped us create a more direct and close relationship with the people we wanted to serve.

One night, while Vera and I were peacefully sleeping, the phone rang. It was three o'clock in the morning and I was sure it was a wrong number. Vera was not well. Cortisone did not relieve her pains. I jumped out of bed and answered the call. It was Hedvah calling from Los Angeles at midnight. "Daddy," she sang out joyously. My heart already told me what her good news would be. "Daddy, I just got engaged to be married to Michael Berg. You know Michael. His mother said that you had dated her when you were a young fellow." Hedvah wanted to talk to her mother and then again to me. We spoke to each other for half an hour, and by nine o'clock the next morning, I was on the plane to Los Angeles.

For many months I had been uneasy and concerned about my daughter. She was twenty-four years old and still alone. During the six hours of flight, my mind was centered on my daughter's life. It wandered to San Bernardino, China, Los Angeles, New York, and back to Los Angeles. At last, I mused, my conscience would no longer trouble me for having left Hedvah alone for long stretches of time. Her accusing eyes would not torment me any more.

On my arrival in Los Angeles, Hedvah and Michael waited for me at the airport. What their first meeting with me at the airport led to was two grandsons, Eric and Jesse, who never fail to meet their "Gramps" at the airport when he comes to see them.

While in Los Angeles, I received a call from the manager of our underwriting department that a Mr. Brian Newkirk phoned from Florida. He wanted to know if I would meet him on my next visit to our office in Hollywood, Florida. He had a proposition that "sounded very interesting." Instead of returning directly to New York, I flew to Florida. I had heard of Newkirk in Wall Street. He was a Canadian multi-millionaire, who made his fortune in uranium mines in Canada.

Newkirk and his wife, Lucille, had an only son, who had died from an incurable disease, leaving them two grandchildren. To memorialize the life of his son, Newkirk bought the island of Duck Key and began to convert it into a replica of Venice. He cut through the island with canals and spanned them with decorated marble bridges high enough for small craft to pass underneath. Newkirk asked me to be his guest for three days on Duck Island. I would see the beauty of the site and its potentialities. My association with Wall Street was now leading me to new ventures.

Duck Key lay midway between Miami Beach and Key West, which is the extreme southern point of the United States. I found Duck Key even more beautiful than Newkirk's description of it. With its canals, curved marble bridges, and wide, two-story houses built in the exquisite architectural style of the West Indies, there was nothing like it on the North American continent. Besides Newkirk and his wife, Lucille, there were about twenty other permanent residents on the island and about eight guests from all over the world, most of whom were listed in *Who's Who*.

Surrounded by a view of the blue waters, I could not have wished for better accommodations. There were fifteen people at dinner and a trio played South American music. One of the guests was Roy Cohn. Like many Americans, I could not forget the important role that Roy Cohn played as the chief counsel for McCarthy's Un-American Activities Committee during one of America's darkest hours. Roy Cohn was one of Newkirk's lawyers, and he occupied a beautiful cottage. Newkirk himself was politically a reactionary, but his cool attitude toward Cohn helped to mitigate my uneasiness in getting involved with him and his associates. Newkirk alone, I thought, was bad enough for me, but with Cohn as his lawyer, it was a little too much to take. After a few days some of my fears and suspicions were allayed by Lucille Newkirk.

Lucille Newkirk was as different from her husband as any wife could be different from the man she lives with. She had withdrawn herself from her husband and his opulent way of life. The bottles of Canadian rye standing on the tables of the house helped her retain her inner equilibrium. After our first official dinner, she told me she was glad to have me as her guest because I was different. I repaid her the compliment by telling her that I, too, was glad to have her as my hostess because she was different. She then asked me if it was true that I could read the Bible in its original language, and when I told her that it was true, I was sure she was going to ask what drew me into the company of her husband and his friends.

Lucille knew the Bible and a great deal more. What she knew and understood from the books she read was her consolation in life. She did not like her husband, she did not like her daughter-in-law, and she did not like Roy Cohn. What she did like was honesty, humility, and intelligence. She avoided all the pleasures and pastimes of her husband. I waited for every available chance to sit and talk with her and listened to her expressions of faith with reverence. For over a year, I was to look forward to the days I would spend on Duck Key, both for its beauty and the beauty of the soul of this remarkable woman, old beyond her years. As time went on, my respect for Brian Newkirk increased because of the admiration he had for his unhappy wife.

On the second day of my stay on the island, Roy Cohn, Newkirk, his daughter-in-law, and I went fishing. I was strapped in a high, swirling, steel chair fastened to the deck; Roy Cohn was on my right and the young lady on the left, fastened in the other chairs. Two of the three boatmen provided us with all the necessary gear for an expected catch of marlin and jack fish. I was the first to be engaged in a struggle with a 100-pound jack fish on my hook. The mighty leviathan pulled me right and left. He pulled my line, raised himself above the waves, and plunged back to the depths. This lasted for over an hour. By the time I succeeded in bringing up my catch, with the help of the two sailors, I had no strength left to go after any more. Everyone pulled up at least one fish and called it a day. Newkirk was the only one who brought in a large marlin.

Before I left the yacht, my relations with my three companions with whom I had spent a full day, were very friendly and cordial. Even Roy Cohn appeared in a better light. He was bright and interesting as a conversationalist. He avoided all controversial subjects including anything Jewish, with which I tried to test him. Ironically, Newkirk, who said that he never thought of me as a Jew, always thought of Roy Cohn as a Jew. When I told him angrily, "What, you call Roy Cohn a Jew?" he was embarrassed.

During the two hours it took us to get back to the island, Newkirk told me of his plans for building a large, luxurious hotel on the Key. After using up a great deal of money in the development of the island and laying the foundation for the hotel, he was in need of additional private and public financing to complete his project. I was asked if I could use the facilities of our firm to help him get the financing. I promised to take the plans back to New York and to present them to the people on Wall Street.

On my return, I consulted with underwriters of new enterprises and they agreed to join our firm in raising the funds needed for the building of the hotel. I called Newkirk and he was delighted.

On my second visit, I finished all I had to do quickly. In the evening I had to put on formal dress for what the *Miami Herald* headline described as "International Was Word for Newkirk Party." After the party, which was hilarious, I told Lucille that while I enjoyed it very much, I was not overly impressed with the big name celebrities. She smiled and promised not to tell her husband. Quite unintentionally I derived some profit from Newkirk's reference to my association with him as his "able Wall Street financial advisor." One of the generals and a foreign guest promised to open accounts in our Florida branch.

One other gentleman with large business interests in Cuba told me of the financial possibilities in Cuba for "an alert, aggressive firm." He invited me to

Havana as his guest. About two weeks after I returned to my desk in New York, I received a letter from Andrew, the Havana businessman. He had a proposition to discuss with me. He asked me to come to Havana as soon as possible. While Cuba was one of the last places to which I would normally be attracted, Andrew's invitation made a good deal of sense. Without knowing much about the Battista regime, I was prejudiced against it, yet in spite of this and some of the warnings about Cuba, I flew to Havana.

No one told us during our flight what was awaiting us in Havana. When the plane landed and taxied to a stop, we had to wait fifteen mintues before the gangplank was brought alongside it. The field was abandoned. From a distance we saw three young boys patrolling the area. They approached and asked us to follow them to an empty waiting room. All the personnel of the airport had run away, and there was no one to check passports or to examine our luggage. One of the three boys, dressed in old, ragged clothes, knew a little English. He told us "to wait until Castro men arrive."

We soon pieced the picture together. Castro and his army had come down from the mountains and had taken over Havana and all of Cuba that very day. The Battista government officials and their hirelings fled when the ill-clad army of the peoples' revolutionary government entered the city, shooting and killing anyone on its way. The remnants of the government forces barricaded themselves around the airport. With the arrival of Castro and his ragged, young soldiers, the barricades were completely demolished. Only a few wounded men were left, crying for help that Castro's men were unable to supply. They had very little medical equipment.

About sixty of us huddled in the waiting room for almost an hour. Then a captain of Castro's army strode in. He was a man in his early thirties and was accompanied by six soldiers, who were little older than the first three boys who welcomed us to Cuba. The captain spoke English with a very familiar accent. He had a little trouble finding the exact passenger list, but before turning to that list, he told us that we had no need to fear. He said we had come on the greatest day in the history of Cuba. These reassuring words brought little comfort to the depressed travelers. The captain then proceeded to read the names of the passengers. The Spanish names were the only ones he could pronounce in any recognizable fashion. The more names he read, the more I was convinced that I knew about the man who was Castro's representative to the first foreign guests of the new, socialist, revolutionary country of Cuba. Then he reached my name, and when he said, "Yaakov" in a well-known accent, I began to laugh. My laughter helped to break the tension. The captain looked at me for an instant and there was something in his look that made him pause before continuing with the rest of the names. He told us how and where to register before we were ready to leave the country, what we were allowed to do, where we could stay, and where we were forbidden to go.

When the captain was finished and we were ready to claim our unchecked baggage, I walked over to him and asked him in Yiddish, "*Fun vanen zeit ir a landsman?*" He grinned and said quickly, "I am from Warsaw. Where are you from?"

"I am from Vilna."

"Vilna," he cried with joy, "is where my mother was born and where I spent the last year of the war in the forests when I was a boy." Embracing me warmly, he kept repeating, "*Vilner landsman!*"

In the three years he spent with Castro's army buried in the inaccessible parts of Cuba, he met only one or two Jews and they did not know a word of Yiddish. They had to converse in Spanish. Now for the first time in many years he had found a real *landsman*.

When I told him that I came to Cuba for business reasons, his enthusiasm waned a bit. He couldn't understand how a likeable *landsman* like me could come to do business in the Cuba of the murderous Battista. When I told him I, too, could not understand it, he laughed. He asked me to meet him in a few hours at headquarters. There were no busses running and very few taxis, so Captain Pablo offered me his driver. When we reached the house of my host, Andrew, we were greeted by the solitary servant who remained. Andrew and his wife had left several hours before our plane arrived. The house, except for the cellar, was shut up tight. The driver, who translated for me, asked me where I wanted to go. I told him to take me to the Hilton Hotel, but he advised me that the hotel was only for Castro and his soldiers. So he drove me to the National Hotel. Before he left me, I gave him a note in Yiddish for his captain, Pablo, which I ended with a few Hebrew lines.

The large, old hotel was empty except for the people who came on my flight. Thanks to my driver, who told the solitary clerk who I was, I was given a gorgeous suite. There was no hot water in the hotel, but my cold bath was just as satisfactory.

When Pablo called, I treated him to the cognac I had brought with me. Much as he enjoyed the brandy, which he drank for the first time in his life, he told me he enjoyed the two lines of my letter which I wrote in Hebrew even more. They reminded him of the time he studied Hebrew with his father in Warsaw before the Nazis destroyed the Jewish quarter. During the years he was in the Soviet Union after the war and later on in Cuba, he never saw any Hebrew writing.

After our drink, Pablo took me to the Hilton Hotel, where Castro and his lieutenants were having a celebration. The lobbies and all the open rooms were filled with soldiers, the majority of whom were under twenty years of age. From their dirty fatigue uniforms, I was unable to tell who was an officer and who was a private. Pablo took me to Castro and introduced me as an "*amigo*" from Poland. Castro, who must have drunk something more than one cognac, was in a jubilant mood. He put his arm around me and told me, in a Spanish that I understood, that Pablo was a brave soldier.

Pablo and I returned to my hotel room and we talked late into the night. He described his remarkable exploits in the forest around Vilna, Russia and in the mountains of Cuba. Before we said good-night, I offered him my small Bible, which I carry with me on my trips. He was sorry, but he could not accept it. I understood. I had another small book of Hebrew poems by Natan Alterman. That he took after I helped him read and understand a poem that even a good Communist would approve. The next day, thanks to Pablo, I had a chance to see all of the beautiful places of Havana before boarding one of the last planes which carried passengers to the American shore.

No one except Hedvah and my secretary knew about my trip to Cuba. When I called Hedvah from my office and told her of my exploits there, she said, "Daddy, you sure know how to pick all the wrong places to go." I corrected her. I never pick the places; they just happen to be in my way.

My deep-sea fishing expedition in Duck Key had reawakened in me the appetite for the joys of outdoor life. Before leaving New York, I inquired about a house on Fire Island. Among the messages on my desk, I now found a note from my lawyer saying that a friend of his wanted to sell her home in Fire Island. This was during the first part of May, when there were still very few ferries between Bayshore and the slumbering, peaceful island, which was cut off from Long Island by three miles of water. I took the first available ferry to Fire Island. From the landing area, I walked to Seaview to see the house. On my return to New York, I advised my lawyer to buy the house. This house played an important role in the next eight years of my life.

I loved all my homes and apartments from my very first house in San Bernardino. None of them, however, brought me the solace and peace that I found in this simple, frame building nestled among trees and shrubs. Whenever I needed a refuge from the hectic pace and strenuous life on Wall Street, I made my way to Seaview, Fire Island.

There, surrounded by the Atlantic and the bay which divides it from Long Island, we led a quiet life. There were no cars and no asphalted streets. We used the wooden pavements for our walks and for our small shopping carts. It was here that I was able to return to some serious reading and devoted myself to fishing or swimming. One kind of fish we were always sure of catching was the blow fish. They could be brought up in any quantities for any number of unexpected guests, and the fish salad and black bread minimized our trouble in the preparation of wholesome, enjoyable meals. We also had an abundance of wild blackberries during the early months of the fall. They were added to our morning cereals and were the main ingredinet in the pies and fruit salads.

Many years later, my son's wife, Ada, and my grandson, Jonathan, came to live with us during the summers. Ada wrote to my son, who was studying in the University of Florence, that Fire Island "is the loneliest, Godforsaken place in the world." Then, after a few days, she left her son in our care and went off to the city.

With Vera well enough to travel, I approved the arrangements for the kind of a wedding that Hedvah wanted. She was against any large, pretentious affair. She had had enough of that during the years when she was one of the steady bridesmaids. Her wedding was celebrated in a pleasant setting at the Beverly Hills Hotel, the way I had anticipated it. The rabbi who performed Hedvah's wedding was the man whom I replaced twenty years earlier as the executive director of the Soto and Michigan Community Center in Boyle Heights. It was the first time in twenty years that I saw Jed Cohen, who had mellowed a great deal. The academic world in which he spent his time lent dignity to what he said. Michael Berg, Hedvah's husband, who was a sensitive young man, torn between his passion for the piano and his father's determination that he should be a lawyer, was the finest match for Hedvah in my opinion. Fortunately, he heeded the advice of his father instead of accepting the advice that I had given him to be a concert artist. Now that Michael is a Superior Court judge and has a rented piano near his chambers, I am pleased with his choice of a profession. Like me, he also guards and shields a spark that struggles against the ill winds of a chilling, legalistic world. My son was unable to attend his sister's wedding. He was in his last year at the university in the charming city of Florence, Italy.

After the wedding, I returned to my active life, which continued unabated for a full year. Some of the older firms did not like the way we had grown. They disliked Montor and the way he had started our operation with large advertisements in the *New York Times*. They began to whisper about some accounts and personnel that moved during the years from their offices to ours.

Within less than a year and a half, I retrieved all the losses which our firm incurred during Montor's three-and-a-half-year operation. More than $600,000 were added to the assets of the firm, of which I owned over sixty percent. Wall street is one of the most competitive markets in the world. Some of the contacts whom I had no time to cultivate began to ask questions. Fortunately, we ran a clean operation and the Federal Securities Exchange Commission, the chief policeman of all financial operations on Wall Street, had not once found any fault with the manner in which we did business. While many of the largest firms were now and again called to task for noncompliance to the strict laws that governed every brokerage firm, we were never asked about any infraction of the rules and laws of the Securities Exchange Commission.

One day the head of the administrative department told me that a New York Stock Exchange inspector wanted to check some of our early files, which were left behind by Henry Montor. He advised me not to allow him to go into any files that had nothing to do with the operation of Alkow and Company. I did not agree with him. While I had no knowledge of what Montor's files contained, I saw no harm in the inspector's looking into them. My more experienced associate with years in Wall Street shook his head and reluctantly complied.

A month after the New York Stock Exchange inspector had gone over the early files, I recieved a long letter of accusations against Henry Montor and myself for a breach of a regulation enacted by the New York Stock Exchange. We were accused of paying salaries to people who were training to be stockbrokers, a minor infraction. Some of these sums, according to the reports, were the exact equivalent of the commission which would have been due to the trainees had they been registered representatives. I knew that Montor at the beginning had given various advances and loans to those who trained with us to be registered representatives. They were poor people and needed to buy groceries for their families while they were preparing for a new career. I did not know that the money paid in advance would be regarded as commissions by the New York Stock Exchange. In fact, I knew of one trainee who had a sick child and received much more in an advance from our firm than he would have received in commission for the business he brought in. I had nothing to do with any of those payments. Montor was in full charge during the first three years. In the eyes of the New York Stock Exchange, however, I was Montor's accomplice.

The New York Stock Exchange made a serious issue of so-called infractions, which were known to have been made in one form or another by most of the firms of Wall Street. Both of us were punished individually. There was, however, no unfavorable reflection on the sound and correct operations of the company, or upon the integrity of Montor or myself.

When the stock market began to deteriorate in the early part of the sixties, I decided to save our assets and preserve the interests of our customers whose funds and securities were entrusted with us. I began the liquidation of the firm. I never envisioned the slow, painful process in the voluntary liquidation of a New York Stock Exchange firm. With only a skeletal staff of professionals, I had to come every morning to the vast, empty floor and supervise the dismemberment of the firm. We owed people money and people owed us money. We paid every legitimate claim.

However, one claim against us was as unbelievable as that which happened to Montor and myself. A gentleman, with the Legion of Honor button in his lapel, claimed that our firm owed him some $6,000. He had originally presented this claim to Henry Montor on the basis of the letter that incriminated Montor with the New York Stock Exchange. Montor disclaimed owing him the money. I certainly had no reason to recognize his claim. He took us to court. Some time passed before the case came up for trial. After listening to the arguments of the lawyers on both sides, the judge asked me directly if the copy of the letter which the plaintiff presented was the one pulled out of our file by the inspector of the New York Stock Exchange. I said, "Yes, your Honor," and proceeded to tell him what the letter and the plaintiff's claims had done to my firm. The judge listened most attentively to everything I said without interrupting or allowing the lawyer of the plaintiff to interrupt me. When the trial ended, I was fully vindicated of having known or having been responsible for the letter. My lawyer said, "I hope that now you will do something with your victory." While I was happy with the verdict of the court, I had no interest in doing anything with it. Wall Street was now a dead issue for me.

All I wanted to do was to finish the liquidation of the business. The closing of my business was a blessing in disguise. It prolonged my life and preserved my health. More than that, it returned me to the appreciation of the great values to be derived in sharing my life with those who were not primarily interested in material values. It took me back to the world I came from.

Like the bee that accumulates its nectar in one place and turns it into honey in another, I accumulated what I could in the winter and brought it with me to my home in Seaview when the frozen canal was opened up to navigation. After some hours of reading, I worked in tending and shaping the shrubs, junipers, cypress, and holly trees. This native vegetation in my backyard was similar to that in Fire Island's unique sunken garden. No garden created by man could equal the beauty created by nature. With gardening, fishing, and the bracing ocean air, I never slept more soundly.

After eight years on Wall Street, Fire Island brought me the sleep and allowed me to discard all the tranquilizers. My "infectious laughter" which had vanished during the previous years, had also come back to stir other people to laughter that they, too, withheld. A few of the people who could laugh remained on the island with me to the very end, after the cold rains and gales had driven the others back to the city. Now that my life had returned to normalcy and sanity, I spent many hours exploring all the hidden, inner light of the island.

After nine years on the island, Vera clung to it until the last minute. She loved it as much as I did. What was good for her soul, unfortunately, was not good for her body. Her crippling rheumatism and arthritis compelled me to remove her on a stretcher on the first of August, when all hope of remaining on the island for the rest of the summer was gone. The incurable illness had driven her out of her paradise. On the ferry that took us to the mainland, I saw her sorrowful eyes look back at the island for the last time.

On one of the hottest days of the summer, we moved back to the city where, in addition to a nurse, I also engaged a woman who helped take care of Vera. The nurse was very fussy. I had to look after her and prepare both her meals, because she absolutely refused to have anything to do with cooking. She insisted that her breakfast eggs be boiled precisely three minutes, and not a second longer.

After five weeks I took Vera to a special institution where she stayed for a month. Five weeks with a woman who was in constant pain was a trying experience. With Vera in a sanitorium, I went back to Fire Island for the Jewish New Year, where the Jewish community in Ocean Beach conducted services for the last remaining residents. The services with a rabbi and a cantor added very little enjoyment of this meaningful holiday in my empty house. The flickering candles, which I lit on the eve of the New Year, glittered sadly.

On the second day, the small congregation was advised that since the holidays fell late in the year, the Yom Kippur services would be suspended and the Torah would be removed to the mainland. This caused great dismay to two of the worshippers, who were avid fishermen. They were confronted with the choice of returning to the island during the weekend of Yom Kippur and omitting Yom Kippur services, or remaining in their permanent mainland homes and attending services. When there is competition on Fire Island between God and the sea bass, the sea bass wins.

The two religiously minded fishermen noted that I was quite conversant with Jewish ritual. While they both suspected me of unorthodox leanings, they regarded me as better than nothing at all. They approached me and asked if I would run a service on Yom Kippur for at least ten people.

The Yom Kippur services were held at the home of an attorney, whose wife served as sexton and hostess. Remembering what she had learned from the Jesuit fathers in her Catholic convent before she converted to Judaism, she lit memorial candles, which she must have brought from a church. She also brought two tall, silver candlesticks and placed them on a white, satin scarf. Since our Torah scrolls were taken to the mainland, I brought my silver, Hebrew Bible and a *shofar*, ram's horn, which she also laid on a white, satin scarf.

Our preparations were made with great reverence. Everyone received a prayer shawl, though only four people knew what to do with it. The prayerbooks were as strange to the worshippers as were the services I conducted for them. Including the wives, there were about twenty-six people present.

In looking at the haphazard congregation, my heart sank within me. I wrapped the prayer shawl around me tightly and in a sad, plaintive voice I chanted the introductory lines of the service, *Al daas hamokom*. These lines originated during the time of the Spanish Inquisition. Their meaning is to forgive the Marranos for their duplicity in living ostensibly as Catholics while secretly practicing the faith of their ancestors. The Marranos gathered in hiding to observe the Yom Kippur holiday, even though the church threatened those who practiced their Jewish rites with death at the stake.

As the service progressed and I had the occasion to look at my audience, I was elated by the warm response of nearly all those present. When two people repeated to me very movingly what I had said, that "God seeks the heart," I knew that the services went off better than I had anticipated. Thirty years had passed since San Bernardino, where I last conducted services.

The following day almost everyone returned to join the morning services. Word had gotten around and many more residents left their rods and reels and came to what they were told was "something different." With more people there were more spirited explanations, discussions, and group participation in the improvised service.

To this day the words of the Reconstructionist prayer ring in my ears: "May life never be empty and without meaning, a weary procession of worthless days."

What started for me in a low, sad mood of utter personal despair on the previous night of Kol Nidre, ended on a high note with the traditional prayer of hope, Next year in Jerusalem

When all had left and the light of the candles was snuffed, I remained with my host and hostess for the breaking of the fast. There was no trace of herring, so we broke the fast on hot oatmeal. At dinner I listened to a prayer of the lady who was my sexton. For one raised a devout Catholic, she spoke exactly like my mother. "God willing," she said, "that we should all meet next year and enjoy such beautiful services as we had today." Though my heart prompted me to say "Amen," I was unable to do it. This was to be the last time I would conduct religious services. Worst of all, it was the last day of my happy life on Fire Island.

The next morning I packed the rest of my belongings and turned the key in the door of my house. It was never the same again.

Jacob Alkow presiding at the annual dinner of the Histadruth Ivrith, 1956.

XXII

A NEW LIFE

Vera did not like Los Angeles; she called it an "overgrown village" without the intimacy and warmth of the community life that a village offers. But Vera loved New York. Withdrawn from the hub of social life, she found pleasure in the life that New York presents in abundance.

In New York she could walk out on the street and effortlessly become part of the city. Within a few blocks of our home, she could be in the heart of nature with birds, squirrels, and children in Central Park. When she was able to get around without difficulty, she strolled along Madison Avenue, gazing at its fine shops and pulsating life on the sidewalks of Lexington and Third Avenue.

This was the city we had to abandon. The treatment of Vera's illness demanded a more even climate. I had no choice but to return with her to Los Angeles, where Hedvah and our grandchildren would help sustain her morale. I found a charming home on a *cul-de-sac* removed from traffic noises, with a peaceful atmosphere about it.

My greatest difficulty was to find a woman who could take care of Vera. Her pains made it difficult for her to change positions and she needed continuous help. After special medication, her ailment subsided a bit, and this gave me enough peace to concentrate on my studies and on my business. I did most of my work in our library, which had a picture window facing a kidney-shaped swimming pool. By turning to the pool, I found relaxation in gazing at the water and the plants alongside the wall.

Aside from courses I gave at the University of Judaism, I found satisfaction in a Hebrew-speaking organization which I had founded in Boyle Heights when I was principal of the school. Most of its members belonged to a world which had passed. In the main, they were old Hebrew teachers, only a few of whom were still involved in the work they had pursued since their early days of manhood. Outside of their Hebrew classrooms and their books, they knew no other life.

At first their speech seemed strange. In Israel, modern Hebrew was as different from their stilted forms of speech as modern English differs from the Elizabethan. I did not really know whether I wanted to fit into this world, where the main interest of the members was to guard their "inner light." But I loved them for their integrity and their untarnished faith in the ideals of their youth, and I agreed to return to my old post as president.

Generally, Los Angeles offered me nothing more than memories. Many of those close to me in my youthful days had passed away. Others had moved to different parts of the country. None of those whom I knew in the film world were still associated with it. Hollywood belonged to a new, young generation with no place for those who preceded it. The few organizations where I was not entirely forgotten had neither appeal nor interest for me. I don't know how long my retreat would have kept me at peace in this relatively inactive life, as I had never known this kind of passivity. Have I come to an end, I questioned, or have I still some vitality left to surge forth to a more challenging life?

What brightened the first year of my return to Los Angeles was the arrival of Dr. Kaplan, who came to southern California to avoid the wintry months of the eastern seaboard. Dr. Kaplan, although eighty-six years old, was in no mood for retiring. Within a few days, he had arranged a full schedule of writing, teaching, and lecturing. I was happy to help him round out his planned activities. I organized some lectures for him and increased their attendance by addressing small groups on the philosophy of Reconstructionism.

"If we have an enthusiasm for living, a passion to surmount limitations, and a striving for a better world, we are consciously or unconsciously believers in God," said Dr. Kaplan. To hear it from his lips again in the same, familiar voice lifted my spirits.

Vera's illness, which had been held within bounds for a while, now flared up in its worst form. There was nothing that could be done to help her. She was compelled to begin her wanderings from hospitals to nursing homes, which lasted till her dying day.

To distract me from my loneliness, I went to a garden benefit party. Standing in line for the buffet supper, I saw a lovely young woman ahead of me. We filled our trays with food and sat down on the grass to eat together. Neither of us knew anyone, but we were both happy in knowing each other. She told me her name was Virginia, and that she was a former dancer, part-time writer, and had a sailboat. When I called her the following week, Virginia's voice was alive and cheerful as it was when I first met her.

Vera died. Her beautiful hands and her fine features, twisted by illness beyond recognition, were a painful reflection of what life does to us.

After a period of mourning, the strong urge to live fully and enjoy life's benefits strengthened my bonds with Virginia. We married. Virginia felt that as a wife, her greatest contribution would be to return me to the orbit of creative activity. She knew that Los Angeles offered very little to quicken my pace. She knew that one does not build one's home in a graveyard.

There was one place where I would be able to start anew. That was Israel.

To share in my new life, she made plans to sell her beautiful home, leave her two lovely daughters and three grandchildren, and go with me to the promised land.

Virginia was not raised in a Jewish environment. Most of her family, who had lived for generations in America, were assimilated, both her daughters married non-Jews, and nearly every other cousin had a non-Jewish spouse. Virginia had never gone to a synagogue and knew nothing of the Jewish rituals. I brought her to Judaism and she brought me back to the world.

It was on Virginia's boat that I found a new dimension to the ocean and a new life that I had never known before. I took navigation courses in the evening and practiced during the day in the endless activities of handling the sails, maintaining the boat, taking it in and out of tight places in the marina, rolling up the sails, washing the boat, and keeping it bright and shiny. A day's outing on our sailboat, without the use of the auxiliary motor, was the greatest cure for the depressed state in which Virginia had found me.

Once we started out on a trip to Catalina Island. It was approximately an eight-hour trip, depending on the winds. We invited a guest to come with us. Stan was the leader of our writers' workshop and a poet, who devoted his life to literature. In addition, he was a fine critic and very helpful to those writers attending his weekly sessions at the Unitarian Church.

Stan and I had different views on many matters. Kind and tolerant toward most of his friends, he was bitter and intolerant of anything that had to do with the establishment. I suspected him of being a Trotskyite, but he never allowed himself to be labeled. Stan had no idea of my capitalist background, but given the friendship he forged with me, I think he would probably have found a way to condone it. As an out and out radical, he was anti-Zionist as well. Here I did not allow him to make any mistakes and made my views on Zionism very clear to him. On large issues which affect our lives, we cannot hide our convictions from anyone.

Stan's writers' workshop consisted mainly of economically and socially ill-adjusted but talented people. Like Stan, the majority were also anti-establishment. Most of them were poor and worked in offices or in menial trades to support themselves while they were not earning anything by their writings.

During the first hours of our peaceful sailing with kind winds, I had an opportunity to talk with Stan very freely. I told him that even though I enjoyed the meetings of the workshop and liked the people, their outmoded Marxist views depressed me. I compared the dogmatic members of the writers' group to some of the old, disillusioned people in the Hebrew Speakers Organization, who could only identify themselves with an outmoded set of pseudoreligious values and culture.

After our long conversation and a dinner of fish which we caught, the winds changed and the sky became dark and ominous with evening gloom. Stan had very weak eyes and wore thick glasses. Perhaps this was why he walked so unathletically, to the point of being clumsy. Our compass was attached to the deck just in front of the cabin. On the way to the cabin Stan tripped over the compass. Stan was all right but the compass was torn from its seat and the screws were broken. We needed more tools than we had on board to re-secure it. Virginia thought that perhaps we should turn back while we were still in sight of land. While she was considering this, I fixed the compass in place with sticky tape. It was a patch job but it seemed to hold and the alignment looked right. We passed another boat and requested its bearing. By this we saw that our compass was functioning and decided to go on with our voyage.

After several more hours we should have been close to Catalina, but the light winds gave us no progress. In spite of our compass check, we feared we were off course. There were small spits of wind which did not seem to come from any one direction. It was past midnight and six hours beyond our estimated time of arrival when I sent Virginia down to the cabin for some sleep. Stan and I remained on deck, pushing the sail from one to the other, trying to cup any breeze that would come up.

Finally a breeze arose. Stan and I took turns on watch, but I was very uneasy, and all I could do was to hope and pray that we were not lost at sea.

Then the sun rose through the mists and I heard Virginia shout, "Land! I see land!" Soon strong winds rose and filled our sails. Within a short time we were close to shore. It was the same Catalina Island where forty years earlier I had helped DeMille's Jesus perform miracles.

This trip was our farewell to the excitement we had as sailors. We sold the boat and made all necessary preparations for a new kind of navigation in the land of Israel.

On our arrival in Israel, Virginia refused to become a part of the foreign community where only English, French, or German is spoken. She wanted to be as much integrated in the Hebrew-speaking community as I was. She undertook a full year of intensive study of the language. For Virginia it was a lot of fun. In learning the words and sentences, she learned much of the country in which she chose to live, and whose history is probably the most fascinating of all humanity. Through learning about the life and country of the new and old Israel, she came closer to my interest and to my passion for the archaeology of the land.

Virginia has a Master's degree in psychology, which she had never made use of in the United States. In Los Angeles, she was content with normal, family life, women's clubs, charities, and the dance troupes she appeared in. In Israel this kind of life didn't appeal to her. Here she felt she was needed for other ends. At the age of sixty, she removed the dust from her diploma and succeeded in obtaining a teacher's credential. With the license, she found a position as a teacher of English in a special school for emotionally disturbed children.

Israel does not allow one's valuable experiences to lie dormant. A country that has to be built rapidly and strongly to survive cannot afford to lose or discard anything which can be of help. Retirement from a productive, creative job is accepted with deepest regret. As long as one is fit to work and contribute, the job may be changed but not ended.

I returned to the educational and archaeological interests of my youth. In these and other interests I have never been disappointed or disillusioned.

My intended involvement in archaeology was not fully realized during the first years of our well-adjusted life in Israel. Other fields of endeavor, which no longer existed for me in America, began to consume my time. They were connected with the new film industry which was slowly developing in the country. Because it was known that I had been a film producer in America, people started sending me scripts. There were two very promising young men who came to see me. They brought me a script. One was the writer and director, Nissim Dayan; the other was his cameraman, Shmuel Calderon.

The script was honest and true, and it contained a message. I was, however, not ready or willing to get involved in production. Besides, the script lacked the experienced touch and know-how of a professional scenarist. It was too long and the dialogue was not clear or sharp.

After weeks of hesitation and continuous calls from Nissim, I finally agreed to produce the film on condition that Nissim would allow me to help him restructure the script. He agreed readily. The more I worked on it with Nissim, the more I liked it and I began preparations for its production. The title of the film was taken from a well-known line of Chaim Bialik, "Light out of Nowhere." Encouraged by the acceptance of the script by the Government Film Center, which provided special loans for production, I started to produce the film, which was to absorb my full time for over a year and a half.

With a small budget, which included the government loan, my investment, and the investments of Nissim Dayan amd Shmuel Calderon, I supervised every detail. To avoid the expenses of construction sets, interior and exterior shots were made on location in the poor, neglected area of Shabazi. When the city was young, Shabazi was the most prestigious section of Tel Aviv, but when we came to film in the area, its crumbling, one-story houses barely retained any of the early pioneering grandeur of the city.

Working in the neighborhood, we came in close contact with its residents, most of whom had settled in it after the Second World War. They were mainly from Morocco and Rumania. Even without a common language, the mixed population of the older people adjusted surprisingly well. The little Hebrew which they learned from their children enabled the poor residents to create a friendly, tolerant community. We were warmly welcomed by the people living here and they competed for the honor of allowing us to use their poor quarters as sets for our production. In the community, we also found the young people we needed who were to portray their typical lives.

The story of the film concerns a traditional Jewish family, uprooted from its rich cultural heritage in Morocco. The father, a religious, learned Jew, and a widower, is unsuccessful in trying to bridge his life with that of his two young sons. The older son is drawn in by a neighborhood gang of hoodlums and drug pushers; the younger wavers between his father, whom he admires, and his brother, whom he worships as a hero. The younger son is the protagonist and he is shown as a fine boy, interested in his studies, who withstands the temptations to join his comrades in their incipient delinquency. He finally succumbs to their pleas to help in a small burglary. Their venture into crime does not materialize when they get frightened by a cat.

Much of the plot could have been transcribed literally from the lives of the people in the area. My mission in producing the film was to bring an awareness of the life of the people who were unable to integrate in the land without the assistance of the rest of the community.

I saw the objective of Zionism as principally the re-creation and the rebuilding of a people, without which the rebuilding of the land is of secondary

Jacob Alkow with his son, Michael, 1962.

value. When an entire, proud generation of North African Jewry was allowed to rot in abandoned quarters after the War of Liberation, I felt that this was a negation and a betrayal of Zionism. In America I had rebelled against the slums and poverty-stricken areas of New York and Los Angeles. Now I was despondent to see the same thing happening in the new state of Israel, which I had hoped would serve as a model for the world.

Shabazi and its disillusioned residents was the first serious challenge I encountered in the country. Driving home each night and entering my spacious, bright villa in a beautiful suburb near Tel Aviv, I could not put out of my mind what I faced during the day in Shabazi, with its unemployment, crime, and neglect.

I found myself becoming involved with the personal lives of the residents of Shabazi. I gave some of them modest loans, all of which were repaid. At the request of a worried family, I went to the police to inquire about some boys who were rounded up during the night. I used my position at the Tel Aviv Rotary Club to help increase its support of the poorly equipped community centers which it had established. I raised money for that purpose by donating the proceeds of the premiere showing of Ingmar Bergman's *Cries and Whispers, Scenes from a Marriage*, and *The Magic Flute*, films which I brought to Israel for distribution in the theaters here.

The contribution which gave me the greatest satisfaction lay in a different direction. A wooden shack served as a synagogue for some of the North African Jews. The roof leaked during the rainy season and a crude, wooden box served as the Holy Ark for the three precious Torah Scrolls, which were brought from their ancient synagogue in Morocco. For years the worshippers hoped that someone would help them construct a Holy Ark for their prized treasure. When I offered to contribute the sum of money to build the ark, I asked whether it would not serve a better purpose if the money were used to repair the roof. The unequivocal answer from young and old, men and women, was that the Holy Ark should come ahead of any other need.

Because of the low budget and financial limitations, our work on the film stretched out over a longer period than was contemplated. My working hours were usually from six in the morning until six in the evening. Virginia, who was busy teaching and studying, maintained that she never saw me looking better and younger during all the years she had known me in America. In Israel, she said, you found something to live for.

The film was finished just before the Yom Kippur War and opened the first week after hostilities broke out. Nothing could have been more catastrophic. Although the serious Israeli press received the film with favorable and even laudatory reviews, and the critics of the leading daily, *Haaretz*, hailed it as one of the most important, authentic, and original productions in Israel, others were troubled by the "heavy plot" and "grim seriousness." They questioned whether it would succeed at the box office.

After several heroic attempts to present it to the depressed Israeli public during the following months, *Light out of Nowhere* was a major financial failure. In addition to the loss I sustained, my two young colleagues, whose optimism and unlimited faith in the financial success of the film had buoyed them up, were now victims of its failure. One of my colleagues lost his small, old car; the other saw his furniture attached by the local sheriff. I was co-signer on their loans and was compelled to pay for both of them.

Three years after my initial failure in Israel, I attended the Cannes Film Festival and was surprised to learn that Rosselini wanted to see me. Rosselini, an outstanding film director, was chairman of the Festival. This was one year before his death. He had seen the original Hebrew version of *Light out of Nowhere*, which had been selected by the French Cinémathèque as one of the best films of its genre. The news of Rosselini's interest in the film spread quickly at the Festival. The Israeli representative helped circulate the good word. My wife and I were invited to a French television station to appear on their program. The belated publicity and recognition in the milieu of this international film festival revived some commercial interest. A dubbed version in Spanish saw some light in South America. The return which we received was, however, too small to reduce our original losses to any extent. More than the return of our capital, both Virginia and I were gratified with the acceptance and approval of my first artistic and business venture in Israel.

Fortunately my losses were fully retrieved for the Ingmar Bergman pictures which I distributed in Israel. *Scenes from a Marriage* ran for twenty-eight weeks in a major theater and brought in more than five times the amount that the film had cost me to import. My other Bergman films, *Cries and Whispers*, *The Magic Flute* and *Autumn Sonata* all succeeded beyond my expectations.

The Yom Kippur War was the main interruption to our happily adjusted life in Israel. On Yom Kippur 1973, I returned home for a short afternoon nap. The long walks to and from the synagogue in the warm weather were tiring and I fell asleep. In less than half an hour I was awakened by the loud sounds of the emergency siren. The radio is normally silent on Yom Kippur, and a shiver passed through my body when I turned it on and heard a news broadcast. Virginia ran into the bedroom, startled to hear that the Egyptians and Syrians had made simultaneous surprise attacks on our northern and southern borders. All reserves were ordered to rush to their stations. I dressed quickly and ran back to the synagogue, carrying my small transistor radio close to my ear. All along the way I saw men running and being picked up by cars to be conveyed to their assembly places.

The news was garbled and ominous. In spite of the censorship, reports from the two fronts were disastrous. When I arrived at the synagogue I found it as full as it had been the previous night of Kol Nidre. The rabbi, with tears streaming down his face, ordered the cantor to end his service and report to the station where he was mobilized. Until nightfall, the services were continuously interrupted by the news we received when we listened to our transistors outside the synagogue.

After the closing service, we emptied out of the synagogue to hurry to our families through the dark streets and the already blacked-out homes. Special squads had been quickly organized to warn all residents to cover their windows, and for nearly a month no light was permitted to escape from any home.

Older men and women who were not mobilized reported for special duties to guard the beaches and all public places round the clock. Many of our neighbors, as well as my wife and myself, volunteered to drive to the fronts and deliver food and drink and convey some of the straggling soldiers from place to place. During the first days, we drove as far into the Sinai desert as we were allowed, and after leaving sandwiches, chocolate bars, and cigarettes near the lines that separated all civilian travel from the armies, we took some soldiers back to the towns where they lived.

Most of them were so tired that they fell asleep as soon as they piled into the car. One thin and haggard young boy, who had come from America, felt a compelling need to talk. For hours he poured out his experiences at the front. He told us of the dogs of Egypt, poor, starved creatures, who followed the troops, howling pitifully for any scraps of food. Again and again he returned to the dogs. So vivid were his words that we could almost hear the whimpering animals in the background like an obligato to his story.

The whole nation was fully mobilized. All private and personal activities ceased. The entire population was involved in the struggle for its existence. Long days and nights passed without our knowing what the real situation was.

After more than a week of anxiety and worry over our great losses, we were heartened by the news of our armies driving the enemy back beyond their borders. Israel crossed the Suez Canal and penetrated deep into Egyptian territory. At long last, we were able to breathe freely and follow events without shuddering.

Soon after the showing of *Light out of Nowhere* I was approached by the Polish director, Alexander Ford, in regard to a contemplated, major production of the life of Dr. Janus Korchak. The film was to be made in Germany and Israel. He had inquired about me among Israeli film people, and after a discussion with Arthur Brauner, the producer in Germany, he asked me to serve as co-producer. I agreed to meet with Ford and read the unfinished script which he had brought from Berlin.

The script had been reworked by many writers over a period of years, and in my opinion, was not satisfactory. It was a case of too many cooks who spoiled the broth. Ford and I hit it off well. He agreed with me and assured me that with the help of a new scriptwriter and our joint participation, we could come up with a satisfying scenario.

I knew about Ford through his fine Polish films. He struck me as a sincere, knowledgeable, creative director and a fine, gentle, human being. I was not convinced that Alexander Ford was the best man to direct the film, which would have worldwide distribution. He knew very little English and all of his good work belonged to the old European school of the forties and fifties. On the other hand, he was the only film director who knew Dr. Janus Korchak intimately, and he had personally been involved with the last years of the greatest Jewish martyr in modern times. The thought of being able to work on the filming of the last chapter of Janus Korchak's life was intriguing and exciting.

I telephoned Berlin and spoke to Arthur Brauner. He was friendly and relaxed. In a Yiddish-Polish accented English, he told me that he had heard good things about me. He wanted me to come to Berlin for "serious discussions" about the production, which was the "dream of his life."

Arthur Brauner was a native of Poland. He passed through the concentration camp under the Nazis, and after the war, arrived in Germany as a penniless immigrant. It took him only fifteen years to rise to the highest rung of financial success. He became the largest German producer of popular, commercial films. Through the returns on his films, he acquired real estate holdings in Berlin at a period when the country was in an economically distressed state. At the time when I spoke to him over the phone, Brauner was a multimillionaire who could easily afford to invest the considerable sum needed for the major production he envisaged. Through the press, I learned that the land he owned in Israel alone was worth over five million dollars.

Alexander Ford, who knew Brauner well, assured me that Brauner was not making the movie solely for profit. Ford was convinced that Brauner would not stop at any cost to make the filming of Janus Korchak the greatest and finest production of his life.

A few days after my telephone conversation with Brauner, I found myself in his luxurious villa on the exquisite estate in the richest residential quarter of West Berlin. Alexander Ford arrived in Berlin, and the three of us settled down for sessions in connection with our respective duties, responsibilities, the final script, the actors, and matters pertaining to production.

The contracts were ready and I was asked to go to Hollywood and New York to negotiate for the best talent available. We had spent many hours poring over the photographs of leading actors, and after careful study had agreed on five whom we considered could best portray the role of Janus Korchak.

For the other leading parts, the more desirable actors were also in America and England. Since English was to be the language of the film, all actors had to be native English speakers. In spite of my admiration for our Israeli actors, I made it clear to both Brauner and Ford that because of the language barrier, no Israeli should qualify for any of our important roles. After Brauner agreed with me in principle, he began to mention names of some likely, inexpensive Israeli actors for the secondary roles. I began to suspect his motives.

In America, my first task was to contact the agents of the five actors we had selected. Three of the five were available. They were Dirk Bogarde, David Niven, and Mel Ferrer. I delivered the scenario to the agents, all of whom approved of the script, and the long haggling began. I was finally able to obtain Mel Ferrer. I phoned Arthur Brauner. He was delighted with the terms and told me to formalize the negotiations with the well-known agents of the actor, the William Morris Agency. I asked that the agency confirm and sign the contract directly with Arthur Brauner who, I explained, was the main investor in the production. The agency told me that they knew Brauner and would complete all arrangements with him.

In Israel I received a call from the William Morris Agency. Ferrer and his wife had left California for Berlin to meet with Branuer and to begin working in Berlin before coming to Israel. Pleased with my successful negotiation, I informed the Israel press of Mel Ferrer's participation in the film on the life of Dr. Korchak.

One week later, I was awakened in the middle of the night by a frantic call from Beverly Hills. Mel Ferrer had telephoned his agents from Berlin and advised them that Arthur Brauner had canceled the agreement on the strength of some ambiguity. I called Brauner the next morning. He casually mentioned that in the meantime he had found an English actor who was "just as good," for half the money that we would have had to pay Ferrer. The actor was Leo Genn. I was stunned. I knew nothing about Genn.

After some thought, I decided to withdraw from my agreement with Brauner. I was advised by my lawyer that since Brauner had canceled the contract with the William Morris Agency because of a technicality, I had no grounds to break my contract with him.

Unaware of my dilemma, Brauner called me a day later in regard to the preparations in Israel, as though nothing had happened. I hired my staff and the technical personnel and actors for minor roles. I also engaged the composer for the music of the film, Moshe Vilensky, who is well known in Israel. Vilensky was a find. As a young man he taught music at the orphanage in the 1930s and knew Korchak intimately. He wrote the haunting score for the picture.

I then began my search for a suitable building that we could reconstruct as an orphanage similar to Korchak's. I was advised that on the road from Tel Aviv to Jaffa, a building existed which people called "the red house" because of its red brick construction. It was about to be demolished by the city to make room for widening the street. When I met the head of the department in charge of the building, I was informed that it would be impossible for us to use it. The city had already issued orders for its demolition, which was to start within a week.

Without wasting time, I went to see the mayor, Yehoshua Rabinowitz. He also came from Vilna. Mr. Rabinowitz (who became Minister of Finance a year later) received me warmly as his *landsman*. He listened carefully to what I told him about the historic significance of the film and of the need to get the right setting for Korchak's orphanage.

Without saying a word, he lifted the telephone receiver and made a round of calls to his department heads and his principal contractors. The building was ours.

Within two weeks the electricians, carpenters, painters, and grips were on the site, working two shifts in order to ready the location in time for shooting. When I called Ford in Berlin to tell him the good news about the orphanage, he asked me if he should send something to the mayor. I answered that Rabinowitz was not the usual kind of mayor, and besides, he told me that as a young man he had known Janus Korchak.

The production, which had begun filming in a poor neighborhood in Berlin, now continued in the red house of Tel Aviv. It was a precise replica of Korchak's orphanage in the Warsaw Ghetto. In addition to the minor parts, which were given to local actors, one hundred children were carefully screened. They were to play the parts of the orphans who were cared for and taught by the man who was their inspiring mentor, their physician, and their surrogate father.

Among these children were two of my grandchildren, Semadar, aged eight, and Jonathan, aged eleven. Watching the portrayal of their last days of joy, fright, and anguish was for me the most moving experience that I had of the Holocaust. Hearing Korchak's words, I felt as if I were an eyewitness to his superhuman struggle to protect and save his children from their inevitable death in the gas chamber. Leo Genn was fairly convincing in his portrayal of Korchak. He acquitted himself better than I had expected. He caught some of the spirit and heroic dimension of the man.

One of the strongest scenes is when Korchak's friends in the underground advise him that there is no way in which the children can be saved. The underground can only save Korchak's life, for which they obtained special documents.

Combining his philosophy with his sublime loving kindness, Korchak refuses and prepares his children to follow him to the Treblinka-bound transport train. The last march of the orphans, carrying on high the flag of their orphanage, and led by Korchak, was the most poignant scene of the drama. Leo Genn was fine, but the part required a much greater actor, the greatest of all time. Brauner was too blind to see it.

After some weeks of smooth sailing, Arthur Brauner appeared on the scene in Israel. It was aggravating trying to quench the fires lit by Brauner in his obsession with all sorts of petty economies. One day I was late coming on the set. When I arrived I found that all activity had stopped. Brauner was puffing and fuming and the air was filled with bitter accusations and recriminations. Ford, the director, and Genn, the star, had both walked off the set and retired to their hotel rooms. I rushed over to see them. Separately I listened to their complaints. Then I called Brauner. I finally convinced each one to meet the other half way, and only then Ford and Genn agreed to return to work.

One day previous to Brauner's arrival, I had given an interview to *The Jerusalem Post*, in which I had said, "Our film is not made with the idea of profit. It is made to try to help ensure that the new generation in Israel and the world will never be allowed to forget the Holocaust." This is what Brauner, himself a victim of the Holocaust, had told me.

After many delays and changes, the film was finally completed and opened in the Jerusalem Theater. 2,000 people attended the gala premiere, including Golda Meir, who sat next to me and wept through most of the showing. As I viewed the film with an audience, I thought that under the circumstances the movie was better than I had expected it to be. The public felt otherwise. I was saddened but not surprised. What hurt me most was that on account of false economies, we missed the opportunity to create a fitting memorial for one of the noblest souls of our century.

I soon managed to shelve these memories. Israel does not leave us much time to reflect on our past achievements or failures. One activity follows another. We are regarded more by what we do than by what we have achieved or failed to achieve.

The great task of rebuilding the land and re-creating the people, which began about one hundred years ago, may require many, many more decades before it is accomplished. In the interim, there is much to be done, not the least of which is achieving a better understanding among the varied parts of the population.

As I look back to the time when I first saw this land, I marvel each day on the unbelievable progress that it has made. There is more hope for Israel today than at any time in the past. Though its economy is beset by rampant inflation and the Jewish populaton is fractured, each pulling in a different direction, it has, nevertheless, made formidable strides. Nowhere have I found joy of life and creation as I do in this land that has never disappointed me.

One who transplants his old roots into a new soil may find an excitement and refreshment which had been lost over the years. This depends greatly on the love with which we embrace our new surroundings.

In enlarging my home to accommodate my art, I have also expanded and restructured the area surrounding our house. I turned it into a more unique garden than the one I left behind.

There is hardly a day when my wife does not go to the sea. In its calm or billowy waves, she finds her greatest relaxation. I also love the sea in the early hours of sunrise and in the late hours of the day. But it is in my garden and in my house that I derive my greatest peace and serenity.

My worldly interests consist of varied investments in the United States. In spite of the little attention I have paid them, they have increased in value over the years. My Israel investments also have not fallen far behind. When there is no crisis, I seldom give them much thought. Israel, unlike other capitalist countries, has favored me by removing from my mind the engrossing concern with material possessions.

My son migrated to Israel from California and increased his family from four children to six, with two more little boys who were born in Safed. He established himself as an architect, devoting a great deal of his time to the restoration of old synagogues. His wife is managing their newly built modern art gallery in the artists' quarter of Safed.

In Israel, I find I am drawn into diverse activities far removed from the beaten path. My interest presently include the restoration of the ancient gates of the city of Lachish, destroyed by the Assyrians in 701 B.C. I am also involved in a model children's hospital that is being built in Jerusalem with the help of *Variety*, and somewhat afield from these undertakings, a sculpture garden in Herzliah which will be a home for the preservation of the art of Israeli and Jewish sculptors.

At eighty-one years of age, my participation in community activities is not attenuated. I cannot expect my involvement in the life of the country to be entirely free from the effects of the disconcerting religious and social forces, but in spite of all this, I am in consonance with my wife. When Virginia is asked why she continues to live in Israel, away from her children and grandchildren, she answers, "I live in Israel because I love Israel. It is here that I feel most needed."

Sitting at an archaeological dig, where history is unearthed, I think of my own vagaries through Lithuania, America, Germany, France, China, Japan and Cuba. In coming to Israel, I have made my own history, and a new beginning.

Jacob Alkow and Virginia, 1975.

922.96   88-66
Al 1
         Alkow, Jacob M.
AUTHOR
In Many Worlds
TITLE
            919294576   13.95

922.96   88-66
Al 1

The Temple Library
UNIVERSITY CIRCLE AT SILVER PARK
CLEVELAND, OHIO 44106